Chicken Soup for the Soul®

Find Your Happiness

Chicken Soup for the Soul: Find Your Happiness
101 Inspirational Stories about Finding Your Purpose, Passion, and Joy
Jack Canfield, Mark Victor Hansen, Amy Newmark. Foreword by Deborah Norville

Published by Chicken Soup for the Soul Publishing, LLC   www.chickensoup.com
Copyright © 2011 by Chicken Soup for the Soul Publishing, LLC. All Rights Reserved.
No part of this publication may be reproduced, stored in a retrieval system or transmitted in any form or by any means, electronic, mechanical, photocopying, recording or otherwise, without the written permission of the publisher.

CSS, Chicken Soup for the Soul, and its Logo and Marks are trademarks of Chicken Soup for the Soul Publishing LLC.

The publisher gratefully acknowledges the many publishers and individuals who granted Chicken Soup for the Soul permission to reprint the cited material.

Front cover photo courtesy of iStockphoto.com/TimeFoto (© TimeFoto).
Back cover and interior photos courtesy of iStockphoto.com/jpsdk (© Jens Stolt).
Deborah Norville photo on back cover courtesy of Timothy White.

Cover and Interior Design & Layout by Pneuma Books, LLC
For more info on Pneuma Books, visit www.pneumabooks.com

Distributed to the booktrade by Simon & Schuster. SAN: 200-2442

Publisher's Cataloging-in-Publication Data
(Prepared by The Donohue Group)

Chicken soup for the soul : find your happiness : 101 inspirational stories
  about finding your purpose, passion, and joy / [compiled by] Jack Canfield,
  Mark Victor Hansen [and] Amy Newmark ; foreword by Deborah Norville.

    p. ; cm.

  Summary: A collection of 101 true personal stories about how people found happiness by pursuing their passions, recognizing their purpose, and finding joy in their lives.
  ISBN: 978-1-935096-77-1

  1. Happiness--Literary collections. 2. Happiness--Anecdotes. 3. Conduct of
life--Literary collections. 4. Conduct of life--Anecdotes. I. Canfield, Jack,
1944- II. Hansen, Mark Victor. III. Newmark, Amy. IV. Norville, Deborah. V. Title:
Find your happiness

PN6071.H2 C455 2011
810.8/02/0353   2011934312

PRINTED IN THE UNITED STATES OF AMERICA
on acid∞free paper
20 19 18 17 16 15 14 13 12 11   01 02 03 04 05 06 07 08 09 10

Chicken Soup for the Soul.
Find Your Happiness

101 Inspirational Stories about Finding Your Purpose, Passion, and Joy

Jack Canfield
Mark Victor Hansen
Amy Newmark
Foreword by Deborah Norville

Chicken Soup for the Soul Publishing, LLC
Cos Cob, CT

Chicken Soup

www.chickensoup.com

for the Soul

Contents

❶

~Counting My Blessings~

❷

~Back to Basics~

❸
~Finding My Passion~

❹
~Attitude Adjustments~

❺
~Overcoming Adversity~

❻

~The Joy of Giving~

❼

~Finding My Purpose~

8

~Simple Pleasures~

9

~Making the Best of It~

10

~Jumping Off the Hamster Wheel~

Foreword

Some people pursue happiness, others create it.
~Margaret Bowen

We're all familiar with our constitutional right to pursue happiness. As a child, I recall more than once telling my not-at-all-amused mother that I was "pursuing my right to happiness" when I made a particularly large mess. She very cleverly informed me that if I wanted to enjoy life or liberty, I would clean it right up too! Who doesn't want to be happy? Not only does being happy beat the alternative, happiness has some pretty attractive benefits. Research has found being happy adds about nine years to your life!

Chances are you picked up this book in hopes of reading some stories that can help brighten your own day or put you on a new path that's got a bit more joy or a little more laughter than the road you currently travel. Inside this book are 101 stories specifically chosen to show you there are many roads to happiness. After you read these stories, you'll be much better equipped to find the path—and the destination—that's right for you.

Some people pursue happiness, others create it. Take a look at Margaret Bowen's quote and ask yourself, "Who's more likely to be happy? The person chasing, or the one creating?" If you need a hint, you may find a clue in these words by Henry David Thoreau that I had on a poster on my wall during high school and college:

Happiness is like a butterfly: the more you chase it,
the more it will elude you, but if you turn your attention to other things,
it will come and sit softly on your shoulder.

As much as you may *try* to be happy, your efforts probably only serve to make you frustrated. "Don't Worry—Be Happy" was a cute idea in a song, but as advice for those who've lost their zest for life, it doesn't work. You can't just "be" happy. But turn your attention to other things—the *right* things—and you will find that happiness has found you. What are the right things? We'll get to that in a moment. But here's a central truth: When it comes to being happy, the journey IS the destination.

It's funny that the Chicken Soup for the Soul people came to me to write the foreword for a book on finding your happiness because there was a period in my life when I was profoundly unhappy. Perhaps I was even depressed. I was too down in the dumps to seek professional help to find out. My career was in the toilet. My telephone had stopped ringing. I didn't think I would ever work again. So what happened? Did I wake up one day, put on make-up and hop over to a TV studio, saying, "I'm back! Put me on the show!"?

Hardly. Instead, I got out my sewing machine. In the depths of my unhappiness, I pulled out my old Kenmore machine, dug out some lengths of fabric, and started making curtains and slipcovers. You can work out a lot of aggression on those long seams as you floor the foot pedal. When you see the results of those hours with the machine—slipcovers that make an old chair new again, curtains that warm up a bare room—you can't help but feel pleased about your work... and yourself.

That long-ago search for happiness led me to reconnect with a long ignored passion. I had been sewing, doing embroidery, and knitting and crocheting since I was eight years old. Dusting off that machine, reminding myself of the many pleasant hours I used to spend stitching, helped brighten my spirits. *Some people pursue happiness, others create it.* That I was happy after returning to my long-lost hobby was an unintended consequence of engaging in something that I had once enjoyed. Without expecting to, I had *created* my own happiness.

The surprise factor has a lot to do with happiness. If you look up the etymology of the word "happy," you see that it stems from the Old Norse word *happ*, which meant "chance" or "unforeseen occurrence." By chance, we stumble into happiness. Like that butterfly, we rarely catch it if we are chasing it.

Here's another secret: You won't find happiness by always striving to be the best. Good enough is, well, good enough. Research conducted by Professor Barry Schwartz of Swarthmore College found some notable differences between those he calls "maximizers," people who have to have the best and are compelled to research every possible choice, and those who are satisfied more easily. Because they insist on the "best," those maximizers do tend to earn about $7,000 more annually, but they feel worse. They're not as happy as the rest of us who are willing to "settle." The ordeal of making the choice, coupled with the potential for regret over the decision made, mitigated any pleasure they might have enjoyed from their increased spending power.

So what can help you Find Your Happiness? Here's my recipe:

- **Count Your Blessings** — Happiness operates in an upward spiral; it feeds on itself. People who keep track of the "good things" in their lives are healthier, more active, more productive — and held in higher regard by others. That would make me happy, wouldn't it you? So take note of what's right in your life and see if things don't change for the better. This book is filled with examples of people who say it has worked for them.

- **Foster Connections** — There is no question it is the connections with others that bring richness to our lives. Strong social connections and shared experiences create the foundation on which happiness can thrive. Pick up the phone; e-mail an old friend.

- **Know Yourself and Pursue Your Passion** — To "Find Your Happiness" you must first know what makes you happy. Perhaps the words of the German philosopher Goethe are helpful: *As soon* *as you trust yourself, you will know how to live.* Pull out your notebook and a pencil and try to answer these questions: What are your passions? What pastimes give you joy? What are you good at? What long-ago dreams have you put out to pasture because they weren't practical, were unrealistic, "could never happen?" Forget what all the naysayers may have said in the past. The answers you supply can help you plan a new journey and find your happiness. The joy is in the doing as much as it is the "done."

- **Keep Learning**—The day you stop growing is the day you start going. There is no question that people with goals and challenges find life more zestful than those content with the status quo. You'll love the story of Jane Congdon, who gave up a career that had stopped making her happy, and at age sixty-six will have her first book published.

- **Find Meaning**—People who have found meaning and purpose in their lives are happy. Period. You might find meaning by getting outside yourself in service of others as Shannon Anderson has with her "good deed a day." You'll read her story about how she first taught her family the benefits of doing good deeds, and then inspired her whole first grade classroom to do good deeds and keep a diary of them. The kids loved it! Ralph Waldo Emerson urged: *Make yourself necessary to somebody.* You lift yourself when you lift others. Perhaps you fail to see the meaning in your job or profession or maybe your job's not right for you. Even hospital cleaners, at the bottom of the ladder in both pay and prestige, see their work as challenging and skilled when they are shown that their contributions are central to the hospital's mission.

- **Find Quiet**—The Chinese have a wonderful expression: *Only the stillness can still.* No matter how noisy and hectic it may be where you are, close your eyes for just this moment and imagine you are deep in a lush green forest, sitting on a moss-covered stone, listening to the distant sounds of water tumbling down a stream. Breathe. Sit. Forget about all the "stuff" in your life. Don't worry about the jam-packed schedule. Just breathe. That small momentary exercise has likely left you feeling just a bit more in control, a bit less frazzled. Remember that butterfly called happiness won't come and sit softly on your shoulder if you are rushing about madly.

The people who have shared their stories with you in this book have all found their happiness through variations of this "recipe."

Betsy Franz knew only one way to live her life and that was at full speed. The way she described a trip to the grocery store, you almost wanted to warn the other shoppers to stay home. She flew around the corners on two wheels hurling her purchases into her cart. Then one day Betsy's life coasted to a halt. Literally. She was so busy she forgot to check the gas gauge and she ran out of fuel on the way to an important meeting. Being the sensible woman that she is, Betsy did the obvious: She screamed and pounded the steering wheel.

Then she stepped out of the car to flag down some help—and saw something she hadn't seen before on her morning commute: the sunrise. It was a glorious, awe-inspiring sight. She eventually made it to work with a lighter heart. Today Betsy Franz moves at a slower pace, one that allows her to be present, to notice the small things, and hear the small voice deep in her soul that had been muffled. She is happy.

Michelle Smyth found her happiness and an unexpected purpose when her son was diagnosed with autism. She became a mom on a mission, researching everything she could learn about autism, elated when she heard about a new therapy that held promise. She hit brick walls at every turn. "Too expensive." "We don't offer it here." But this mom was not to be denied. Michelle cajoled her way into observing some training sessions, convinced a respected specialist in the field to coach her, and turned her basement into a therapy center, all so she could work with her little boy. His progress was incremental, but real. Small accomplishments were celebrated and more challenging tasks tackled.

Before long, other families struggling with autism heard of Michelle's efforts and asked if she'd help their children. A support group was born that has since blossomed into a full-fledged autism center serving kids throughout her area. Michelle says she has "an indescribable joy," excitement for the future, and happily believes she is fulfilling her destiny.

Jennifer Quasha thought her destiny was to be constantly depressed. She probably hadn't heard that researchers believe that forty percent of our sense of happiness comes from our own activities. She'd had a difficult childhood, lost two friends in a car accident, survived a mugging at gunpoint and was brutally assaulted—all before her mid-twenties. Depression ran in her family and she just assumed it was to be her lot too.

Then she decided to confront her depression. She'll tell you all the things she's done, including what she calls her "little secret." It's the small datebook in which each night she writes down the one thing that made her happiest that day. It's working. As Jennifer puts it, "The spin on my life has changed. I actively seek the positive."

Alexander Brokaw tried to see the positive in his college studies. He really tried. With two parents on Wall Street, he figured he was supposed to pursue a career in business, but his heart wasn't in it. His books went unopened until just before finals, which he somehow squeaked through. On winter break his sophomore year, a friend got into a bar fight and Alex rushed to defend him. Two guys attacked him and Alex ended up in the emergency room, being examined for a concussion.

The CT scan revealed no concussion. It was worse. The scan had picked up a brain tumor. Alexander had to withdraw from school and undergo chemotherapy. During his forced break from school, he resumed a childhood pastime he'd discarded years before. He began playing pretend, conjuring up epics with adventures and storylines that he put on paper. When Alex recovered and went back to school, he switched from finance courses to a creative writing major. He says, "Being successful is doing what makes you happy. Life is too short and uncertain to do anything else."

It is the uncertainty of life with which we begin our stories, with the incomparable wisdom of Angela Sayers. One of Angela's greatest wishes was to be published as an author. In this book, she is. Sadly, it was one of Angela's last wishes, as she had been battling osteosarcoma since she was fourteen. You'll notice I said one of her "last" wishes, not her "dying" wishes, because as this very wise young lady put it: "I'm living. Every day."

Angie wrote her story for this Chicken Soup for the Soul edition as she was nearing the end of her long cancer battle. She'd already lost one of her lower legs and most of her lungs to the disease, which doctors had just learned had spread to her brain. Yet twenty-year-old Angie had not an ounce of bitterness. Listen to her perspective:

"I'm still here. I'm still living. Life is precious, whether you have a straight road stretched before you as far as the eye can see, or whether, like most people, your road turns and bends into the undergrowth and you have no idea where it leads. Follow that bend, and your heart, no matter where it goes. Mine may go on, to places unmentionable, but everyone's does, eventually."

Angela Sayers' journey ended on July 15th, 2011, as this book was being completed. She was only twenty. But while her body has gone, her incredible wisdom lives on. We start and end the book with Angie's wisdom, including Story 1, in which she describes her happiness as she continues to live her shortened life, and Story 101, her final letter to family and friends, which her family found after she died. Turn the page to see the gift that Angie left you in her inspirational stories and ninety-nine others that show you how to *find your happiness*.

~Deborah Norville

Find Your Happiness

Chapter 1

Counting My Blessings

*Better to lose count while naming your blessings
than to lose your blessings to counting your troubles.*

~Maltbie D. Babcock

Chicken Soup for the Soul

My Epiphany

With the past, I have nothing to do; nor with the future. I live now.
~Ralph Waldo Emerson

t seems that when something awful happens to me, my mind just shuts down. These things change the way I think for a period of time after they happen. Somehow, I find a way to keep it all together by reverting to my "one day at a time" motto, but really, inside, I'm freaking out. Sometimes I'm freaking out and I don't even realize it yet. I've discovered lately that moving on from those difficult times really is a process.

These days, I am in the final stages of my long battle with osteosarcoma, a bone cancer, which made its appearance when I was fourteen years old, claimed one of my lower legs and a lung along the way, and recently spread to my brain. The doctors found three or four new tumors in my brain. This news was a terrible blow since it meant two huge things. It meant that one, along with the nodules that I already had in my single lung, the Thalidomide I have been trying isn't doing a single thing for me. And secondly it officially marked me as terminal. The doctors told us that they thought I probably had less than a month to live.

It has now been longer than a month, and I am still here and still feeling well. Nothing has truly changed about my situation. I am still taking medication for the headaches, and sometimes my breathing is a lot more strained than it used to be. Although I do have a cold, which could be part of it, it's most likely that the cancer *is* progressing.

There is nothing in my situation that has changed. I know that I probably won't make it, still. But there is something different now about the way I look at things. I *feel* different. I feel inspired! I feel invigorated! I don't feel like I'm just sitting around waiting to die anymore. I feel infused with life. There's a reason I have already beaten the odds. There's a reason it's not time yet.

I don't know what came first—the changes to my daily routine, or the changes to my perspective. But somehow they're working together to be just what I needed. During the past week or so we've been making small changes to my medications since I've been doing so well. The first thing we did was drop the nausea medicine I'd been taking on a schedule with the pain medication. It turns out that I don't really need it at all, since I haven't had any nausea since. We also started weaning me off the steroid I'd been taking to control swelling, which makes me eat everything in sight and makes me swell up like a balloon. Somehow, and the only thing I can think to attribute it to, is that by getting rid of those two medications, I am feeling a little more like myself. I haven't had to take a nap in ages! My eyes, which had been blurry and unfocused, are doing so well that I finished a book that I was reading... on my Kindle! My computer screen no longer tries to flip letters around. But that's not all—a few days ago Mom convinced me to put my prosthetic leg on for a while. It didn't take too much cajoling, since it was something I'd been meaning to try since I have been feeling better. It doesn't quite fit right because I haven't worn it in a month. Right now because I haven't been wearing it, I have no leg muscle to even hardly hold it up. But I can kind of walk on it, with my crutches, and I have hope and faith that before long I'll be able to use it again for a short time. :)

I'm not sure where it came from, this sudden epiphany I've had. But something inside me has clicked. It reminds me of a story my pastor told me when he came by for a visit, about a man who was pronounced terminal. Another person asked him, "What are you doing right now?" And the man who was dying answered, "Well I'm terminal, I'm dying." The first man either asked him again what he was doing right now or informed him somehow that he was wrong.

The man who was terminal wasn't dying just then, just at that moment he was living. And as long as he was breathing he would be living. That's the epiphany I've had. Right now, regardless of the things to come, I'm living! I'm not sitting around waiting to die. My entire perspective has changed. I'm alive right now. I'm living.

So, today I leave you with this message, one that I can hardly believe that I went this far without. Cherish every single day. It is one of those things that is easier said than done. The way that something feels is all about perspective. Sometimes our hearts don't need a miracle. Sometimes there just aren't any miracles and the world around us feels like there can never be any happiness in it again. I know how that feels. I have had some dark days these last few months. I won't lie. It's difficult to know that eventually I won't feel good. It's hard to know that essentially I'm just sitting around waiting for the cancer to progress.

I can't think like that anymore. I have to think about the things that I can do. The life that I can live. I may not be able to go on the ski trip this month, but I'm still doing better than expected. I'm still here. I'm still living. Life is precious, whether you have a straight road stretched before you as far as the eye can see, or whether, like most people, your road turns and bends into the undergrowth and you have no idea where it leads. Follow that bend, and your heart, no matter where it goes. Mine may go on, to places unmentionable, but everyone's does, eventually. All roads lead to the same bend, and although we can't see around the corner, I know there are people who have gone before me that will help me when I get there. But for now, I'm not there yet. Today I'm living, and my heart sings with joy for the days that follow.

For anyone going through a difficult time, I want to pass on the list of ten steps that I composed. These steps have helped me move forward in the past. I'm not a professional and I have no claim to fame, but these steps have helped me and I want to share them with other people. Here are my Ten Steps to Moving Forward:

1. **Cry, Yell, and Grieve:** The first step can make you feel like you are

taking a few steps back, but it is necessary. I think when something happens that reroutes your entire life and the direction you were going previously, it is normal to grieve and be sad. Because I believe that whenever you go through a difficult time, it changes you. It changes the way you think and perceive things, and the first step to acceptance of the new reality, whatever it is, is to mourn the past and the person you used to be. So, let yourself grieve for as long as you need to, and when you're able, you'll find the next step.

2. **Talk When You're Ready:** Sometimes you feel like talking things through and sometimes you don't. When you're ready to talk, find someone who you can talk to as an equal and whose opinion you value, and pour your heart out. Sometimes, just having someone who cares and who is there for you, no matter what, gives you the boost you need, to move on from the first step (even though you may feel still the need to grieve from time to time).

3. **Escape When You Need To:** but not too often. Sometimes life just takes a dump on you, and your heart and mind are too full to process things in a healthy way. In these moments, escape is essential; watch a TV show or movie, read a book, or veg out on the Internet. Take a break from the things that are weighing you down, and come back to them later with a fresh outlook. But I caution you on escaping too often, because escaping never makes your problems go away, and you always have to deal with them eventually.

4. **Start Small:** If the big things are too overwhelming at any given moment, start small. Instead of worrying about a huge appointment next week that you're afraid might hold bad news (perhaps similar to where you just were) try to focus on smaller more attainable goals. Rather than brooding about the appointment, focus on your exercises, your chores, or even your homework assignments. You'll get there in the same amount of time, whether or not you worry about it.

5. **Find Your Muse:** Your muse is the source of your inspiration. Find the thing, or things, that inspire you the most, and absorb them into your world. These could be anything. For some, it could be their children, others music or nature, and for people like me, poetry or literature.

6. **Reach Out:** Interaction is an important thing in any person's life. Reaching out doesn't necessarily mean telling everyone about your struggles, rather it means finding people you enjoy, and spending time with them. It can mean laughing and teasing each other, but it also means support. Maybe not support like that of step two, but support that lets you know that they care and that they're thinking of you. This kind of support is a bulwark that can bolster you through any storm. These are the people who know how to cheer you on, when you're going through a hard time.

7. **Channel Your Nervous Energy:** Often you may find yourself stressing out and worrying. The best way to prevent this is to throw yourself headlong into another project, albeit a more relaxing one. For me, this usually means writing, scrapbooking, or artwork of some kind. I actually find that some of my best poetry is written when I'm trying not to freak out.

8. **Help Someone Else:** Helping someone else is actually a great way to help you deal with tough things that are going on your own life. It may sound selfish, in an ironic way. But not only does helping someone through their problems distract you, it also fills you with a pleasant satisfaction. Plain and simple; it feels good to help someone else out.

9. **Focus on the Good Things:** If you go through life with a "woe is me" attitude, things can seem harder than they really are. Granted, I'm finding that optimism comes more easily to me than most, but I cannot help but feel that some optimism is imperative

to dealing with any situation. By focusing on the good things in your life, you can muster up enough strength to hope. And I believe that hope is ultimately what allows you to move on.

10. **Take One Day At a Time:** We spend so much time worrying about things that are far in the future, that we miss the things that are happening in the moment. Even if the moment you are in seems difficult, and there are things on the horizon that seem even more difficult, it is important to focus on the moment you are in. We can't worry about things that haven't happened yet, or that may or may not happen. If you must worry, worry about the day you are in, and worry about tomorrow, well, tomorrow. But remember also, no matter what you're going through, that you will get through. No matter how hard it seems in that moment, or how bleak the future looks, time will move you forward against your will. Eventually you'll find that things don't seem as hard, or hurt as bad, and life will take on a new routine. And you'll be okay. Or... at least that's the way it's been for me.

~Angela Sayers

The Great Thanksgiving Challenge

I can no other answer make, but, thanks, and thanks.
~William Shakespeare

My friend Marilyn and I had just settled into a booth at our favorite coffee shop. "BookTalk is at my house next month," I said. "I hate getting ready for it."

"I know what you mean," Marilyn answered. "I spent a week cleaning when it was my turn in February, not to mention baking two cakes."

"Not to mention that it's all over in a couple of hours. All that work for two hours!"

Marilyn nodded as we sipped from steaming cups of latte.

"And if that's not bad enough," I said, wiping foam from my upper lip, "my entire family is coming for Thanksgiving this year. I love them dearly, but you know what that means?"

"Yep. Cooking and cleaning, changing sheets, wondering what to feed everybody for breakfast. I go through the same thing every year."

The chimes on the coffee shop door jingled and a bedraggled woman entered, carrying two super-sized shopping bags stuffed with odds and ends. Twists of gray hair escaped from the ratty scarf covering her head. Nothing she wore matched, and one black canvas high top had a hole at the big toe. As she passed us, it was evident she hadn't bathed in days.

"Would you listen to us?" I whispered, feeling ashamed of myself. "We sound like two ungrateful curmudgeons."

"That poor woman probably can't pay for a cup of coffee."

"Do you think she's homeless?" I asked.

Marilyn shrugged her shoulders. Then she grabbed her wallet, and headed for the counter where she paid for the woman's coffee and an apple fritter. The woman smiled, showing bad teeth. I heard Marilyn invite her to join us, but the woman shook her head and settled into a soft chair in a sunlit corner of the shop.

"That was nice," I said when Marilyn slid back into the booth.

She rolled her eyes. "That was guilt."

I nibbled a piece of chocolate biscotti. "You know something? Some days, all I do is complain."

"Me, too."

"Take BookTalk for instance. Those women are smart and funny. I'm honored they asked me to join the club. The last thing I should do is complain about having them come to my house for a few hours."

Marilyn glanced at the woman thumbing through a tattered *People* magazine. "I don't know why I always see the glass half empty when it's more than half full," she said.

"We should stop complaining—it's a bad habit." I said this with more conviction than I felt.

Marilyn set her cup down just as a megawatt smile broke over her face.

"What?" I asked.

When Marilyn gets that look, it always means some bold plan has taken hold of her brain—usually one that includes me.

"We'll give it up. Complaining. We'll give it up for Thanksgiving."

"You mean Lent. That's months away."

"No—I mean we'll stop complaining and start being thankful.

Just in time for Thanksgiving. It takes thirty days to drop a habit and thirty days to start a new one."

"So what's your plan?"

Marilyn leaned back and crossed her arms. "A challenge. We'll keep a diary. Write down every complaint. Then think of something to be thankful for, and write that down too."

"What if we can't think of something to be thankful for?"

Marilyn pointed to the old woman who had fallen asleep in her chair. "You can think of something."

"Then how will we know we're really keeping track? It would be easy to cheat."

Marilyn stuck out her little finger. Now it was my turn to roll my eyes. Pinky swear. We'd been doing it since junior high.

"Challenge accepted," I said.

Thanksgiving Day was a month and a half away. Could we really drop a bad habit by then? And replace it with a new one?

The next morning I poured my cereal and picked up the milk carton only to discover it was empty.

"I can't eat cereal without milk," I muttered. Then I caught myself, not believing the first words out of my mouth that day took the form of a complaint.

"Great," I said, talking to the cat. "Can't even start the day right."

And there it was: complaint number two.

"This is going to be harder than I thought," I said, searching the desk shelves for a notebook. "Why can't I ever find what I need when I need it?"

Welcome to my world, complaints three and four.

I grabbed the phone and dialed Marilyn's number.

"What's up?" she asked, way too perky for early morning.

"I've been awake fifteen minutes and all I've done is complain," I complained. "This is hard!"

"No kidding. Jim forgot to make the coffee last night—his job—and I had to wait ten minutes for the pot to brew."

"Did you write that down?"

Marilyn laughed. "Can't find a notebook."

"Neither can I!"

"Okay—quick—what are you thankful for?" she asked.

"I'm talking on the phone with my best friend and the cat is purring in my lap. What about you?"

"I'm drinking coffee in a warm kitchen and about to go work out," Marilyn answered. "See? This won't be so hard after all."

But it was hard. Hard to believe I complained so much about trivial things. Hard to believe I wasn't more thankful for my family, my friends, and my health. My mind kept wandering back to the homeless woman, and I caught myself saying little prayers for her.

BookTalk met at my house the first week of November. In preparation, I cleaned and cooked and complained. But I recorded the blessings, too: my husband cheerfully moved furniture to accommodate thirty women; the cheesecakes I baked were perfect; my friends in the book club complimented my beautiful home—and I realized they were right.

As weeks passed, I noticed my notebook recorded more blessings than complaints. Marilyn reported the same phenomenon. That's not to say we didn't complain—we did. Just not as much. Maybe the complaints dwindled because we realized we had so much to be thankful for.

The Monday after Thanksgiving, Marilyn and I met for coffee again, comparing stories of the holiday weekend and sharing what we'd written in the pages of our notebooks.

"It's interesting," Marilyn said. "I don't complain as much now. And when I do, the complaints sound more like problem statements than whining."

"I feel better about myself, too. And about life in general." I took a sip of creamy latte. "I guess we owe that homeless woman a bushel of gratitude, don't we?"

"Yeah," Marilyn said. "We sure do."

~Ruth Jones

Finding My Joy

Joy is a flower that blooms when you do.
~Author Unknown

I have a confession to make. I lose things all the time. You know my type. I'm the lady who drives out of the restaurant parking lot with her take-out on the roof of the car. The one who leaves the windows open during thunderstorms. The one who needs three duplicate sets of keys hidden in rocks and crevices all over her property.

By now I've even lost track of how many things I've lost.

I'd like to blame it on the fact that I'm a mom to six children. Or to pretend it's the stress of home-schooling that causes my forgetfulness. Plus, I've got the added responsibilities that come with being a pastor's wife. All good reasons, don't you think? But the truth is, I was this way long before we married, started a family, entered the ministry or taught the first home-school lesson.

If you ran into me on the street, you'd never guess I'm so scatterbrained. I can do a pretty good imitation of competence. But chances are I'm probably standing there doing a figurative head scratch while I ask myself the question: What was I doing again?

See what I mean? Even my train of thought gets lost.

People like me need a strategy for coping with such forgetfulness, and I've developed an excellent one, if I do say so myself. It's very simple. I never panic when something goes missing and I never look for it. My theory, however unscientific, is that it will turn up the minute I stop searching for it.

Library books, driver's license, car keys, cell phone, birth certificate, wallet, plane tickets—you name it, I've lost it. I've also found every single item, because eventually this stuff resurfaced. Granted, sometimes it took as long as three years, but still. I found the things I lost. Every time. Without fail.

My theory worked like a charm.

Until the day it didn't. That was the day I lost something and couldn't find it again.

I lost my joy.

As usual, I waited a while for it to return. But as the weeks passed, I began to panic. I wondered how long it would be before I felt happy again. In place of light, there was darkness. Anxiety rooted in my heart where contentment used to live.

As the weeks turned into long months, I struggled to ignore the depression that was bearing down and smothering me. I knew it was one of those things women may experience after childbirth, but my baby was six months old. Exercise, sunshine, even a trip to my doctor wasn't helping my heavy heart. Given that I used to look forward to each new day, this change was a hard pill to swallow.

I tried to grit my teeth and power through until the fog lifted and the burden eased. After all, everyone has bad days now and then, right? In the meantime, I spent a lot of time sitting on the bathroom floor, leaning against the tub and crying while the bath water ran.

I had to do something.

So I did the one thing I'd never done before, and went out in search of what I'd lost.

I started by closing my eyes and praying for joy. Only then did I begin to see where it had been hiding. It was first spotted in the pages of my Bible. Then later, I found it in the rocking chair with my baby in my lap, and even more when I felt my toddler's arms around my neck.

The fog began to lift. After that, when I learned how to say no, the clouds cleared and the sun came out. I realized my older children didn't have to be in organized sports if it meant extra stress. My seven-year-old could learn Spanish in high school as opposed to the first grade. The house didn't have to be perfectly clean. I could let go of the smaller things to gain much greater things.

Little by little, it came back.

Joy.

Contentment.

Peace.

And a truly grateful heart.

Of course, I still lose things all the time. Just the other day I lost a prescription on the way to get it filled, the dog's medication, and the check register.

I still use my old theory and say with a shrug, "Eh. It'll resurface eventually."

But I use my new theory, too. I search with eyes shut and hands folded in prayer.

Because if it's really something I need, I know God will bring it back to me.

~Debra Mayhew

My Own Happiness Project

Happiness is an attitude. We either make ourselves miserable,
or happy and strong. The amount of work is the same.
~Francesca Reigler

When you find yourself sobbing unexpectedly in a bookstore, you know something's wrong with your life.

I was snuggled into a puffy chair, focused on the book in my lap, Gretchen Rubin's *The Happiness Project*. It told the story of the author's yearlong journey to examine her life and make happiness-promoting changes recommended by scientists, philosophers, popular culture, and friends.

As I read the opening pages, I found myself nodding, relating to her ideas. She warned readers that her experience was unique, but I saw reflections of myself in her personality, her marriage style, and her interests. I read quickly and eagerly, thinking I could improve my life, too, and suddenly I was stirred by a long-forgotten feeling, hope.

When my husband and friend found me, I was a sniffling, emotional mess with tears soaking my cheeks. I was overwhelmed not only by a desire for change, but also the realization that I was ready to succeed. I pulled myself together and clutched the book possessively on my way to the checkout counter.

Over the next few weeks I savored the author's words, sometimes reading in bed or in a coffee shop, always with a pencil and paper nearby for notetaking. After I finished, I spent hours sitting at the desk in my study, designing my own happiness project. I considered what happiness meant to me and decided what behaviors to change or keep, how I would make that happen, and what attitudes I would cultivate. It looked like a lot to take on, but I had a plan. Getting more sleep, making time to relax with my husband, seeing my friends frequently—all these could be accomplished by better time management, right?

Not so fast. The moment I put my plan into action, I was immediately reminded that if it was all so easy, I'd have done it long ago. Sure, some changes were manageable, but I still only had twenty-four hours a day. If I wanted to expand time for my goals, I had to cut other priorities. How was I supposed to say no when everything was important?

Despite that struggle, life began to change—but not because I'd mastered time. I'll probably always wrestle with the clock. Instead things were looking up mainly because of two attitudes I embraced regardless of what was on my calendar: gratitude and presence.

Gratitude and I go way back. We're like old friends who rarely see each other but always click when they do. Years ago, I'd started a gratitude journal, recording little joys like mint mochas and scented lotion as well as thankfulness for life-defining things like good health and loving relationships. At first I wrote often, then less so as time passed. I didn't give gratitude much thought until years later, when major surgery reminded me how much I needed it. There was nothing like being mostly helpless for months to remind me to appreciate the things I still could do.

The lessons of that time never left me, but, just like my attention to the journal, they faded into the background as life directed my attention elsewhere. It was time for another reminder.

I was running through my gym's parking lot during a rainstorm, preoccupied as usual. As I entered the gym, the desk clerk asked how I was.

"I'm soaked," I complained. "It's pouring out there!"

Instead of commiserating, he asked me an unexpected question. "Do you like the rain?"

I was taken aback. Actually, I had always liked rain. I thought it was comforting, loved its sound, appreciated that it made everything so lushly green. Why was I complaining?

"Yeah, actually, I do," I said, feeling thankful he'd made me think about it. It was a simple moment, but it was an effective reminder that cultivating gratitude is like cultivating a friendship. The more effort I put into appreciating and acknowledging it, the more rewarded I feel.

To keep gratitude in my daily life, I started playing a game called "five things." I think of five things to be thankful for in the moment, with no generic answers allowed. Instead of "I'm grateful for my health," I'll say, "I'm grateful my leg feels well enough today to exercise." This game is particularly helpful when worry sidetracks me, such as when I'm driving home from my job, pointlessly dwelling on workday problems. To distract myself, I focus on five current things to be grateful for, for example, a project finished early, praise from my boss, a favorite song on the radio, a storybook-blue sky ideal for a late-afternoon walk, and the fact that my husband will be cooking his famously mouthwatering hamburgers that night.

Playing "five things," with its emphasis on what's right, right now, works well with its companion attitude—presence. It wasn't until I started making an effort to live in the moment that I realized how much time I'd spent fretting over past actions or worrying about future events. After struggling for years with anxiety, I was shocked to find that eliminating stress was often as simple as focusing on the present. You can't wander into traffic if you've stopped to smell the roses.

I discovered something delightful, too—like scissors cutting paper or rock crushing scissors, presence quashes worry. If I'm truly in the moment, I'm not worrying. I'm too busy taking action or having fun. If I start to worry, I can stop it by assigning a time to take the next step to solve the problem and then letting it go until it's time to act. If there's nothing I can do, I skip straight to letting it go. I've found it's not bad situations that sour my life, it's the related worrying that's most toxic.

I'm not saying I'm always happy. Interpreting my world through a prism of gratitude and presence takes practice, and sometimes I need reminders. Recently I was grumping around the house, knowing I should exercise but feeling uninspired. My right leg, which has periodically bothered me since my surgery, was aching.

"I need motivation help," I said to my husband, Frank, who had just gotten home from work. "Will you go on a walk with me?"

"I can't," he said. "My foot's hurting again, and I need to get off my feet."

I must have looked disappointed, because he glanced at me and said, "You look sad! You can't be sad! You're happy now, remember?"

I smiled at the fantasy that I could eliminate all unhappiness. Still, even as I complained that I'd been putting off exercise for days, and you can't just do that—sure you can, the King of the Couch argued—my perspective was changing. Frank's comment reminded me that point of view is a decision I make. With that reminder, I knew I was going to walk. I'd appreciate the fresh air, the cold, clear sky, and my ability to take each step through the neighborhood. As I put on my walking shoes and my winter coat, I felt better already. Grateful. Happy.

~Alaina Smith

The Color of Happiness

I would not waste my life in friction when it could be turned into momentum.
~Frances Willard

After nine years of indecisiveness, I finally decided to paint our home's entryway and hallway. At least, "indecisiveness" was the explanation I gave. But, looking around the other painted and decorated rooms of our home I finally realized there were many other reasons it took me so long to decide on a color for these supposedly welcoming areas of our home.

Moving away from my hometown with my new husband, I had entered our home—a blank slate at the time as we were its first owners—feeling overwhelmed by the fact that I knew no one in this new town and had no idea how I would decorate the three bedrooms, two bathrooms, kitchen, breakfast nook, and living room. I so badly wanted our house to feel like a home, but at that time, it all felt so foreign—marriage, living on my own for the first time, a puppy. I was so terribly homesick, that for a little while, I was convinced that we would move back to my hometown and away from this over-whelming house.

Yet, over the next couple of years, our bedroom was painted, as was the bathroom (twice), the breakfast nook and kitchen (also twice), and ultimately our firstborn's room. Our son's room was beautiful, with a light green cha ⬛ ⬛ s, jungle-themed bedding. His room was the ⬛ ⬛ the house. I always kept the entryway and hallway on my "to do" list, but our second baby (and beautiful room) and two jobs later, lack of time always seemed to be the excuse not to finish this project.

Over those years, my once close relationship with my parents cooled for a variety of reasons, their health began to decline, and their visits to my home became less frequent. The rejection stung, so to avoid feeling the pain of this loss, I busied myself with my children, housework, and other activities and put the entryway and hallway project on the back burner. It just seemed easier to do that than make a decision on paint—or to deal with my feelings.

After a couple of years, I realized I could no longer bury my feelings of rejection, hurt and loss, and sought the help of a counselor, who guided me through a process where I ultimately found happiness—and began to focus more inwardly on my own family, and less outwardly toward the family I once had.

And then one day, upon returning home from picking up my son from school, we walked into the house, and I realized how unwelcoming it looked to us—the white walls, the lack of pictures, and the lack of warm window coverings. It was as though—through the pain, rejection, depression and more—my feelings didn't allow me to take the final steps to making our house a home. It was as though I was waiting for my parents to tell me that they were planning to visit, and walk into that entryway again—which was the "perfect" excuse I was seeking to finally finish this project. But, my journey toward acceptance—accepting that my parents may never visit my home again, that I may never be fully accepted by them again, that my husband and children were the most important members of my family—finally revealed what I needed to do: paint away the past and look forward to a beautiful future with my family.

It seemed that my husband was just as excited about this final transition. He happily helped me paint over those white walls, removed the white blinds from the windows in preparation for warm colored curtains, and reveled in the transformation that our home underwent, with a simpl[e] — "Harvest Brown." It was then that I realized that it did[n't take me] nine years to decide on a color—it took me nine years to finally look inside my home for happiness, and not outside of it.

~Heather McGowan

The Lucky One

A daughter is the happy memories of the past,
the joyful moments of the present, and the hope and promise of the future.
~Author Unknown

Our daughter is a child of the Army. Her mother is an Army nurse; I am an Army lawyer—a "JAG" officer. Through three individual deployments to Afghanistan and Iraq I've learned that our greatest path to happiness is the unifying joy of our five-year-old, who over the course of many trials and separations continues to redeem us—she is what makes us lucky.

Emma was born in January 2006, during a bitterly cold upstate New York winter, ten days before I deployed to Afghanistan. Five months later her mother was deployed there also. Emma landed, like so many other military children, with her grandparents, the youngest resident of the Bethany Village retirement community in Mechanicsburg, Pennsylvania, the ward of my eighty-six-year-old father and seventy-seven-year-old mother. She became one of the community's most popular residents, the instant delight of grandmothers and grandfathers alike, who are drawn to the youth and smiles of a five-month-old.

It is difficult to articulate the all-consuming guilt a parent feels when leaving an infant behind. It was particularly hard on her mother. Of course we chose this life, despite its inconveniences and separations, out of a genuine belief that military service was something that mattered—to be part of the large moral reserve where values like sacrifice, honor, selflessness, and integrity still matter. Our fidelity to those values would be dearly tested. If you have ever left a baby behind for a combat zone... well, it just isn't easy.

I returned from Bagram and Kandahar eight months later to reclaim a child I hardly knew, and was arguably unqualified to care for without some sort of adult supervision. It was Emma, me, and two Wheaten Terriers, 370 miles from the nearest family member. I will forever be grateful for the support from my boss's wife who graciously checked in, providing advice such as not to feed hot dogs to an eight-month-old, and otherwise made sure I didn't do anything shockingly stupid.

And yet, despite the endless days, the bottles and diapers, the lost weekends and sleepless nights, missed meetings and a worn-out BlackBerry, I ended each long day feeling as though something meaningful had happened between Emma and me. We survived, we thrived, and we would wake up the next morning to do it all over again. In truth, I felt almost indescribably lucky for the time alone with her.

So each night from those days forward, while we awaited her mother's return from Afghanistan the following year, I would look down in utter amazement at this gorgeous daughter of mine and quietly ask her, "Why am I lucky?" And then I would softly answer, "Because I have you." I had Emma. Mom was a world away. The family was a day's drive away. In the cold and snowy Watertown winter of 2006-2007 it was just the two of us and the dogs. Looking back it was one of the most indelibly memorable periods of my life.

Over time, as Emma learned to talk, she gradually picked up the refrain. I still remember the exact moment, lying in bed after *Click Clack Moo* and *If You Give a Mouse a Cookie*, that she rolled over and said, "Dad, you're lucky because you have me." Indeed I was.

It has been, and I am ever prayerful that it will always be, one of the heartfelt narratives of our relationship: the simple but sublime acknowledgement that I am fortunate because of the blessing of my daughter in my life and her awareness of how I feel about us; what we had, and what we shall always have.

I am lucky because throughout the preschool age of princesses she always allowed me to be her prince; she would dress up in a rotating collection of about a dozen dresses, glass slippers and all, and we would dance through the house as she sang theme songs from *Beauty and the Beast* and *Cinderella* with joyous abandon.

I am lucky because Emma inspires and fortifies me to be more than I am: a window on a world I never fully imagined before she came into my life. In the early days when it was just the two of us, and ever since, I wake up early as much for her as for myself. Fatherhood brought a new imperative to support and provide and make something of this life so she can be proud. She is the high school coach we all ran an extra mile for because the victories were for him as much as us—a coach in size 3 slippers and a Hello Kitty nightgown with a laugh that melts whatever egocentricities remain in her father.

I am lucky because she unifies us as a family. Emma is the connective tissue that brings purpose to the sometimes tumultuous rhythm of our lives. She reinforces the relationship that brought her into the world, sustains it with meaning, and focuses it on the future.

On about her fourth birthday the old refrain added a new line. "Why am I lucky?" I would ask. "Because you have me," she quietly responded. Then to my surprise came the question, "Dad, why am I lucky?"

"I don't know sugar bear, why?"

"Because I have you, Dad. Because I have all of you."

But the lucky one... the really, truly, lucky recipient of the magic that is our father/daughter love affair, is me. She is the lantern that guides my feet along the path of happiness. One day she will find that prince and hopefully know the utter joy of little fingers wrapped tightly around her own hand. And the magic will continue through her. Lucky until the end.

~Colonel George R. Smawley

The Happy Book

Every day may not be good, but there's something good in every day.
~Author Unknown

I've spent a lot of my life unhappy. Looking back there were times that it was okay to feel that way, for example when my parents got divorced, when I was mugged at gunpoint during a vacation, when two friends died in a car accident when I was in high school, and when I was brutally assaulted in my early twenties.

But there were the other times, too. In middle school I didn't think that I was as smart as everyone else; I didn't have cool enough clothes; my mother dropped me off at school in a beat-up car. Junior high was the same. I wasn't as tall and thin as all the other girls; my baby teeth hadn't fallen out yet; and where were my boobs? Fast forward to high school. Still the boys had eyes for others; still everyone was smarter; still everyone dressed better. Yes, my boobs had finally arrived, but somehow that paled in comparison to everything else. In my first job out of college I wasn't making as much money as my friends; my apartment wasn't as nice; when I looked around there was always something to feel miserable about.

I come from a long line of people who have suffered from diagnosable depression. When I was single, I assumed that was just who I was—it was the genes I had been dealt.

When I was twenty-four I met my husband. We got married three years later, and three years after that I had my first child.

Once we had kids, my excuse of "it's-in-the-genes" didn't work so well for me anymore because that meant my kids were going to be depressed. And although I realize that that still might be the case, I began looking at my unhappiness in a new way.

It was something I had to work on myself.

Over the years many things have helped me fight depression: healthy eating, exercise, fresh air, friends, volunteering, church, therapy and medicine. It all helps.

But I have a little secret, too.

It's an exercise that I do every night before bed. By the side of my bed I have a small datebook. It covers January to December, but it's small—every day only has enough space to write one line.

Every night I ask myself this question: "What made me the happiest today?"

Because I don't have space to write very much it seems easy, and it only takes me a few seconds. But in those seconds I replay my day and decide on its happiest moment. Some days I come up with answers I expect, and other days I find myself surprised.

Some days it's: "my husband came home early," "reading before bed with the kids," "laughing with a friend on the phone," "getting a parking space when I was late... right in front!"

And some days aren't as easy and it's: "finally getting to get into bed," "being able to stay calm during a fight with my daughter," "not having to cook dinner—again."

But the spin on my life has changed. I actively seek the positive. Every day.

And sometimes, if I have a sour day, I look back through the book, read, and remember those happy moments in the past.

In fact, I wish I had started my happy book back in middle school. Entries might have been: "I don't need braces like everyone else," "I caught Charlie S. looking at me today," and "I didn't trip when I went up on stage to receive my Most Improved Player award."

~Jennifer Quasha

Asperger's and Friendship

A friend is someone who understands your past, believes in your future,
and accepts you just the way you are.
~Author Unknown

As far back as I can remember I was the odd one out at school and for me it meant a lack of friends. However, those who were willing to be my friends tried to help me, and I had a core group of friends who stuck with me through the storms of elementary, junior high and high school.

When I was diagnosed with Asperger's syndrome in the ninth grade, I was told that I would have to go to a special school for autistic kids. My resource teacher at that time said it would be a bad idea, and then he asked me if it was okay for him to talk to my class about my diagnosis. For those who do not know what Asperger's syndrome is, it is a high functioning form of autism characterized by a special interest, sensory integration dysfunction, lack of social skills, communications, and executive function.

I thought we were giving them more ammunition with which to tease me. Well, I was mistaken. Instead, they rallied around me, teaching me what was socially acceptable and how to study better.

I wound up being on the Academic Decathlon team for three

years; in my senior year I was team captain. I helped lead the team to Most Improved and received the Most Inspirational Participant award. But I will never forget the high point of senior year—I was asked to be a starting player at the senior alum game; when I went on court my peers started to stamp their feet and call out my name. The game was slowed down, and I was passed the ball. When I missed the first shot, my peers stamped harder and called my name louder. I landed the second shot and scored two points. I will never forget the cheering of my peers. I was voted MVP even though I had scored only two points.

When I moved on to college I found another group of friends at the University of La Verne and these friends have been with me now for five years. I will never forget their kindness. As an Aspie, I don't deal well with surprises; I need to rehearse possible scenarios. But on my twenty-second birthday my university friends decorated the door and hallway of my dorm. I was overcome by the surprise, but surprisingly, I didn't have a meltdown from the surprise! They surprised me again on my twenty-fourth birthday.

But the real moment I found happiness, and really understood what was meant by happiness and friendship, was yesterday—April 9, 2011. It was a joint birthday party for me, my cousin who I call my big sister, and her sister's boyfriend. I had invited thirteen people and only five showed up, but the five that came included an old friend from elementary school, a friend and mentor from high school, and two friends from the university. I was nervous and scared because I had no idea what to expect, but when the party was over I had received a true gift. I realized what makes me happy and stronger is having a large group of friends. Just having a friend is highly unusual for someone with Asperger's, but I have a large support group: a core of five friends that have stayed in contact since elementary school; a group from secondary school, and now friends from the university.

I have two other friends with the same diagnosis and they don't have friends like I do—friends who support me, who guide me, and who are not afraid to tell me when I have done something incorrectly. My friends make me happy, and they make my life worth living—because I am rich in friends.

~Richard Nakai

Happiness Is Being a Parent

Happiness often sneaks in through a door you didn't know you left open.
~John Barrymore

The thing that stood out about my family was the fighting. My mother was a fierce, volatile, and determined woman who insisted on being right. When I was five, she left my father in Hong Kong and brought me to the U.S. to start a new life. My stepfather was so emotionally wounded as a child that he lied about his age to join the Navy in order to escape his family. He dealt with his pain by plunging himself into a sea of alcohol. While growing up, I witnessed these two in knockdown, drag-outs that made the Ali/ Frazier bouts seem like polite tea parties.

I learned from my family that I shouldn't have kids; I didn't have a clue how to be a parent. My mother and stepfather showed me the devastation two people could inflict on each other, and the thought of doing that to my children scared the hell out of me. Besides, who needed that kind of responsibility? So I bailed on the whole concept of being a parent. Deep down, I was afraid I'd be a miserable failure in the most important role anyone could undertake—raising a child.

My wife, Quyen, and I dated two years before getting married. Throughout the course of our relationship, I told her I didn't want to be a father, and she never tried to change my mind. Still, I understood her desire to be a mother. She came from Vietnam and lived through the horror of the Vietnam War. In the aftermath, her family lost their home, the restaurant business that supported them, and all their possessions to the Communist government. All they had left was each other.

Quyen grew up in a family of eight children and helped take care of her siblings. She cherished the role. Her dream in coming to America was to start a family so she could raise her own kids, yet she still married me knowing my stand on being a parent. This thought always leaves me humbled beyond words.

I remember the day my life changed. Quyen and I attended a friend's party. Among the guests happened to be a couple with a baby boy. When my wife caught sight of him, she lit up like the angel atop a Christmas tree. She asked to hold the infant and gently cradled him, her expression of unadulterated joy readily apparent at the bundle of life gurgling in her arms.

Quyen stayed with the baby as his parents mingled, and I marveled at how he gazed into her eyes while she sang lullabies. She dabbed dribble from his mouth with a Kleenex. When he cried, she retrieved a bottle from his mom, fed him, and patted his back until he burped. My wife was utterly enraptured. I watched her slowly rock the baby to sleep, his head nestled upon her shoulder like a kitten on its mother's belly.

I made a decision that night; I would be a father. I still didn't trust myself to do it right, but I knew Quyen would more than make up for my shortcomings. When we arrived home after the party, I conveyed this to Quyen, and let's just say a child's first glimpse of Disneyland wouldn't have held a candle to the radiance bursting forth from my wife. She pulled me to her and cried the kind of deep, sobbing tears that well up from the core of your being when you experience something that truly matters.

After a time, Quyen clasped my hands as if to impart meaning through her touch. Then she looked at me with an unwavering smile. The sureness in her eyes communicated to me before she spoke. "You're going to be a great father," she said.

Today, we are blessed to have ten-year-old Kevin and seven-year-old Kristie in our lives. We named our son after Kevin Costner because Quyen and I loved *Dances with Wolves*. Kristi Yamaguchi's grace and artistry on the ice gave us the inspiration for our daughter's name.

Kevin can spend hours on his Nintendo DS Lite, Wii, or anything video game related. Quyen and I have to set strict guidelines or he'd be playing 24/7. He's a chatterbox who can't get enough company. His favorite food is Kirkland macaroni and cheese. He is so sensitive that his eyes tear up when his cousin from Hawaii departs after staying with us for a week.

Once, Quyen and I were discussing our ideal careers at the dinner table and I asked Kevin what he wanted to be when he grows up. My son thought for a moment before proclaiming in complete earnestness, "I want to be a free man. That way I can stay home and play games with my kids all the time."

Kristie snuggles next to me as I read her children's books. She unleashes a lilting medley of exasperation if I don't tell her a bedtime story every night. She teases me by pretending to fall asleep in the car whenever we are driving home from Costco. Her favorite food is microwaved chicken nuggets. When I'm feeling down, she somehow senses it and spends time with me. My funk immediately disappears.

Kristie asked me a question last week. "Daddy, there's a Father's Day and a Mother's Day. How come we don't have a Kid's Day?"

To say my children mean the universe to me is an understatement. Put simply, they give my life a purpose and I thank the heavens each and every day for the two most precious gifts a father could ever receive.

~Ray M. Wong

Happy New Year

Patience is the ability to count down before you blast off.
~Author Unknown

There they were. Two pink lines... on my home pregnancy test. It was confirmed: I was pregnant. This wasn't exactly news I could sit on, despite the fact that it was a quarter past six in the morning. I had initially ventured into the bathroom to take a closer look at our humidifier, which appeared to be on the blink.

I padded back to bed with bare feet, crawled across the bed, and nudged my husband, Scott, who was snoring and motionless under more than his fair share of the comforter.

"Babe," I began, prodding him relentlessly, "two things: the humidifier is indeed broken..."

Not surprisingly, this declaration didn't elicit a response.

"...and we're pregnant," I finished.

That one, however, did the trick.

Scott awoke with a start and switched on the lamp, his eyes wide and inquisitive. "Really?" And then his mouth formed into a large smile.

I proudly scurried back to the bathroom to produce the evidence, brought it to the bedroom, and showed Scott.

His smile cooled. "The line is... really light," he said with a hint of disbelief.

"Light still means pregnant," I replied in my best I-am-too-pregnant tone.

"Hmmm, I don't know," he said, planting a hint of doubt inside my own head.

Cut to the office of our family doctor two hours later. Scott had an appointment for a routine check-up, and he had goaded me into coming along so that the nurse, Sherry, could give me a blood test.

"Exciting!" Sherry exclaimed as she withdrew the needle from my arm. "I'm off tomorrow, so the next time I talk to you, maybe…" her voice trailed off into a roller coaster of anticipatory squeals. "This is going to the lab today. Call back tomorrow morning. The results will definitely be in by 10 a.m."

But they weren't. I checked. Twice. Then I spent an inordinate amount of time pondering what could have possibly come between my test results and their timely—promised!—delivery to my doctor's office. Not knowing was doing a number on my already shaky conviction.

Maybe I wasn't pregnant.

That day, my yoga practice saved me from was-I-or-wasn't-I limbo. I deliberately lost myself in an invigorating self-practice at home, and then I drove to a friend's home to teach her privately. This brought me back down to earth, and the benefits were twofold: It was preparation for the upcoming final exam in my yoga instructor training program, and it served to calm my nerves by reminding me to live in the moment. This moment.

The next day, New Year's Eve to be exact, I tried the doctor's office again. I was equipped with a level head, but my breath caught in my throat when an unfamiliar, albeit chipper, female voice filtered through the line. "Good morning, how may I help you?"

"Yes, my name is Courtney Conover, and I'm calling to obtain the results of my pregnancy test," I said, the rising intonation of my voice surely disclosing my hopefulness.

"Please hold."

It had been a full forty-eight hours. The results had to be there. As I held the phone, a parade of never-before-experienced milestones ran through my head: What I would look like with a swollen belly;

Scott and I bringing our baby home from the hospital; our child opening presents on Christmas morning.

And then the proverbial needle scratched the record.

"Hi, Courtney? Um, yeah, well, the results are here... but we can't give them to you. You see, the doctor must be in to verify them, and he won't be back until Monday. Sorry."

I had hit the nadir. My stomach gave a lurch and then immediately began turning about as if on spin cycle. This couldn't be. Wasn't it inhumane to expect a possibly pregnant woman to remain in left field about her status? On New Year's Eve of all days? I wanted to proclaim this—no, shout it—but an imperfect combination of shock and outrage choked back my words. I hung up.

Frustrated and nearly incoherent, I then dialed Scott at work. Scott, bless his heart, calmed me down and said that he'd call the doctor's office to see what on earth could be done.

In the meantime, I had to get my act together so that I could go to work myself: I was bringing my mother along to a burning bowl ceremony I was covering for my weekly column, and it was set to start in thirty minutes.

Consider the irony: I fancied myself a positive thinker; I was this close to becoming a yoga teacher so that I could help others live healthier, more peaceful lives; and I was en route to a burning bowl ceremony, a ritual that encouraged people to let go of old, unproductive thought patterns in order to make room for useful, promising ones. Yet here I was, fit to be tied over something beyond my control—despite having so many blessings in my life.

And the cherry on top?

There was still a chance that I could have been pregnant.

I spent the next three hours among a wonderful group of men and women who wanted nothing more than to make 2011 bigger, better—happier—than the year that preceded it. The moderator gave us two sheets of paper, one for writing down things we wanted to release and another for writing down what we wanted to attract into our lives. It was a powerful exercise, one that shed enormous light on all that I already had to be thankful for: my health; a loving husband; a supportive mother; the ability to pursue my passion as a writer. My list, admittedly, was rather long. If that wasn't reason enough to be happy in the new year, I didn't know what was.

Still, I could think of something I needed to let go: My fervent desire for things to always go the way I wanted.

I consider it more than coincidence that my day started looking up after the ceremony. As soon as my mother and I entered my car, my cell phone's voicemail alert chimed; it was Scott. I felt a frisson of excitement as I called him back. Maybe—just maybe—he had some news.

He did: I was pregnant.

Scott had somehow contacted Sherry, who had somehow reached the doctor so that he could give the aforementioned clearance.

So, there, on a rainy New Year's Eve, in the parking lot of the burning bowl ceremony, with my mother by my side and my husband on the phone, I learned that I was expecting my first child.

At that moment, absolutely nothing else mattered.

Talk about putting the happy in Happy New Year.

~Courtney Conover

Happiness—
A Study in Contrasts

Happiness and sadness run parallel to each other.
When one takes a rest, the other one tends to take up the slack.
~Hazelmarie "Mattie" Elliott

In the early morning hours, I like to sit at the bay window in my kitchen and watch as the first rays of sunshine creep across the field behind my home. I love the contrast between the shadows and the startlingly clear patches of sunlight. It seems as if the sunshine is made brighter and clearer because of the stark difference between the light and dark.

Sitting there, I can't help but reflect that the same is true in my own life. Those times when I have been most happy have usually occurred after a trial or challenge experienced by me or a member of my family.

When my son, who has fragile X syndrome, was young, he was unable to tie his own shoelaces. No matter how hard he tried, the laces would always slide away like Jell-O through a baby's fist.

I feverishly sought alternatives. We created our own set of flexible laces from sewing elastic. These would allow us to stretch back the tongue of his shoe and then slide in his foot. But young boys lead adventurous lives. Puddles of mud, piles of snow and backyard sand often left the laces dirty, limp and stretched out of shape, needing frequent replacement.

When shoes with Velcro tabs came onto the market, I celebrated. Here was our answer! This sticky wonder solved our dilemma—that is until shoes with Velcro lost their coolness and were not produced for a time.

While other mothers were worrying about what college their sons would attend one day or whether they would find a nice girl to marry, I was worried about my son's shoelaces. My recurring nightmare was seeing my son as a fifty-year-old man still unable to form the necessary bows, his shoelaces flapping behind him as he walked. Irrational? Yes. But the mind and heart of a mother with children with special needs is not always a rational thing.

And then, finally, one day, when my son was seventeen, I heard the front door bang as he came running into the house. On his face, he wore an ear-to-ear triumphant grin. "I did it," he said.

"Did what," I asked.

"I tied my shoes."

We cried, rejoiced, and applauded with joy as he tied his laces over and over for us. Looking back, I can see that the joy of that moment was magnified because of his earlier struggles.

Happiness doesn't always fall casually into our lives. It isn't something that can be purchased at a store. Quite often it is experienced the most profoundly when it follows challenging experiences. I believe that true happiness, and its even purer form, joy, is found in simple blessings—sometimes something as simple as tying a pair of shoelaces.

~Jeannie Lancaster

Find Your Happiness

Back to Basics

Life is really simple, but we insist on making it complicated.

~Confucius

The Tent

We tend to forget that happiness doesn't come as a result of getting something we don't have, but rather of recognizing and appreciating what we do have.
~Friedrich Koenig

Water hit me in the face and trickled down my shirt. "We've been attacked by munchkins!" I hollered at my husband as I ran after our five-year-old son and three-year-old daughter. We were a family armed with water guns and giggles, and somehow the kids always got their best shots on me. My mom's eyes crinkled with delight as she watched us play while cradling our infant son.

"Lindy," she said, "you and Tom are more like older siblings to your kids than parents." This was an observation, not a criticism and Tom and I received her words like a badge of honor. We didn't take life as seriously as we probably should have. Our marriage was easy and our children a delight. We let the kids stomp in rain puddles and stay up too late. We felt we had been given this amazing gift of three little personalities and we were privileged to know these beings before anyone else. It was like we were harboring three beautiful secrets that we would introduce to the world one day.

When Tom and I married we knew we wanted to have kids and experience America. We had our own design business and could set up shop anywhere, so we did. We lived in some of the best tourist spots in the country. We lived in Atlanta, Georgia through its gorgeous spring months. We enjoyed Colorado's delightful year-round climate.

For a time we lived in a two-story farmhouse, rich in character, on a pumpkin farm in Illinois and helped with several harvests. In the Northwest we chose to live in a little fishing village in the shadow of Mount Rainier. Later we moved to Montana where we were literally surrounded by mountains and taught our kids how to ski. The houses in which we resided varied widely. One was expansive with all the amenities, while another was a little duplex in desperate need of repair. Each one enriched our lives differently, but none as much as when we lived in the tent.

"The tent." Whenever I say those words my husband smiles knowingly. That was the one place in which we did not choose to reside. Tom and I had been living in the most impressive house we had ever rented. It was a two-story in Washington State with picture windows all the way up to the vaulted ceiling. We had bedrooms enough for everyone plus a writing room and a room for me to do my illustration work. The windows looked out on a lush, green meadow bordered by tall pines. We were often surprised by deer that were curious enough to peek into our family room window. We would have stayed there forever if it hadn't been so wonderful.

Now, we like wonderful. We like amenities and everything that this house had to offer, but so did the realtors, and because they liked it so much they were able to sell it right out from under us.

Although this complicated our lives and added to our expenses with deposits and moving costs, we were not worried. We had one really good design client. This company not only kept our bills paid, but also took the majority of our design time. They had us create newsletters, brochures and advertising pieces. We hadn't needed to pursue other clients, so we didn't. That, however, turned out to be a mistake.

The same week that we got the call that we had thirty days to move out of our house, we also got the call from our one and only client. He told us he had hired in-house designers and would no longer need our services.

Difficult circumstances, but not insurmountable. We planned to get in the car and hunt for a new place and new clients. That is when the final blow came. Literally! Our car's engine blew up and we were done. We were thirty-four years old, had three kids and found ourselves without a car, without a job and without a home.

As we had always done before, Tom and I put our heads together and brainstormed survival plans. We borrowed a beater pick-up truck from his brother-in-law and when the deadline came for us to be out of the house, we moved most of our belongings into a storage unit. We had still not found a place to rent so we took our tent and our sleeping bags and a few changes of clothes to a state park and set up camp. The kids were delighted! We had been on many adventures with them and this was just one more, but not for me.

The tent was meant to be a weeklong stopgap measure, but new work and another house were not forthcoming. The reality of being without a home was setting in and I began to feel fear and frustration. We weren't camping, we were surviving, and as the days rolled on with no income, our checking account dwindled. The prospect of having the required deposit and first month's rent to get into a new place was fast diminishing.

My husband began each day by driving to his office in town to buy a newspaper and searching for housing and jobs. Daily I shook out sleeping bags and amused the kids with nature walks and berry picking. My job was to keep them happy while I hid my own fear of the future. As long as the weather stayed warm we could continue this way, but early fall frosts were not far off. The days of no work and no house turned into weeks of anxiety.

One night when the three children were asleep in their bags, Tom and I talked quietly about our worries. I was feeling the full burden of our homeless and jobless situation and could not stop the tears from rolling down my face. Tom rubbed my shoulders and leaned in close. "We are the most blessed of people, you know," he said softly. I looked at him incredulously.

"What do you mean?" I sobbed. "We have nothing!"

Then he gently replied, "Honey, we have everything that matters right here. We have the kids, we have a roof over our heads, and we have each other."

It seemed so simple—too simple—but I knew he was right. I told him, "If anyone heard you say that they would think you had lost your mind!" We began to chuckle and then we began to laugh! We laughed and hugged until our tears of desperation turned into tears of tenderness.

We lived thirty-three days without a home that year. Miraculously, the landlord of a duplex trusted us to move in without having a dime of deposit to give her. Since that summer we have moved less often, and made contingency plans for unexpected hardships, but we have never forgotten our days in the tent. That was where my husband and I became grown-ups in our hope, in our faith and in our love. We make a point to vacation in the tent every summer just for pleasure. It is there that we remember we have everything that matters.

~Lindy Schneider

True Contentment

I like to walk about among the beautiful things that adorn the world;
but private wealth I should decline, or any sort of personal possessions,
because they would take away my liberty.
~George Santayana

He called himself a permanent camper—not homeless, not a bum. His living and working arrangements were by choice, not circumstances. He didn't use drugs, he wasn't an alcoholic, and he didn't take handouts.

The man had prosperous siblings who had urged him to return to his home state, take their money, and maybe even establish his own business. But he didn't like the strings attached to the arrangement, and besides, he'd left home thirty years earlier specifically because of his family. So instead of pursuing a college education like his brothers, or becoming a corporate workaholic like his dad, the Permanent Camper opted for his own free style of living. When just a teen, he began wandering until he eventually settled in the woods located in Central Florida. For the next thirteen years, his dwelling arrangement remained tucked out of sight, and he survived by working odd jobs as needed.

Somewhere along the line, the Permanent Camper and my husband became friends. Maybe it was the Permanent Camper's work ethic and abilities or maybe it was the intelligent dialogue that attracted them to each other. I'm sure the Permanent Camper's lifestyle and reduced responsibilities appealed to my husband. And the

Permanent Camper's experiences, which ranged from living with the Navaho Indians to becoming a chess champion, certainly provided fuel for conversation.

As a result, the Permanent Camper frequently visited our home, often helping my husband with yard work (the camper knew all about irrigation systems), or organizing the garage (the camper worked twice as fast as my husband), or hanging Christmas lights (the camper was younger and more agile). Following the work projects, the two would sit in the driveway and chat over a cold drink, or come inside to watch some sports event.

Over time, the Permanent Camper joined in on family activities—dinners, movie night, holidays. Our grandkids enjoyed playing Frisbee with him, and he showed our granddaughter how to bead. It was following one such family activity that the Permanent Camper reminded me of an important life principle. Until that time, I'd not envied him.

We sat in the living room watching a football game and enjoying a variety of finger foods. The camper leaned back in his chair and patted his stomach. "I never imagined having so much in life," he said.

I know I must have looked at him with a perplexed expression. He continued. "I have no wants and my life overflows with blessings. God has given me more opportunities and relationships than I ever imagined I'd have."

I was flabbergasted. His heart was full of joy and gratitude. This man who lived in a tent, read by candlelight, rode a bike to get around, showered behind gas stations and shopping strips, was totally content with life. He had all he needed or really cared for: his own "home," practical education from hands-on experience as well as knowledge from his extensive reading, opportunities to play in chess tournaments, and fellowship with good friends. "Things" mattered little to him, and he was satisfied with twenty-five-cent T-shirts from the thrift store or inexpensive fast foods. He actually preferred sleeping in his own tent rather than spending the night in a friend's house, and he didn't mind walking or biking miles to a destination.

I seldom heard the Permanent Camper complain. If he did, it was mainly about politics or the "bums" who expected others to provide for them rather than making every effort to be self-sufficient—like him.

I had so much to be thankful for, but too often, I worried instead of expressing my gratitude. I was always trying to gain more, rather than being satisfied and content with what I had. But I had to admit, sometimes I'd felt the same way as the camper—my heart full of joy and gratitude because God had provided more than I could ever imagine.

From that moment on, I saw the Permanent Camper through different eyes. I accepted his hippy-style appearance, his life preferences—and his worthiness. And now, he's not just my husband's handyman or friend. For me, the Permanent Camper has become family.

~Georgia Bruton

An Eight-Hour Drive

Simplicity is making the journey of this life with just baggage enough.
~Author Unknown

ne would think it impossible to eventually derive happiness from a death... especially a death of catastrophic proportions. I will never forget the Thursday night I received a call saying that my dad had committed suicide.

I was devastated. Evidently, the man who had labored for forty-one years to overcome so many obstacles had finally admitted defeat.

Early the next morning, I left my home in Virginia for the eight-hour drive back to my boyhood home in Ohio. During such a mind-numbing trip, the brain screams through a roller coaster of emotions. Of all those differing lows, I felt anger the most. Part of me was so mad at Dad for just tossing in the towel like that. Was this the same former Marine who had taught me to never quit? Secondly, part of me was so angry at Dad for the way that his selfish suicide had wronged my mom. She had given my dad too many loving, devoted, and submissive years to deserve such a tragedy. She was far too young to spend the rest of her life alone.

As I continued the drive, I began adjusting my attitude about my own life. As a boy, I had watched my dad build a successful heating and air conditioning business completely from scratch. His persistent drive, stubborn ambition, and tireless work ethic were truly exemplary to me. Thus, I embraced those traits and went into the Marine

Corps. But now as a man, I doubted if those attributes really paid off.

By the time I hit West Virginia, I began seeing my life in a whole new light. I had always seen so much of myself in Dad — and now that scared me. Was my own relentless drive and blind ambition leading me down the same path? I needed to step back, take a breath, and pursue a simpler lifestyle.

Thus, as I crossed the Ohio River, I experienced an epiphany about my own life. I had always thought that — in five years — I would retire from the Marine Corps, return to Ohio, and run for Congress. From there I was going to be a one-man dynamo and climb the political ladder to eventually become a Senator. But now I was saying, "Why bother?" Dad's suicide had completely taken the wind out of my sails.

Later that day, I arrived home to the hugs and kisses of my family.

That Saturday the first viewing of my dad's body was held at a local funeral home. The number of people who attended that viewing was a real testament to the caliber of man that my dad was. The line stretched out the front door of the funeral home and all the way down the block to the corner.

At that viewing, I was proudly decked out in my Marine Corps Dress Blues uniform. I wanted to look like the pillar of strength that I felt my family needed. When it was my turn to view the body, I stood over the casket and stared down at my dad. I stroked his cheek and rubbed his shoulder — after saying a silent prayer that begged the question "Why?"

Then I answered my own question. I honestly believed that Dad had driven himself to death. I vowed to be happy and not let that happen to me.

My family held two more viewings on Sunday. Again wearing my Dress Blues, I was the next-to-last person to view Dad's body at the end of the second viewing. Obviously, Mom was last.

Before allowing Mom to step to the coffin, I placed my head upon my dad's chest and cried, praying to God that He forgive my dad for taking his own life. Dad really was a great man, and didn't deserve to rot in Hell for one mistake.

Then I replaced the prayer with yesterday's promise. Again I vowed to be happy, and not make the same mistake.

After Mom viewed the body, they closed the coffin.

Dad's funeral Mass was held at ten o'clock on Monday morning. After his burial, a luncheon was held at the local Knights of Columbus hall, where my dad had been a loyal, dutiful member.

Then my family returned home and went mushroom hunting in the woods—because that's what Dad would've done on such a gorgeous spring afternoon. That night, we sat around a fire in our backyard and simply talked. Dad loved fires too.

I returned to Virginia that Wednesday and resumed my life.

Fifteen years later, I retired from the Marine Corps in Beaufort, South Carolina. But I didn't return to Ohio and pursue a career in politics. Instead, I remained on Hilton Head Island and took up a writer's simpler lifestyle.

I'm happy.

~John M. Scanlan

A Miracle

Pleasure is very seldom found where it is sought.
Our brightest blazes are commonly kindled by unexpected sparks.
~Samuel Johnson

A miracle has occurred in my life. One of many that have occurred in my sixty years. Some I am aware of and others wove their way into my existence so quietly that I hardly noticed, until looking back years later. This one started eleven years ago and as I look back I realize our ability to hear the intuitive whispers and step out into the unknown was a major factor.

My husband and I were semi-retiring. He owned a pest control business and I taught African drumming. Our children were grown with lives of their own. We were living in a tiny home in Seattle, our family's home for the past twenty-five years. We had remodeled our house while raising our kids and had decided that it would be a perfect size for two semi-retired adults. The house was minutes from all the amenities: malls, theater, Mariners baseball, and restaurants.

On past vacations to wilderness and rural areas of the United States, I had often wondered what it would be like to live in a remote area, so different from our own lifestyle. I didn't think I could live so far removed from civilization, but felt it must be very peaceful.

In 1999 my father-in-law passed away, leaving us his rambler in Wilkeson, an hour away from us. Wilkeson is an old coal mining and logging town with a population of 450. To me, Wilkeson was an adorable piece of history, but I couldn't imagine who would want to live in such a small country town.

My husband and I spent every weekend clearing out his dad's home and found it to be a treasure trove of family history and antiques. We spent many enjoyable weekends working and cleaning. The house was on a half-acre of land that bordered a twelve-acre lot. Locals told us, "You will fall in love with Wilkeson and move here someday." I was horrified at the thought of moving from my beloved suburban home with all the necessities for an industrious, productive, creative life.

Months passed. Each Sunday night when we returned to our Seattle house I felt boxed in and stressed as we re-entered the world of freeway traffic and congestion. We longed for the next weekend so we could head back to the hills, forests, and friendly, gentle people of Wilkeson. Finally we decided to keep the Wilkeson rambler for a weekend retreat.

At this point, events started to move quickly. I felt swept up in a current I could not control. I felt unsure about our decision, mainly because the house would be an added expense and it didn't feel like my home. Looking out the window of Dad's house one day, I asked God to let me know if we were making the right choice—within three minutes a rainbow appeared across the pasture beyond our window!

We learned that the town of Wilkeson was trying to purchase the twelve acres adjacent to Dad's house, with the intention of building a large housing development. We accompanied the neighbors to County Council meetings to fight this and felt if this occurred the peaceful country atmosphere we were starting to crave would be ruined.

One morning, after a council meeting, my husband and I woke up, looked at each other, and said in unison, "Let's buy the twelve acres and build our dream house." Where did that come from? Now I know it was just another step in the unfolding miracle. The twelve acres has a protected salmon creek (I need to be by water), a wooded hillside with old-growth cedar (my husband needs to be by forests), an old barn (my husband has always loved old barns), herds of elk and deer, eagles, coyotes, quail, and beautiful pastureland. Along with this decision came the realization that we wanted to be in the country full-time! Without too much intellectualizing, we sold our house in Seattle in one week, cleared out twenty-five years of clutter, and moved into the Wilkeson rambler to live there while building our new home right next door.

We decided to take our two-week vacation that year and spend it clearing blackberries on our new property. We planned on arriving September 12th of 2001. On September 11th, our world as we knew it came to an end with the terrorist attacks on our country. I am so thankful we had our beautiful pasture and hillside to work on in the following days. It was a truly healing experience. One hot afternoon we were sitting on the hillside, drinking water and resting for a moment when the bells in town tolled for the victims of 9/11. My heart swelled with a mixture of sadness, joy and peacefulness—life's smorgasbord of emotions.

After that our lives became a blur… finding plans for a dream house—we wanted a covered porch, windows so big you could see the stars, a loft, a Jacuzzi tub, and French doors from our bedroom out onto the porch… getting plans drawn up and approved, finding the excavator, builder, subcontractors—shopping for appliances, carpet, lighting, plumbing fixtures, paint, cabinets… and coordinating all of it. My husband and I provided some of the sweat equity and for two years built our dream house. It literally went off without a hitch—we had none of the disasters you hear about when people build their own home. The process unfolded so smoothly that I knew it was meant to be. At each stage, all the pieces fell effortlessly into place. We were able to build this beautiful home for the same amount of money we got for our little 1,100-square-foot house in Seattle!

I need to mention that I was sitting on the front porch, in the midst of construction, one summer day, marveling at how I had come to be at this point in my life and thanking God for this turn of events. I had my eyes closed and when I opened them a deer was standing so close I could practically touch her.

We sold our father's house easily and now live on the twelve acres, in our dream home. This unbelievable series of events happened because we allowed ourselves to step out of our comfort zones when the inner voices nudged us on.

As I sit at my desk, I look out at the hillside and the neighbors' horses, listening to the quail's song. I'm awaiting my daily visit from the elk and deer. I am so happy that we listened to our hearts and let this miracle happen. We are living our bliss!

~Margie Pasero

16

Life Lessons from the Lab

Be content with what you have, rejoice in the way things are. When you realize there is nothing lacking, the whole world belongs to you.

~Lao Tzu

Several years ago in Oregon, three climbers on Mount Hood slipped off a ledge and slid more than five hundred feet in the ice and snow. After spending the night on the mountainside in whiteout conditions, with winds swirling at up to seventy miles per hour, the signals they beamed with a live transmitter were picked up by rescuers down below.

Despite the nifty technology that helped to pinpoint the climbers' location, one of the rescuers gave credit to Velvet, the black Labrador Retriever that had accompanied the climbers and huddled with them throughout the bitter night. "The dog probably saved their lives," he said.

What I love about this story—besides the fact that they were all rescued safe and sound—is that Velvet became a hero by virtue of just being a dog. There was no mention of the Labrador's extraordinary valor or intelligence or training. Apparently, Velvet's big life-saving technique was The Huddle. There she was, along for the climb, and when the going got rough, Velvet the Life-Saving Dog just lay there in a heap with the climbers, sharing warmth on a cold night.

Although my own black Lab has never rescued me from an 11,239-foot mountain, she has saved the day more than once when I've felt a frown coming on. And just like Velvet, what Lizzie does comes as naturally and instinctively to her as licking the dirt off her paws or rolling around on her back spastically when she has an itch to scratch.

When life gets too complicated, when the demands on my time are more numerous than there are hours in a day, Lizzie will rush up to me with her suggestion, tail wagging, leash in mouth. Somehow she knows there's nothing like a walk for slowing down your day, for taking in a breath of fresh air, and, as they say, for stopping to smell the roses — although I don't think that's quite what Lizzie stops to smell along the way.

Every day, she reminds me that when someone comes through the door, returning home from work or from school or just stopping by for a visit, there's only one way to respond. Put on a happy face. No matter what kind of day she's had, whether she's been out for hours or cooped up in the house all day, she never fails to run to the door and shower whoever enters with all the drooly affection of her canine heart.

In Lizzie's world, there's no time to waste on fussy little details that could eat up time when there are so many more satisfying things to, well, eat. Just throw some of those nuggets from that giant bag of food in one bowl, pour a little water in the other and watch it disappear. Same food, same bowls, same enthusiastic response night after night. Why not be happy with what you've got?

She pulls out her best mood-altering tactic when I'm sitting at the little round table in the alcove in our kitchen. There I am, helping with homework or sewing ribbons onto ballet shoes, paying bills or just kicking back with a book. The next thing you know, this warm mound of fur plunks herself down at my feet, wrapping her front paws tightly around one of my ankles, as if to say: "It's about time you're sitting down. Why don't you stay a while?" I like to think of it as a hug.

In fact, if all else fails, Lizzie's solution is as simple as it is effective.

Wherever you are, in the middle of the morning, in the middle of a movie, in the middle of anything—except, of course, dinner—it doesn't matter. Just nod off. Take a nap. And when you come back to join the rest of the world, surely you will have regained your stride.

There's nothing like a dog to remind me that in this complex world we really need to stay in touch with a simpler existence. As Velvet showed us, just being who you are is enough to make you a hero. And as long as you've got food in your bowl, a warm bed to curl up in and someone to wag your tail for, I mean, come on. Life is good.

~Rita Lussier

Wanting Versus Having

If a man could have half his wishes, he would double his troubles.
~Benjamin Franklin

"Mom, I can't wait to own a fast Porsche someday and peel out and lay rubber in front of my friends," announced sixteen-year-old Steve, as he drove our old family car home after he passed his test for a Florida driver's license. I studied my son's excited face as he fantasized about his future transportation.

"I hope you get your dream car, but a Porsche is expensive," I replied. "You'll have to work hard to earn one."

Over the next several years Steve excelled. After high school he received a full scholarship to the prestigious Coast Guard Academy and graduated as an Ensign. Later he earned an MBA and a master's degree in engineering and got a job with a large corporation. The demands of working long hours competed with family obligations to his wife and young son.

One day he called and sounded happy.

"Hey, Mom. I'm inviting you and Dad to spend the weekend with us. Andrew is eager to play with his grandparents and Stephanie wants you to come for dinner on Friday."

"We'll be there."

We arrived to a round of hugs, and then Steve asked me to stand in front of the garage. I noticed a mysterious look on his face.

"I want to show you something, Mom."

He opened the garage door.

I shrieked and my mouth dropped open. I stared at the silver Porsche convertible, with the top down.

"Oh Steve! What a gorgeous car! It's your dream come true!"

My son grinned. I noticed tears of happiness in his eyes.

"It's a used 911 Carrera 4 Cabriolet, in mint condition, and one of the fastest cars on the road. I got a good deal, for less than half its original cost of a hundred grand. C'mon, let me take you for a ride and show you what this car can do. I'll take Dad later."

After I buckled up in the jazzy sports car, I studied my son's excited face, as I had the day he got his driver's license and fantasized about this car. Then he started the engine and we sped off. When my head was thrown against the headrest I clutched the door handle for support.

First, we roared from zero to sixty on an open stretch of road. Next, we raced up a steep bridge where I feared we'd go airborne, until Steve downshifted the engine. Finally, we executed a fast 180-degree turn in a deserted parking lot before we headed for home.

"Wow! That was a white knuckle ride!" I gasped, as I climbed out of the bucket seat.

"This car exceeded all my expectations," Steve said with pride.

Months later, during another visit, I stood next to Steve in his garage and admired his immaculate sports car. I was unprepared for what came next.

"I've decided to sell the Porsche," he said.

"Why?" I asked, in disbelief.

"I don't have time to enjoy it, and it's too small for our family."

Then, after a thoughtful pause, Steve shared an important lesson.

"I have discovered wanting a Porsche... was more fun than having one."

~Miriam Hill

A Detour to Bolivia

When you come to a roadblock, take a detour.
~Barbara Bush

Once upon a time, I had an amazing job. I went to work every day enthusiastic and eager to enjoy my job. Then I'd do it again the next day just as excited as the day before.

This wonderful ride lasted about eight years. Then things changed. My dream job became a nightmare. Swinging-door leadership turned our once congenial and cooperative staff into disgruntled and disgusted employees. As for me, I was a walking pity party, inviting family and friends to listen to how miserable my job and life were. You can imagine how popular I was.

About that time, something I considered insignificant happened. I had recently returned from an amazing six-week exchange trip to Mexico and presented a program to the local Rotary club that had sponsored me.

My minister was in the audience that night. After the program, he came up to me and said, "Linda, I didn't know you could speak Spanish. You know our church sends a medical and construction team to Bolivia every year. We've never had anyone who could speak even a few sentences of Spanish. I'd like you to think about going with us this year."

I knew about the trip—and I also knew the trip was rough,

rugged and not my kind of travel. But, to be courteous, I told him I'd think about it.

As he left, he said, "I'll check back with you."

He did. At 8:15 the next morning, he was sitting in my office. He told me the plans for that year: staffing a medical clinic and working on a church in Colqueamaya, a poor village high in the Andes Mountains. He said, "We will float a river on a raft, walk to and from the job sites and sleep on straw mats. Maybe there'll be latrines and maybe not. It'll be exciting, and I know you'll enjoy it!"

I listened politely, but on the inside, I was rolling my eyes and thinking, "No way." At that time, I was a sissy, prissy traveler. Camping and roughing it were for my husband and sons, avid campers and backpackers. I told my minister I would think about it.

In spite of my travel misgivings, I began to consider going. The idea my minister had planted began to flourish. I thought, "I'll go on this trip so I can put some time and distance between me and my job. Maybe it will help me decide what to do."

I decided to go on the trip for very selfish reasons. It would be a break from my job and unhappiness. I made a deal with myself: If things were better when I returned, I would know that I was the problem and I would have to leave the job.

My husband and sons thought, "They'll life-flight her back on the first plane. She won't make it. She can't handle it."

But I did make it. I surprised myself and amazed my family. I loved the experience!

On the trip, we experienced all the adventures my minister had promised and more. I worked with people who lived in extreme poverty. Most were herders or subsistence farmers. They lived in adobe brick houses with thatched roofs, slept on hard-packed dirt floors with a few blankets for warmth, and often ate only one simple meal a day. In spite of all this, they were happy, even joyful, and lived as if they had no cares in the world.

Their happiness puzzled and confused me. They had nothing and were happy. I had everything they didn't have, and I was miserable.

I took a long, hard look at myself in the mirror. What I saw was not pretty. I asked myself, "What's wrong with this picture? What's wrong with you?"

The truth was ugly. I was all about ego, status, money and show. My priorities were upside down. I had some serious thinking and changing to do.

When I returned to my job, another surprise awaited me. Instead of the situation being better, it was much worse. I hadn't considered that possibility. My decision to leave the job was easy; the financial consequences were not. Fortunately, my husband was supportive, and we downsized before it became popular.

I didn't have another full-time job for two years. My 4,000-mile detour to Bolivia had derailed me from the fast track and the road to fame and fortune. I had many moments to consider what I had learned on the detour.

I realized that money is only a thing. People—family, friends and relationships—are more important than things. I learned that for me, a simple life is best. I am now blessed with less. My current job pays much less and has few perks—and I'm happy. Interestingly, the people around me are happier too!

Another plus—I've learned to rough and tough it with the best—and I like it! I go back to Bolivia as frequently as I can for a refresher course on what's really important in life and for the right reasons.

So, if you find yourself on a rough, rocky road in life, keep putting one foot in front of the other. Maybe you'll come to a detour like I did that will lead you to simple, happy experiences and adventures in your life.

~Linda E. Allen

Living Life Full-Time

A little simplification would be the first step toward rational living, I think.
~Eleanor Roosevelt

My heart pounded as I waited for her to answer the phone. "Vicki, hi. How's that new baby of yours?"

"Oh, he's amazing, Kim. Actually, he's the reason for my call. I wanted to talk about my options for coming back to work. I can't imagine leaving him to go to work all day, every day."

I rambled on about how much I loved being a mom. As she listened, I gushed about how I was enjoying the time with my baby, taking him for walks, seeing him smile, and feeling his chubby fist grasp my finger.

When I finished, I pitched my proposition: part-time Mall Marketing Director, job sharing with another part-time marketing director.

Continuing my spiel, I told her about an article I'd read about job sharing and how it was becoming a viable alternative for moms who wanted to "have it all"—family and career—yet simplify their lives as well.

She was silent.

When I finally finished my inventory of excuses, I hoped I'd convinced her how complicated it would be working full-time in such a demanding job while trying to raise a child. I held my breath to hear her response.

"Vicki, here's what I think. I think you should be there for your baby, and if you choose to, you could return to freelance writing. I know you've wanted to be a mom for a long time, and I think you should grasp this opportunity. You and I both know that the marketing director position is a full-time career, not a part-time job."

I felt overwhelming relief at that moment. Letting out a deep breath, I smiled at my husband who was waiting next to me, watching for my reaction. As I held the phone under my chin, I pumped my fist and mouthed the word, "Yes!"

"Okay, Kim, I suppose you're right," I feigned disappointment. "I just had to talk to you about that option, because I know I'm not ready to return to work full-time."

"I understand, Vicki. I think you're making the right decision, and we'll miss you, but I think it's for the best."

She was compassionate about my decision to downsize my life. It seemed as if my boss almost knew I was going to give up my position as marketing director of the mall, because she outlined the procedure for filling my position and offered to act as a reference.

As I hung up the phone, I ran to my husband and hugged him, knocking the bottle out of baby Luke's mouth, who looked up at me with wide eyes. I grabbed him and held him in my arms, dancing around the kitchen with him as he held on tight.

And that's what I've been doing for the past ten years—"holding on tight," as my new more simplified life has meant changes I could never have imagined.

The day I resolved to simplify my life was more than ten years ago. Even though it meant giving up some luxuries, that decision to stay home with Luke, and later, Lisette, filled my life with a richness I could never have imagined.

My morning no longer consisted of whizzing through a drive-through restaurant for a quick but expensive breakfast. It no longer meant spending too much money buying vast amounts of clothing, only to struggle with coordinating the perfect work outfit. It now included cuddles, stories, and a mid-morning walk to the park.

Afternoons meant naptime for Luke, and time for me to write and play the piano that had been gathering dust in our basement.

My days no longer consisted of meeting with stressed-out store owners, crunching numbers in the marketing budget, or running around during Bridal Shows and Sidewalk Sales trying to please hundreds of people while wearing myself down.

Before Luke and Lisette, lunch meant expensive catered meetings with mall merchants and employees around a long conference table. Now, it's a picnic blanket spread out on the grass with peanut butter and jelly sandwiches and sippy cups of apple juice.

My former afternoon brainstorming sessions about how to stretch our $90,000 marketing budget have become brain building sessions for my four-year-old about the letters of the day on *Sesame Street* and *WordWorld*.

Our "budget talks" involve discussing how our bike ride to the local bakery didn't have to end in an argument over the 75-cent custard-filled Bismarck versus the 30-cent cake doughnut with frosting and sprinkles. The end result (and it only took us five minutes versus weeks of budget talks): the cake doughnut is a much better investment.

The big difference in my afternoons: I pray for long naptimes for my two little staff members so that I can write.

Sure, my days run longer now. Compared to my 9-to-6 days at the mall, they now run from about 8 a.m. to 9:30 p.m., when it's bedtime for my two little staffers. But now, my days end with a sense of accomplishment that I have improved the lives of the two little ones who bless mine.

My nights now consist of dinners at home with my family, instead of waiting in line at the mall food court—eating on the run again—while checking my watch to be sure I have time to finish my "to-do list" and still make it home before six.

But for all the "exciting" things I used to do, I now have new activities to replace them, and even though we have cut our income nearly in half, we have more money saved, and have paid off our home—simply by cutting back on frivolous expenses.

Expensive vacations and new vehicles no longer excite me. I have enough excitement in my simplified life with first words, first steps, and even first falls—all followed by big hugs and kisses on plump cheeks.

I now look forward to leisurely bike rides to the park and shopping excursions in, yes, our minivan (gently used, not new), which has much more interior room than our former sporty, but gas-guzzling SUV.

Nights are filled with baths, Lego-building, and on special occasions, Disney movies filled with princesses and wishes come true.

Sure, my life used to be busier before that crucial day when I made the call to my former boss, but I wouldn't trade my new—and simpler life—for the world.

~Victoria LaFave

Cupcakes and Karma

We have to learn to be our own best friends
because we fall too easily into the trap of being our own worst enemies.
~Roderick Thorp

For most adults, managing the daily demands of a job, spouse, kids, home and community can be challenging, not to mention stressful. Since I was one of those mom-wife-employee-homemaker types who couldn't say "no," I soon developed combat tactics to dispatch my duties with military precision and efficiency.

A two-hundred-page report by morning? No problem! Five thousand cupcakes for the kindergarten class by noon tomorrow? Can do! I formed a battle plan, launched my attack and took no prisoners. Bring it on: the school board, the homeowner's association, the Cub Scouts. I felt invincible. But where was the joy?

Yes, I was super-productive. But in spite of everything I did for others, at considerable cost to my health and sanity, I felt empty, angry and unappreciated. I know now that I was the only one to blame.

After getting knocked on my keister with a diagnosis of breast cancer, I decided to take stock of my life—or what might be left of it. On my doctor's orders—reduce stress and take better care of myself—I finally realized I needed a gentler approach to life. And that's when I discovered an amazing phenomenon called "Karma."

I don't know who came up with the idea that the energy you send out into the universe each day will be returned to you in kind, but two thumbs up for that guy. He was light years ahead of the rest of us.

At first I was skeptical—surely it couldn't be that simple—but I was fresh out of ideas and desperate to turn my life around. So I made a slight adjustment to my morning routine. I looked in the mirror and asked myself what feeling I wanted to have returned to me that day. And the answer was always, "Joy!"

Before I could share joy, however, I needed to find some. And that's exactly what I did. First, I had to let go of years of pent-up anger in order to make room in my heart for happiness. Next, I changed my career to one that is more fulfilling and nurtures my creative spirit.

Given my recent health scare, I realized that time is too precious to waste. I now spend my treasured moments only with people I enjoy, surrounding myself with mentors and close friends who share inspiration, laughter and fun, and provide a strong support system for life's ups and downs.

Donating my time and talents to help others is still high on my priority list. When given in the right spirit, it's an investment that pays big dividends in joy. Instead of saying "yes" to every request, however, I carefully choose the projects that are closest to my heart. So please don't ask me to make cupcakes. I love eating them; I just don't enjoy making them. But I'd be glad to help with an art project instead.

Old habits are hard to break, especially when you reach my age. But even though it took me more than fifty years to discover the path to a happier life, I feel an overwhelming sense of gratitude. Every day I look into that mirror and ask myself the same question, and the answer fills my heart with joy. And if that joy arrives in the form of a cupcake made by someone else, it's even better!

~Gloria Hander Lyons

My Little Town

Kindness is the golden chain by which society is bound together.
~Johann Wolfgang von Goethe

While most college towns are crazy, mixed-up, wonderful places, Arcata, California is probably a little more crazy and mixed-up and wonderful than most. Arcata is the home of Humboldt State University, a throwback to the 1960s, and a haven for students, professors, hippies, artists, musicians, cannabis farmers and dreamy-eyed mystics. A lot of "senior citizens" live here, too. It's commonplace to see elderly women sporting belly button jewelry, pierced tongues, and eyebrow rings, and old men with a matrix of tattoos and gray Rasta hair. Arcata welcomes everyone.

People who visit Arcata come back again and again. Either that or they stay for good. The town has a way of drawing you in and making you feel good about life. It's something a person can't explain, like a climber getting a hit of oxygen at altitude, or a duckling that's fixed on a dog because it thinks the dog is its mother. It's called imprinting.

There's never a dull moment in Arcata. The place teems with an infinite array of hacky-sackers, Frisbee-flingers, bongo-beaters, skateboarders, earth mothers, and alcohol-modified transients. Most of them hang out at the Co-op or on the plaza, next to their brightly colored busses and chicken shack pick-ups, while their dogs run around in loose orbit. A bronze statue of President William McKinley stands in the center of everything, and an intonation-challenged guitar player often sits nearby, singing a folksy ballad that makes little, if any, sense.

Some folks call this place Sillyville. Others call it Haight-Ashbury North. I like to call it home. For me, real happiness boils down to one simple thing: the town where I live.

Arcata is a town with a big heart. It's always been a good place for folks down on their luck to find a job, or at least a handout. People who live here can't stand to see anyone go homeless or hungry. Everyone is out to help their fellow man and save the planet. There are movements to save the toadstool, feed the snail darter, and help the hairy-eared spotted owl. Arcata residents install solar panels on their roofs, brew their own biodiesel, and hang rainbow flags outside their front doors. At various places in town you will find Food for People (the food bank of Humboldt County), a hemp and beans farmers' market (where veggies and hugs are exchanged in equal volume), and the annual Arcata Bay Oyster Festival (where lots of shucking and even a little jiving takes place). You will also find such strange and diverse celebrations as Anti-Valentine's Day, Stop Road Rage Week, Future Sea Level Rise Awareness Month, Unicycle to Work, Kill Your TV, and, my personal favorite, Free Your Breasts Day.

The citizens of Arcata don't make their living through stock futures, tanning beds, or exploitation of third world workers. They do not wear Prada suits or expensive designer eyeglasses. Nor do they drive Hummers, wear fur, or turn their thermostats up past sixty-eight degrees in the winter. Citizens in this town live on vegan diets, petition to de-pave their streets, build homeless shelters, and drive their bicycles back and forth to the tofu store.

Arcata folks are green to the core. They recycle everything from gray water, plastic, and aluminum, to glass, cardboard, food scraps and fingernail clippings. They natural birth at home, eat vegan quinoa salads, drink ginseng tea, and make their own soap. They pick litter off nearby beaches without being asked to, march for peace, and celebrate equality and diversity in its many forms. Arcata residents have been called everything from heathens to hippies to lily-livered environmentalists. They consider such names to be supreme compliments.

You might say it doesn't matter if places like Arcata still exist. After all, embracing peace, love, and diversity in a town of fewer than ten thousand souls is just a small step in the right direction, not a full-blown manifesto. But for those of us who live here, life is about love and brotherhood, and the tickle you get in your spirit when you discover that good people still exist.

It's a feeling that leaves a lasting impression on all those who visit this town. Not because it teaches them something new. But because it teaches them something they might have forgotten: If you want to change the world, you have to start somewhere.

~Timothy Martin

Find Your Happiness

Chapter 3

Finding My Passion

Follow your bliss
and the universe will open doors where there were only walls.

~Joseph Campbell

Playing Pretend

Go confidently in the direction of your dreams.
Live the life you've always imagined.
~Henry David Thoreau

In the middle of my sophomore year of college, I sat down to work at my desk. On one side, my economics textbooks remained unopened. On the other side, unstudied Chinese vocabulary flashcards were piled high. Months of skipping classes, partying and procrastinating had landed me there. I had to learn a semester's worth of knowledge in a week. I was miserable. Trapped and anxious, all I wanted was to burst out of my seat and pace back and forth. I wanted to be somewhere else. But, this was the life I had convinced myself I was going to live.

Somehow, I made it through that grueling week of finals.

While at home for winter break, a friend and I were out drinking at some unrespectable hour. I was in a cocky mood, riding high after surviving the semester by the skin of my teeth. So when another friend appeared in the bar's front window, with blood running down his face, I immediately charged outside to defend him. This is when I got blindsided by two assailants. The first punched me in the face. Then, as I fell to the ground, the second kicked me in the head.

When I wound up in the hospital later that night, a CT scan showed I didn't have a concussion. Instead, I had something much worse: a brain tumor.

Nothing in my life has come close to the fear I felt at that moment.

Death was my first thought. Would it be in six months or a year? How much pain would there be? How soon until I couldn't speak? When would I lose the ability to think?

The next day, my parents and I sat with a team of neurologists. They explained the tumor was located in the middle of my brain. It could not be removed through surgery. At considerable risk, I had a biopsy. It was the only way to determine if the tumor was cancerous. I had gone through life without a single symptom, which meant it could have been there all along, or it could have appeared a month before. When I woke up from anesthesia, my parents stood beside me. Their eyes were teary; their smiles were wide. The tumor was benign.

I returned to college and managed to get my studies on track. Those textbooks were open and read; those flashcards were memorized. But I still lacked passion for what I was learning and the business career that I expected to have. Every three months I would get a brain MRI to check the tumor's growth. It had appeared stable for more than a year. Then, on one beautiful morning, my mom called me. I could tell she'd been crying. The results of my latest scan had come back. The tumor was metabolically active.

Much like that night in the hospital, I felt crushed. My life had been taken from me a second time. By my twenty-first birthday, I had withdrawn from school and was undergoing radiation.

It was a strange feeling to have radiation on a brain tumor that had never given me a single symptom. Friends and family often told me how unfair it was: to be removed from growing up to face something so awful. I had endless stretches of time to think about that particular point of view. It was a surreal time spent on cold tables watching machines slowly circle my head; tired times that left me unable to get out of bed; energetic times once the neural steroids kicked in.

This time-out from life's normal direction gave me ample opportunity to think about grand ideas like happiness, purpose and passion. One morning, I found myself thinking about that long ago week I spent cramming for exams. Why was I so miserable? Why did I feel so lost? I knew there was something important underlying my desire to jump up and pace back and forth. I knew it reached back long before college, all the way back to one single moment of my childhood.

I was five years old, and had come across a book by the young-adult-fiction author, Lloyd Alexander. My father's name is Lloyd, mine is Alexander, and in my kindergarten mind, the coincidence translated as a calling. I was going to become an author. So, I started writing stories. I'd excitedly begin on the first page of my journal, continue to the second, and maybe even reach the third before it was left abandoned on my desk. Most often, the final sentence was unfinished, its last letter drawn down the page as if some monster had dragged me off.

Instead of sticking to the page, I would jump up from my desk and begin pacing back and forth. I'd start speaking my characters' dialogue, acting out their action, and before I knew it I was playing pretend. I played pretend constantly. It was like a drug; I couldn't function without my daily fix. And while playing pretend with friends is part of any childhood—whether as Power Rangers or princesses—I always preferred to play it alone.

Day after day I played out complete epics, building countless worlds with rules and citizens. Often my characters so enchanted me, their stories became so ingrained in my thoughts that after playing out their entire journeys, I'd start them over from the beginning. I'd replay entire narratives, exploring new details and alternate outcomes. So lost was I in these stories that by the time I rounded them all to a close I was an eighteen-year-old heading off to college.

My passion was to create stories. Unfortunately, it was stained with my embarrassment over playing pretend long past the age of five. So, I swore off it. When I sat down to study in my sophomore year, I wanted nothing more than to burst up and start playing pretend. But I wouldn't allow it. I would go into finance like my parents, and conform to my image of what I thought it meant to be an adult. But that too was just a fantasy.

While sick, I began playing pretend again. This time I benefited from the discipline of college. Pages of notes, timelines and sketches began to accumulate. I devoured books. I hadn't felt this passionate in a very long time. And it didn't take me long to realize why. It was clear where in my short life I had found the greatest joy. It was a place countless measures of my energy were already sunk. Only when steeped in fantasy had I been truly happy. Yet it was a passion I had only allowed to exist in the margin.

For fear of rejection, failure and vulnerability, I had resisted what felt most natural. But being forced to face life's fragility at such a young age, I no longer cared. Sure it wasn't easy. When I returned to school, I crammed a four-year creative writing major into three semesters. I lived and breathed reading, writing and editing. I still have plenty of fears and doubts, but I know success doesn't come without risk.

I'm lucky for a lot of reasons. I'm especially grateful for my health—radiation sent my tumor into remission, where it will likely stay for a very long time. Above all, I cherish being given the chance to reevaluate my life. For me it took a brain tumor to realize that storytelling was more than just a childish whim. I've come to understand being successful is doing what makes you happy. Life is too short and uncertain to do anything else.

So I write, and simply hope what I create means to others what it has meant to me.

~Alexander Brokaw

This Is My Stop

Do you want to know who you are? Don't ask. Act!
Action will delineate and define you.
~Thomas Jefferson

My twenty-three-year-old heart was slowly breaking, as it had been for years. "Caitlin," my mother sighed into the phone. She paused. I sat waiting. And then she added, "You're always going to miss the bus."

I looked down into the lap of my favorite suit—the one that had a black skirt and a royal blue top with chunky black buttons. Tears were burning the corners of my eyes, but I was also trying hard not to snap and yell something unfortunate into the receiver. It was lunch hour, but an unusual number of people were milling about the office. My desk was in the heart of the action. What would people think?

As my mother rattled on about why I shouldn't go to graduate school in education and why she couldn't support such a decision, I realized that she was more than 750 miles away but still had an incredible hold on me. That's when I finally had my moment of clarity. It was a moment that had taken seven years to arrive.

I realized that I couldn't keep caring what people thought, even if those people included my mother. At some point, I needed to do what felt right to me, even if I did not have one or both parents' blessing. Going to graduate school in education was something I needed. I knew that, and I had to follow that feeling.

"You know what, Mom? I've got to go. I have work to do."

With complete respect and in total control, I hung up the phone.

It wouldn't be the last time that my mother told me I was making a mistake, and it wouldn't be the last time that she got under my skin. But it was the first time that the stakes were high and I succeeded in saying, "Enough!"

I do believe that my mother always felt that she had my best interest at heart—whether we were discussing my need to lose weight, my choice of college, the sorority I was pledging, or the company I was keeping. Gradually, though, I learned that she was letting what she wanted overpower what I needed. And honestly, her work and life experiences were not always deep or broad enough to justify giving her opinions the weight that I had.

So on that afternoon back in 1994, I returned my acceptance to the Curry School of Education at the University of Virginia. I am so thankful that I did because I'm not quite sure who I would be had I not.

I blossomed during graduate school. One reason that I returned to the institution where I had earned my bachelor of arts was that I wanted to make things right there. I knew that I had not capitalized on my undergraduate experience, in large part because I had not studied what most interested me—education—because my parents made me promise that I would not pursue an education degree. I had studied a lot during my undergraduate years, but my schoolwork was one gigantic, never-ending chore. I had floundered, struggling to find my niche academically and socially.

When I returned as a grad student to study instructional design, I quickly found love: My schoolwork fascinated me, my professors challenged me, and my friends in my program inspired me. The Internet and the Web were gaining a substantial following, and I spent hour upon hour in the computer lab, delighted to be designing Web-based educational tools. My work was so fulfilling that it consumed me, in the best possible way.

The following spring, while sitting in that computer lab that claimed so much of my time, I snagged an internship at Monticello co-developing the first website for Thomas Jefferson's home. That internship determined my future career path. Sitting in that same chair, I also met the man who is now my husband.

Seventeen years later, Mark and I have a happy life. We are the proud parents of two children, and we have built a home that we cherish in a community that we love. I have been blessed with a variety of work experiences that have kept me on my toes and have allowed me to create products that bring me pride. Through the years, I have taught teachers, librarians, and even preschoolers.

By standing up for myself and trusting my gut, I claimed my life and found happiness. I not only caught the bus, but also loved the ride.

~Caitlin McLean

24

How I Found My Calling

*The person born with a talent they are meant to use
will find their greatest happiness in using it.*
~Johann Wolfgang von Goethe

A s I write this, my first book is going to press. I am sixty-five years old. Writing is my calling, and it had to call itself hoarse for fifty years before I answered it.

I hated English classes all through school. Why were we taught the same grammar, punctuation, and usage rules year after year? What could be more boring than diagramming sentences, conjugating verbs, and looking up words in the dictionary? By high school I did know that I liked to write, but I didn't connect it to those classes. I took the yearly doses of English required for graduation without realizing I was good at it. Even in college I suffered through Study of the English Language and wore my pajamas—under a raincoat—to Contemporary Literature. My focus was Art.

I'd grown up in an alcoholic household and had not learned how to plan or how to complete a project. I felt lucky to be away at school, yet I hadn't settled on what I wanted to do with my life. Though I'd done well in high school, my lack of discipline became painfully clear in college. If you'd seen lights on in the Art Department late at night back then, it would have been me, trying to finish all my paintings by morning.

I did my assignments at the last minute, but I did like writing papers for freshman English—even at one o'clock in the morning. In fact, I liked it better than Art. I found a niche with my writing, and a wonderful professor convinced me to change my minor from PE to English. I slowly discovered that I not only had a talent for putting words together, I loved the English language. I had a feel for the mechanics as well as the rhythm of words, and writing made me happy. But I still had work to do before I found my true path.

I agreed to write a lengthy research paper with another English professor as my advisor. It was an honors project to be completed as independent study, and my grade would be A, B, or F. After I handed the paper in, the professor returned it with a single comment at the top indicating that my approach to the topic did not work. In other words: Start over. I was humiliated, and on top of that I didn't know how to dig in and fix my paper. My motivation drained away, and I gave up. I'd been offered the honors course because I was a good student, and now I'd earned an F. I felt the sting of failure, even though the grade was never turned in.

After college I worked as an English teacher and then as a newspaper reporter, in addition to a brief career in commercial art. In 1978 I moved to Cincinnati, unaware that a coal strike was in progress and jobs were scarce. I worked in a box factory and a figure salon before stumbling into a job as a textbook editor. By the time I settled into educational publishing at age thirty-three, I knew that I had found a profession that fit, and I stayed thirty years.

In my fifties I began to think about retirement and a second career. I'd grown up in the hills of West Virginia and hadn't exactly seen the world. I still enjoyed writing and had been keeping a journal for several years. Why not become a travel writer? I was divorced and living alone since my son was grown. Travel writing seemed perfect.

And then I got promoted at work. My new job as Acquisitions Editor involved traveling all over the United States to meet with authors and educators. What could be better as I prepared for my new phase of life? I reveled in seeing new places, always taking the time to tour each city: Memphis, Minneapolis, San Diego, San Antonio, and Seattle; Las Vegas, New Orleans, New York City, and more. Most often I would take a bus tour. I began keeping notes when I traveled, so that I could practice writing about my trips. That was how I learned that I didn't want to write travel guides. Someone else would have to compile the hard facts for tourists; I knew it wasn't my calling.

I read books about travel writing and even found a summer course at the University of Minnesota. I became a fan of the travel essay. That was what I would write!

After a few years in my new job, the cities began to repeat, but that wasn't the game changer—it was this: I developed a fear of flying and came to dread every trip. I was in agony as soon as the plane started roaring down the runway. After I opened my eyes, I spent the time in the air looking at my watch, looking at the map in the back of the flight magazine to see where we might be, and looking at my watch again. The slightest bump would make my heart pound in terror; any new noise would activate dark thoughts like the scene in *Goldfinger* when Oddjob was sucked out of the cabin through a hole.

What would be the career trajectory of a travel writer who hated to fly?

I did long to go to Europe. I hadn't had the opportunity as a young woman, and there was one country I particularly wanted to see: not England, not France, not Italy—but Romania. I'd always loved Dracula and wanted to see the rugged landscapes and castles of Transylvania. Romania could be the setting for my first travel book! Even before I'd seen it, I knew I had the passion to write about Dracula's land. It was an outgrowth of my childhood passion for horror movies. I set out at age fifty-nine and endured ten thousand miles of flying to get to Bucharest and back. I spent nearly three weeks touring Romania with a guide and took thirty-six thousand words of notes. My career writing travel essays was surely launched; all I'd have to do was make sense of my trip notes.

That was the understatement of the year. My trip notes required major massaging, but that wasn't all. My travels in Romania had triggered memories of home and my childhood with an alcoholic mother. What began as a travel book developed into a memoir as I connected my past with the legend of Dracula. As I wove the two stories together, I revisited my past and began to see it in a different light. The result has been newfound peace and happiness.

It Started with Dracula: The Count, My Mother, and Me took five years to complete. By the time it's published in a few months, I'll be sixty-six.

This is my calling: writing my memoir and now the one I'm co-authoring with my brother. My life is exciting. I'm finding adventure in every new phase of being an author; and what I think of, as I close this piece, is the question that I have often seen posed in advice columns about anyone who considered or accomplished something new late in life: How old would you be if you hadn't done it?

~Jane Congdon

25

Why I Still Travel to the Wild

Travel and change of place impart new vigor to the mind.
~Seneca

Friends always ask why I, a middle-aged klutz with no athletic aptitude, travel to perilous places—the jungles of Thailand or Borneo or Papua New Guinea, for example, where the water is often unsafe and the food chancy; places with infectious diseases, malarial mosquitoes, venomous snakes and the wildest of animals; some places where the locals are just a few generations past headhunting.

I never know how to answer. Because I want to wiggle my toes in the mud of adventure? Feel the spine tingle of danger? Run my fingers over the inscription on a rough-hewn beam erected six thousand years ago? Because I want to share in my husband's fearless and irrepressible wanderlust?

My travel decisions assumed a new gravity nine years ago after I suffered a stroke caused by an unpronounceable autoimmune disease that turns my blood to sludge. (It's called antiphospholipid syndrome or APS.) To prevent another stroke, my doctors told me, I'd have to take dangerously high levels of blood thinner for the rest of my life. Any travel remote from medical help would be risky. An infected finger, a slip on a damp temple step, even a minor traffic smash-up would no longer be mere annoyances—they could be life threatening. Not to mention autoimmune flares, overreaction to heat, or a jet-lagged mistake taking more, or less, of those hazardous blood-thinning pills.

I had to think about what was important to me: family, of course, and friends. But then what? No matter how many times I racked it up, no bucket list was complete without travel. Then I had to decide how I might manage the risk. I had to decide how lucky I felt.

My return to travel after my stroke came in baby steps—a symposium in Texas, a visit to my mom in Virginia, a vacation with a girlfriend to England. It all came back, like sliding into the bucket seat of my fifteen-year-old car: the vagabond freedom from routine, the excitement of discovery, the fresh air of change, the thrill of just going.

The first real test of my travel moxie came nine months after my stroke when I joined my husband, Jack, on a business trip to China. Touring near Guilin, we swung like acrobats on a windy chairlift ride for 3,000 feet up Yao Mountain, adventure enough for one day, I thought. But after we'd toured the remains of a Tang Dynasty temple and savored the misty and ethereal view, Jack wanted to ride down on a toboggan that looked to me like a silver husk bobbling on a twisted ribbon lying unanchored on the ground.

Before the stroke it would've seemed like fun. But now? I cringed. I waffled. My mental klaxon screamed warnings about lax safety standards, the consequences of a cut, a fall, a crash. My stomach flipped and flopped for seconds that seemed like minutes. Then, snatching confidence from who knows where, I shrugged my shoulders, crouched and lowered myself gingerly into the wobbly thing, feeling like a human cannonball—and just about as smart.

That flying toboggan ride down the mountain marked my adventure travel comeback.

In the years since then, I've traveled about twenty-five percent of the time—much of it with Jack. We've tracked leopards in Botswana and grizzlies in Alaska, climbed temples and crawled caves from India to China and back again. We've sailed the Yangtze River in China and the Mekong in Laos; visited hill tribes in Burma and Vietnam, Lost Generation cafés in Paris, the opera in Vienna and Prague. Traveling with girlfriends, I've explored Mayan villages in Guatemala, dodged snakes in Costa Rica, discovered the charms of Provence.

I've also walked the floor with two newborn grandchildren. I've traveled to D.C. for one best friend's wedding, to Chicago to celebrate another's sixtieth birthday, to Denver to hold a third friend's hand when she buried her husband, dead too young at fifty-two.

Through it all, my luck's held out—no hippo maulings, no deadly falls, no car wrecks or crushing infections.

For me, adventure travel is a risk worth taking. Travel broadens my world, keeps me connected to the earth's hum, to family, to friends. Most of all, saying "yes" to travel keeps me connected to myself.

After 9/11 and the terror threats and reactions that followed, friends often asked me whether I was afraid to travel. That always got my dander up. If we let ourselves be afraid to travel, I said, then the terrorists win. I guess I feel the same way about my personal terrors, stroke and APS. I'm careful. I watch my medicine like a hawk. I get my blood tested. I weigh the risks. Then, if I decide it's okay, like that toboggan ride down Yao Mountain, I just jump in, let go and savor the ride.

~Anne Sigmon

Never Say Never

Your assumptions are your windows on the world.
Scrub them off every once in a while, or the light won't come in.
~Alan Alda

I was a fish out of water that semester. As a non-traditional college student, a euphemism for older, I was petrified. I was all about English and Communications. I had far more credits than necessary to graduate, but my institute of higher learning would not grant me a degree without a science course. So, I bit the bullet—along with every last fingernail—and signed up for Human Biology.

On that first day of class, visions of a plummeting grade point average filled my head as the professor strolled into the classroom. He was an imposing figure at well over six feet tall. A booming voice that easily carried to the back of the classroom was filtered through a dense, sandy blond mustache. He was all about setting the record straight from day one. "I give four tests a semester. Don't skip any of them. If you miss one, don't ask if you can do a report as a make-up. You don't want to write it and I don't want to read it."

I was certain I'd made a terrible mistake. I should have taken Ecology 101, which involved field trips to the New Jersey shore to watch horseshoe crabs scamper across the sand and to observe tiny aquatic creatures in the tide pools. What was I thinking?

It turned out to be the semester that changed the direction of my career. Who knew I would love science? I came away from the course telling others, "Everyone should take Human Biology. It's the manual for the most important machine you'll ever operate." I had become positively preachy.

My mind had opened. I was greedy for more details about these amazing bodies we inhabit. Next, I elected to take Anatomy & Physiology—Parts I and II. I didn't need them. I eagerly welcomed them.

A surprised friend had asked, "What happened to the Judy who loved literature and journalism?" I had no answer. But fate stepped in as it is wont to do—if you leave yourself open to possibilities.

Shortly after I graduated, my next-door neighbor called. "Judy, I have a friend in need. She's a medical journal editor. Her assistant suddenly left and she's looking for a summer fill-in. I thought of you."

It promised to be a marriage made in heaven. Writing and working with medical journals. Too good to believe. But it was true. That summer job turned into a freelance medical journal career that lasted many years. As a part-time freelancer, I also had time to follow my passion as a journalist. I wrote commentary essays for a large metropolitan newspaper. I had the best of both worlds. I loved them equally.

Just when I thought I would never find another ideal marriage, another proposal came my way. My husband's cousin, Jim, had been a caregiver for his father during the years his dad suffered from Alzheimer's. Jim had used his degree in gerontology and his on-the-job training to gather ten years of research on how to be an effective Alzheimer's caregiver. He had accumulated a paper mountain of facts. Did I have the ability to turn his research into an easy-to-read manual for caregivers? When Jim approached me, it was tempting to say, "Write a book? I can't do that." But, along the way, I had learned to say, "I'll give it a try."

Although it is an accepted truism that nothing ventured is nothing gained, we often are afraid of failure, so we play it safe and say "no." Jim and I had no guarantees that we would find a publisher in a highly competitive market after a year of hard work. It took a while and many painful rejections, but we did it. Our book was published in 2002.

Writing is a great joy. Getting paid to write is an even greater joy. During my long freelance career, I have had numerous assignments, from public relations to scriptwriting television commercials. I approached each one fraught with fear. But I stuck to my mantra: "I'll give it a try."

I've never been sorry. I found my happiness by learning to never say never.

~Judy Harch

Antony's Gift

Follow your passion, and success will follow you.
~Terri Guillemets

The bus rumbles down the street, jolting as it stops and starts. The first rule of riding public transportation in Baltimore is not to make eye contact, but I feel safer when I know my surroundings so I glance up and around quickly. I think I see a familiar face, but that's not possible since I very rarely ride this bus. I turn my gaze to the book I brought to shield me from the world.

Finally, the bus arrives at my stop, down the street from the bookstore where I work my second job. I am a temp at an insurance company during the day and then travel to this book and music shop to work nights in the music department, an ironic occupation since I am basically musically illiterate. But this job is only for the Christmas holidays, to get enough money to buy gifts for the family. I can handle it if I set my mind to it.

I step off the bus and go only three steps before I hear someone calling me, "Ms. Arvidson! Ms. Arvidson!" I haven't been addressed by my maiden name since June, and at first I don't even acknowledge it. "Ms. Arvidson, is that you?" The voice is more insistent now. I can't ignore it, so I turn and see a young man. As his name comes back to me, I am flooded with memories.

•••

Antony was one of my students during my one and only year as a special education teacher working with juniors and seniors at an inner-city high school in Baltimore. I had spent two years in graduate school earning my teaching credentials, but I was miserable right from the start and the year was an emotional blur. On the fifth day, there was a shooting in the cafeteria. In October there was a lock-down that we all thought was due to the O.J. Simpson verdict being read, but was actually due to "gangbangers" roaming the hallways. I sat huddled alone in my classroom for lunch, listening to the sound of heavy running in the halls above me and the voice of a TV commentator in front of me.

The roll books showed twenty to twenty-five students enrolled in each of my class periods. My actual classes consisted of five regular attendees and three or four who came and went. Drug deals occurred in my classroom, but there was no support from the administration or the single police officer assigned to the school. I tried to teach my students the curriculum, but was told by the "powers that be" that I should concentrate on life skills such as filling out job applications because "none of these kids are college-bound and they just need to get jobs to pay bills." The unfortunate truth was that my students were not going to get traditional diplomas, but only certificates of attendance for their four years of high school.

For special education teachers, the goal was to get the students released from their Individual Education Plans, or IEPs, before graduation so they could get a "real" diploma. I found that my students had never been told or educated about their disabilities. I sat down with my regulars, told them what their disability was, and assigned a research project where they learned about their individual disability and discovered ways to cope with it. Many of my students learned about famous people who overcame disabilities and went on to be successful adults.

Although most of the students completed the assignment, few believed that they could overcome their disability. Most believed that they would never escape their environment. One young man actually quoted news stories and explained, "I don't know why you think we should go to college, I'm gonna be dead by the time I'm twenty-five anyway." I didn't know what to say.

But Antony was different. He worked incredibly hard and did an amazing research project. He presented it as a speech and his voice was reminiscent of Dr. Martin Luther King, Jr. His audience was held captive by the resonance and intonations he used naturally. This child who had been labeled as learning disabled had a wonderful gift. I did my best to help him recognize this, and by the end of the year he was released from his IEP. He was the only one of my students to receive a regular diploma that year. I was proud of him, but my heart was defeated. What about the others? I resigned at the end of year.

• • •

"Hi, Antony. How have you been?"

"Ms. Arvidson. I'm so glad I ran into you."

"What are you up to? Buying Christmas presents?"

"Yeah. I have a job and I've been saving up for a while. What are you doing here?"

What am I supposed to tell him? I quit teaching? I'm an emotional wreck? I feel like I didn't get through to my students? I need to re-evaluate where my career is headed? That's why I'm temping during the day and working at a job I hate at night? I'm a failure?

"I'm working a night job to get a little extra money, too," I say, finally.

"That's cool." He pauses, suddenly nervous. "Hey, I wanted to tell you something." A hint of excitement is in his voice.

"Okay," I say, cautiously curious.

"Well, first, I want to say thank you."

"For what?"

"For helping me graduate. For making me believe I could graduate."

My heart skips a beat. "You did that on your own," I say quickly. "You worked hard. You have a gift and you used it."

"But I didn't believe I could until you were my teacher. You're the one who made me see that I could do anything I wanted. That was you, not me." He shrugs and looks away.

"You chose to believe that. I couldn't get through to the others. I couldn't do what I was supposed to do...." My eyes begin to fill.

"I'm in college," he blurts out and gauges my reaction. I can't speak so he continues, rambling. "It's community college, but I'm studying music and speech. My favorite class is English because it reminds me of you and what you made me believe in." I say nothing. If I speak, my voice will break. He goes on, a bit uncertain. "Anyway, I wanted you to know that and I wanted to thank you. So, thanks."

"You're welcome, Antony. I'm so proud of you." These words are whispered. I turn away quickly and enter the music store. I rush to the restroom, unable to hold back the flood of tears. I shake; I sob; I laugh out loud. My mind is spinning like I'm on a carousel. After several minutes, I manage to pull myself together enough to get through my shift.

As soon as I get home that night, I frantically dig out my teaching portfolio. I turn to the philosophy of education statement I had naïvely written in grad school. When I get to the last line, my vision blurs, as I read: "If I can help change the life of one student then I have done my job."

I wasn't a failure after all. I've been a teacher ever since.

~Jenny Scarborough

The Write Life for Me

Any life, no matter how long and complex it may be, is made up of a single moment, the moment in which a man finds out, once and for all, who he is.
~Jorge Luis Borges

The questions came amid a life storm as these things usually do. Who am I? Where am I? Why am I?

And the answer was clear: the only person I ever want to be is me.

Right before my thirtieth birthday I was diagnosed with multiple sclerosis, an autoimmune disease that affects the central nervous system. I read the results from my MRI on the hour-long drive to the neurologist's office and I cried. I cried because I was scared. I cried because I didn't understand what MS was or what was happening to my body. I cried for all the things I said I'd do someday and never did. I thought at thirty I would have it all figured out, and I didn't.

My neurologist was positive, telling me I'd live a normal life, have kids, take vacations and continue to work, but I wasn't so sure. He started me on a five-day IV of steroids to take the numbness in my legs away.

The diagnosis process was long and painful, but the recovery period was worse. I was on medical leave from work and while I was being tortured with an IV and home nurses my friends were at work living normal lives. Depression settled in and some days I didn't even want to function.

My husband reminded me that I had two options. Treat the

disease and move on with my life, or give up. I felt like I was giving up.

The IV treatments left me weak and anxious and I often burst into tears for no reason. I couldn't even sweep the kitchen floor for more than two minutes without feeling exhausted. In a fit of anger I grabbed a pen and a notebook and I wrote a letter to my MS.

I wrote about my fears and frustrations. I told that piece of paper exactly what I felt about the disease. I wielded my pen like a dangerous sword, telling no one in particular just how angry I was. The more I wrote the calmer I felt. The calmer I got the more empowered I became. Anytime I felt dispirited I sought comfort in writing. I started penning letters to the MS. By treating it like a real thing I could attack, I started to heal.

Somewhere in my soul, a spark ignited a long extinguished dream.

I had pursued writing my whole life, working on high school and college newspapers and literary anthologies, as well as graduating from college with a degree in journalism. After two years reporting at a newspaper, that dream was snuffed out and I changed industries.

My doctor released me back to work and I returned with renewed energy and a strong desire to be better than the person I was before. I wanted to show the world that MS didn't beat me and it wouldn't. I turned thirty and celebrated the beginning of a new decade.

And I wrote.

MS took me by the hand and guided me back to writing. By seeking comfort in the pen I have had more success with my writing than I had at any other time in my life and I'm finally living the life I've always wanted.

You have to choose the life you want to live, before life chooses for you. I still have a lot of stories I want to tell and I'm going to use the time I have to tell as many as I can. That's the life I choose. No regrets.

~Valerie D. Benko

Dance Lessons

There are shortcuts to happiness, and dancing is one of them.
~Vicki Baum

The feel of gliding around a dance floor gracefully performing a waltz or romantically moving in a samba is one of my greatest delights. In fact, dance has been a significant part of my entire life, and I have committed considerable time, money, energy, frustration and glowing success to mastering all different types of dance.

Would this passion have been ignited if not for the sacrifice of my mother? I doubt it. I grew up on the other side of the tracks in a very affluent town. What I mean is that while classmates were flying to Vail for the weekend to go skiing, my brothers and sister and I would get cafeteria trays to use as sleds on local golf courses. However, in our community, which is a suburb of a major metropolitan area, there were many benefits even us "townies" could enjoy. We attended outstanding schools and securely patrolled parks and streets and participated in extravagant town-directed summer activities.

But one activity that we could not enjoy by simply living in this town was dance lessons. In the early 1960s, my mother thought that dance lessons, table manners, polite behavior, and etiquette were important skills that her children needed to prepare themselves for their futures.

Her attempts at teaching us herself left her with bruised feet and left us frustrated and discouraged. Then one evening after dinner she presented us with our "church" clothes all freshly ironed and informed us that we were going to the dance school for lessons. There was such joy on her face that no one grumbled about putting on our Sunday best in the middle of the week.

For several weeks, each Thursday night we endured the sneers from our dance partners who commented on the fact that we always wore the same clothes. Their comments brushed right over me because within the first week of dance, I was hooked. The lights, the music and the intricate dance steps captivated me. For that one brief hour, I was transported to a life of gaiety that my wealthy neighbors took for granted.

At the end of the hour, my mother, who had been reading a book in the car during the lesson, would bring us home. There, she would clean up the house, make lunches for each of us for the next day, fold laundry, and review our homework. After we were tucked into bed, she would say, "I'll be back in a bit. Don't forget your prayers, and know that I love you."

This routine went on for weeks until one evening I realized that I had left my sneakers at the dance studio. Since I had gym the next day at school, I had to go back to get my sneakers. My father reluctantly drove me to the studio and just as I was about to knock on the door, I saw my mother on her hands and knees shining the hardwood floor. I was devastated; I banged on the door and my mother approached with a huge smile on her face. "Mama, what in the world…" I stammered, but before I could finish my sentence, she laughed and said, "Don't worry my precious girl, I saw your sneakers here and I was going to bring them home."

"But Mama, that is not what is upsetting me, I'm upset that you are working so hard so late at night," I wailed. She pulled me into her soft arms for a big hug and explained that the dance instructor was giving us the lessons in exchange for my mother cleaning the studio. "This is a wonderful solution, my baby girl," she stated firmly as she held me at arm's length. Looking me straight in the eye, she said, "Don't let anything take away the joy you have for dance. In fact, darling daughter of mine, never let anyone take joy away from you for anything."

As we walked arm and arm back to the car, I vowed then and there that I would honor my mother, I would honor my joy, and I would keep dancing—and I have.

~Judith Fitzsimmons

My Great Escape into Writing

An incurable itch for scribbling takes possession of many,
and grows inveterate in their insane breasts.
~Juvenal

The crack of the nun's hand against my face stung mightily but, unlike my five eighth grade buddies, I refused to cry. Stupidly, I laughed. "You think that's funny?" my diminutive principal shouted in my face as she slapped me again, harder this time.

I finally realized that standing in front of eight rigidly straight rows of fellow students for a very public reprimand was not very amusing.

My crime? Avoiding the cafeteria hot dogs by sneaking off campus to Taco Bell.

My punishment? A 500-word essay on my misdeed on top of the public flogging.

Contritely my pals etched out painfully dull confessions promising never again to break school rules. Me? I started with a title, "The Great Escape," and just managed to get my second wind somewhere past the 500-word mark.

I started out with a vivid description of the cafeteria hot dogs, noting that their remarkably rubber texture made them a perfect substitute for a four square ball if you were in a pinch. I hinted that there was an unnatural chemical makeup in the wieners and that my exit from the school grounds was all in the vein of self-preservation.

Instead of simply walking out the unmonitored side gate, I praised my squad for successfully dodging a rain of bullets from the nun-guards in our church's bell tower. In the clear, I had us shimmying under the "barbed wire" fence for our first taste of freedom in over three hours.

I went on to say that we were constantly looking over our shoulders to see if we were being "tailed." Unlucky for us, we should have been looking ahead because when we arrived at our Mecca... Taco Bell... the school secretary was leaning against her ugly brown station wagon and motioning us to get in. We'd been busted without even one bite of a crunchy taco shell for our troubles.

Needless to say, my composition was not accepted. In fact, our principal, Mother Slap-You-Twice, was outraged by my defiance.

I was taken out of class and marched to the pastor's office in the rectory. In a loud voice, the cranky nun described first my group escape and then... much worse... my insulting essay. Finally, she pulled me roughly by the upper arm to stand before the priest I'd confessed a fair share of my sins to over the years.

In a much kinder voice than that of his female colleague, he asked, "Did you write this?"

Without much remorse, I nodded in the affirmative. Exhibiting my first sign of caution since the Taco Bell epic began, I consciously avoided the utterance of even a single sound lest I dig my ditch a bit deeper.

"She should be expelled for such insolence!" Mother hotly suggested.

"Let me read it first," he replied.

He began reading and started chuckling. Turning the page, he burst out laughing. By the conclusion of "The Great Escape," tears ran down his now very red cheeks and his eyes were filled with mirth.

This appeared to bode well for me. Mother, however, was not grinning. She snatched my essay out of his hands and demanded that something be done about my rebellious attitude.

Composing his features a bit, the priest tried to conceal the silly effect my melodramatic story had on him. At last he lifted one hand and I wondered if he was giving us a blessing or just trying to get the principal to calm down.

"No, we don't want to expel her. She's our best chance at winning the essay contest."

And so my new punishment seemed painless, even intriguing, to me. I was supposed to write an essay entitled "Why I'm Proud to Be an American."

Words of freedom and individuality, two concepts I fervently embraced, flowed effortlessly from my pen. My sentiments must have touched a positive nerve with the judges because my essay took first place for the city of Sacramento and then for the State of California.

Suddenly I was a heroine instead of a hellion. I'd brought honor on my school and my principal valiantly tried to block out our prior run-ins when she greeted my parents under these most auspicious circumstances.

I must confess that I will always be grateful to my confessor who forced me to continue writing instead of hiding both pen and paper from one whose imagination easily treks to the moon and back during the space of a single lunch recess. Once I had a taste of the joy... along with the glory... writing could bring me, I couldn't be stopped.

~Marsha Porter

A Real Turnaround

Chase down your passion like it's the last bus of the night.
~Terri Guillemets

My writing career began ten years ago with my slice-of-life articles published locally and nationally. As a beginning writer, I was happy to be on my way, writing and learning as much as I could. With two little kids underfoot, as well as working full-time, it was a challenge to find time to write, but I managed.

I was soon discovering the power and effect of my words on others, translating to why I was writing; to entertain, inspire, and motivate others. Readers telling me they laughed, cried or were inspired by my personal articles only reinforced these reasons. I discovered WHY I was writing in the first place.

But they didn't know what was really going on behind the typewriter.

I was faced with many challenges, depression being one of them. A series of events had me questioning myself and my abilities, jeopardizing my happiness. I was not a happy mommy, and even though I tried to keep joy in the house, I knew it wasn't the same. I had no spark, and found it difficult to enjoy the everyday little things in life. My writing life stalled, then stopped, and I didn't write much for two years. I lost the passion and reason of why I was writing in the first place, and forgot the joy it gave me and others. And just to compound things, I gained weight—the most I had weighed in my lifetime.

In short, I was not a happy person.

But slowly I crept out of the darkness, one step at a time, one word a time.

I learned I had to be in control of my own happiness if I was to feel better, be a more engaged mom, and have a happier life.

I started walking, establishing a routine—or trying to at least. A few years had gone by during these challenging times so my kids had gotten older, and I was able to escape for short periods. I traded early-morning television news on the couch and sipping tea, for running shoes, rain and sometimes snow. I got out there and walked, rain or shine, maybe not every morning, but at least every other morning. It cleared my head, allowed me time to think, gave me fresh air and fortitude, and made me feel invigorated and healthy. I was eating wisely, and the weight started to go. Slowly the walking gave way to a running-kind of thing; I am not a marathoner, and my style of running was, and still is, not attractive. But it worked for me. It put a spring in my step, and gave me energy and spark to get out and do things with my kids—and enjoy it.

But I was still missing one integral part of myself—my passion.

I started writing again, and rediscovered how much happiness it gave me. I had started a new job, joined a monthly writing chapter, and was determined to keep up my walking/running routine. Finding balance was sometimes difficult in juggling my family, my job, and my walking/running routine. But I was determined to fit in writing time—because it made me happy. Early mornings had me pounding the pavement, not only because it was the perfect solitary time to do it, but because that was the only time I could do it. There was no reason why I couldn't also be writing in the early mornings when the world was asleep. Sure I loved to watch the news and have my tea, but that wasn't my passion—that wasn't what made me truly happy.

The solution? I set the alarm just a bit earlier and either wrote on the alternate mornings when I wasn't walking, or I would squeeze in some writing time after my time outside.

Through all this, I learned that happiness does not take a lot of hard work, but it needs to be worked on—created and controlled by me. I created my own happiness, and in turn, I have been more involved with my kids, more focused on them when they need me. I had to sacrifice sitting on the couch every morning with my tea and the television news playing, and get out there and do something that would foster my happiness.

It has gone full circle. My own happiness has showed through in my mothering and through my family, my job performance and my attitude towards challenging situations. I again have readers telling me the effect my writing has had on them, with some able to get on with their own writing because of my inspirational/motivational articles. I laugh more, and my kids laugh with their happier mother.

It was up to me to make it happen—my own happiness. One step at a time—one word at a time.

And I did.

~Lisa McManus Lange

Find Your Happiness

Attitude Adjustments

The only difference between a good day and a bad day is your attitude.

~Dennis S. Brown

Life in the Slow Lane

The moment one gives close attention to any thing, even a blade of grass it becomes a mysterious, awesome, indescribably magnificent world in itself.
~Henry Miller

I always seemed to be running late. I'd wake up in the morning early enough to have plenty of time to get to where I wanted to go. But by the time I found myself on the road headed for my destination, it was obvious that I was going to be late. So I'd strap on my seatbelt, put the car in gear, and slam the accelerator to the floor in an attempt to make up for the five or ten minutes that I'd somehow lost. The scenery became nothing but a blur as I played chicken with the traffic lights and kept my mental radar on the alert for the men in blue.

This constant rushing also extended into other aspects of my life. When I went grocery shopping, I looked much like the winner of an all-you-can-spend-in-five-minutes shopping spree. I'd race up and down the aisles throwing in items right and left. My cart would take the corners on two wheels as I yelled out my deli order to the startled lady behind the counter.

Or, at the mall, I'd race through the stores like an entrant in the hundred-yard dash. There was no window shopping for me. I'd plan my route before I even walked through the doors and then neither rain nor sleet nor an unexpected sale at JCPenney could keep me from making my rounds.

I had to rush around like that. There just weren't enough hours in the day and I was afraid I might miss something if I didn't hurry up.

And then one day, as fate would have it, I ran out of gas. I had been running behind as usual so I hadn't noticed my gas gauge. As my car coasted off the road, I looked at my watch and slammed the steering wheel in frustration. I had a meeting in fifteen minutes and I hadn't even finished preparing for it.

But as I got out of my car, an amazing thing happened. I looked out towards the east, and the sun was just beginning to blaze over the horizon. There was a low misty fog hanging over the river and some ducks were cutting thick, smooth trails across the otherwise glass-like surface of the water. A few sailboats sat at anchor, their mirror images extending out before them. And as the sun inched up through tiny trails of clouds that stretched across the sky, it extended beacons of glorious, wondrous light that shouted with all its beauty and strength, "Behold world! I have risen, again, for another day!"

I was awestruck. This glorious scene had been going on right outside my car every morning and I had never taken the time to see it. I had been rushing around in such a hurry to not miss anything that I had been missing everything!

I turned toward the road. Traffic was whizzing by at breakneck speed. I wanted to shout at the drivers, "Stop! Look what's happening over here! You're missing it!" But instead, I climbed up and had a seat on the hood of my car. And I quietly, joyfully, patiently watched as the sun painted a brand new day: a day of ducks and sailboats and silvery reflections on a mirrored sea.

When a co-worker finally recognized my car and stopped for me, I had somehow been transformed. My heart, my mind and my soul were all lighter. I went into work but was jealous that my car got to stay behind for a few more hours and watch the transformation of morning into afternoon, as the ducks and the river and the sailors all woke up and moved into their day.

It was as if I had been switched from 78 down to 33 rpm that day. Life went from a fast jitterbug into a slow, fluid waltz. I slowed down enough to see the people I worked with. To talk to them about things other than work. To notice if they were particularly happy or troubled and to see if they needed to tell me why.

I began taking long, slow walks around my yard and neighborhood, noticing for the first time all the mysteries and wonders that were right there for me to see all the time, patiently waiting for me to slow down enough to notice. Not only were there sights that I had been missing, but I began to hear entire symphonies all around me: birds singing, wind blowing, leaves rustling. And as I continued to practice my newfound peace, I discovered, to my amazement, another sound: a still, small voice deep inside my soul. And this voice had incredible things to say, images of intense beauty to point out, flashes of great insight, pearls of deep wisdom and constant words of inspiration, encouragement and guidance.

Life is different now. For years I had been like a hamster in an exercise wheel, running and running and running and never realizing that the destination I was racing to… was exactly the place that I already was. In fact, I've traded in my exercise wheel for a hammock, and this lazy hamster is sometimes quite content to just lie on my back and spend an entire afternoon trying to make clouds disappear. And incredibly enough, the world is still turning. It didn't need my hamster wheel for momentum after all.

I'll admit that I am a few minutes late to work sometimes now. And I take forever in the grocery store. And window shopping and people watching in the mall can take an entire afternoon. But life is no longer passing me by. I am here, fully present, in every moment of life as it unfolds before me. Joyfully, peacefully, patiently traveling this life in the slow lane… and enjoying every precious moment of it.

~Betsy S. Franz

A Matter of Perspective

What we see depends mainly on what we look for.
~John Lubbock

There have been times in my life when I felt like I had the weight not only of the world, but the entire universe, on my shoulders. During those times I was sure life couldn't get any worse, and that I was the unluckiest person who'd ever lived.

That all changed in a heartbeat one cold winter day. I found myself downtown, shuffling along the street with my head hanging, my spirits low. I'd just gotten word the promotion I was hoping for had gone to another person. A year's worth of hard work had come to nothing, and I was looking at another year of grinding away at a crummy job I could barely stand. The icy wind that bit at my face was like a slap from the uncaring hand of fate.

Worse than all that, I was meeting my wife, and I'd have to look into those hopeful, ever supportive eyes and watch the light go out of them as I told her how I'd failed to reach yet another goal. We would have to find a way to make do again, to figure out how to keep a roof over our heads and food on the table, when we'd already stretched our budget to the breaking point.

Why did life have to be so hard? I worked for my living, putting in eight, ten, twelve hours a day, going to school at night trying to better myself and make me look more indispensable to the company I worked for. Didn't I offer to take every thankless job that no one else wanted to touch? Didn't I show up every day with a smile on my face and a can-do attitude? Why was all that effort ignored?

Finally I saw my wife standing there, moving from one foot to the other, trying to stay warm. I immediately noticed her coat, years out of style and beginning to grow threadbare at the edges, her shoes that were not made for such harsh weather, and the hair that she had learned to cut herself to save money. This was the woman that I had to disappoint yet again. I knew that the dreams she'd had in her heart when we first married had not been extinguished, but they had been cut down and reduced to more modest hopes. Even those would have to be dashed this day.

I stood there holding her against the cold as I explained what had happened, and being the person she is, she took it all in with a grace and love that would not allow a trace of accusation aimed at me. She didn't have to. I felt enough of it for both of us. As we walked toward the bus stop, passing by a group of strangers huddled against the cold, I couldn't contain it any longer. I stopped and looked up at the heavens, feeling the anger well up in my throat.

"Why does it have to be like this?" I said out loud, the bitterness plain in my voice. "Why do we have to be stuck renting a tiny little house in a poor neighborhood? Why do I have to have a desk job that pays me minimum wage? Why does my family have to live on beans and rice and bread? Why do we have the same clothes we bought years ago? Why am I down to my last five dollars every payday? Why does it have to be like this?"

My wife was trying to tug me along, but I pulled back, not wanting to take another step further in the terrible life I had. I stood there on the icy street, wanting to just collapse under the weight of my endless problems. I was ready to give up, to say I had been cheated out of a life that I deserved. That's when I heard the voice speak softly beside me.

It was one of the strangers in the group of men we'd passed by, and as I turned to look at him I realized he was one of the homeless people who hung out by the river surviving on handouts. The man was dressed all in rags, his hands and face were red from the cold, and the look on his face was one of the saddest I had ever seen. I stood there and stared at him, hearing the words he'd spoken moments before echo inside my head.

"Man, I wish I had that guy's problems."

In that instant I came to realize all the blessings that had been given to me, all the gifts I'd taken for granted and ignored. As I looked over and stared at my wife trembling in the cold, I realized I was one of the luckiest men on earth. I had a wife who loved me, a family I adored, a job that kept us going, and hopes and dreams for the future that had never been erased.

I smiled at my wife, and the hope I'd been draining from her came back into her eyes. There was a silent question I asked her, and she instantly understood what I wanted to do. She nodded, and I stepped toward the man who'd spoken those words. I reached into my pocket, pulled out my last five dollars, and put them into his hand. Then I rejoined my wife and the two of us walked down the street, the warmth in our hearts keeping us safe from even the bitterest cold.

~John P. Buentello

34

The Reset Button

Attitude is a little thing that makes a big difference.
~Winston Churchill

My co-worker Jan lives in an electric wheelchair. A few years back, a public bus door grabbed her left leg and wouldn't let go. She lost her leg above the knee and her life changed dramatically. As long as I have worked with her, I have had a hard time understanding how she keeps such a good attitude given what has happened to her and how inconvenient her life is now.

But life goes on. Jan is finishing her college degree now, one class at a time.

One particularly stressful day we were working together in customer service. Jan usually runs the bestseller book division at our store. She has a crack memory and is very good at customer service and details. People love to work with her.

But the customers this day could not be satisfied. Finally when there was a lull in the complaints, Jan said she would be gone for a few minutes. "Is it finally time for a break?" I teased her, knowing it was hours past that.

"No," said Jan. "It is time for the reset button." She zoomed off in her electric wheelchair. I didn't recall seeing any reset button on her chair.

It wasn't very long and Jan was back with a smile on her face. Noticing my puzzled look, she asked what I was thinking.

"Well, you said you were going to use the reset button. You came back with a smile on your face, like things have changed."

Jan had a laugh like a fairy. You could hear it ring all over the store. My question had certainly amused her.

"The reset button is my way of saying that I need to stop to reassess things, count my blessings and realize I have a lot to be grateful for. I needed to adjust my attitude to reality, not just a few hours this morning that were miserable. It makes life go much better."

Working with Jan is a blessing for me, even in stressful times.

Jan zoomed in closer to where I was standing and spoke in a low voice. "You know," she said, "it's lucky the reset button never sticks, because some days I have to use it a lot!" With that she zoomed back to her desk laughing.

~Pamela Gilsenan

Happy Today

If you don't think every day is a good day, just try missing one.
~Cavett Robert

My profession as a hospice chaplain is usually a conversation stopper, especially at parties. After all, who wants to talk about death and dying when deciding which dessert to eat? Nope, hospice talk just doesn't seem to go hand in hand with happiness and party talk.

But in fact, some of the happiest folks I have ever known are those I serve as a hospice chaplain. But they are dying, you say; how can they be happy?

Death, or rather the knowledge that your death is imminent, does many things to folks. It causes great denial, grief, agony, heartbreak, and reflection. And rightly so. But after a while, it can provide great motivation to enjoy the last days of your life to the fullest. You don't have a day to waste, a day to complain, a day to hate, a day to not be happy.

You eat the best foods, visit your favorite places, and receive calls and visits from your favorite people. You stop worrying about hair and make-up. Your grudges and resentments are abandoned. There's no more keeping up with the Joneses. Letting the "child within" come out to play becomes a priority. You laugh as you recall old stories. You let go of the bad and embrace the good when you know life is indeed very, very, short.

Often my patients tell me how happy they are relinquishing

their worries, their prejudices, their anger, their fears and really enjoying today, one minute at a time, with its beauty, its simplicity, its love. How much happier would we all be if we recognized these truths: that joy is found in people, not things? That fear of tomorrow reduces the pleasures of today? That grudges burden us and prevent us from embracing grace and forgiveness? That each day is a gift to be given and received with open hands and loving hearts?

Why should the grim reaper have to knock on our door before we open the door to happiness?

On the day before she died, one of my patients asked me to send cards to ten people who she had hated or who she knew had hated her. She wrote these words inside each card:

I have held a grudge against you for many years. Forgive me.
I have wished bad things to happen to you. Understand me.
I have wanted to harm you as you harmed me. Accept me.
I am dying soon. Don't cry for me.

I want you to be happy when you think of me. Smile for me.
Be happy now, for one day you too will die.
Learn to love and then you will be happy.
It is a lesson I wish I had learned long ago.
I love you.

She sent the cards, laughing as we addressed each one, telling me about each person and the now insignificant reasons why she had disliked them so much or they had disliked her.

As I left, this woman looked at me and said, "It's never too late to be happy, is it?"

Nope, it's not. Start today.

~Malinda Dunlap Fillingim

Career Magic

More men are killed by overwork than the importance of this world justifies.
~Rudyard Kipling

The gift I'd been striving for—working day and night to achieve—had finally arrived in the form of a phone call. My heart raced as I listened to the words I'd been waiting to hear: "We'd like to offer you the position of District Conservationist in Mifflin County."

I accepted my first supervisory role, determined to take on any new challenge life threw my way. Already blessed with a position as a trainee in resource protection, the promotion was a real honor. I reported to my new office in Lewistown, Pennsylvania with eagerness and resolve. Ready to save the world!

Applying for the job in Mifflin County took a pole vault of faith. I grew up outside of Pittsburgh, far from the rural countryside where my career had now taken me. The differences in culture and surroundings were astonishing. I soon realized a major traffic jam in Mifflin County consisted of being the third car behind an Amish buggy.

The shopping centers and subdivisions of my old world were replaced by flourishing farm fields, stretching from forested ridge to forested ridge. It felt like I'd found heaven on earth. The community welcomed me with open hearts and genuine delight. Smiles and joy proved to be the norm, beaming from every corner of the county.

Living in this tranquil paradise was beyond my wildest dreams and life seemed to be filled with limitless opportunities.

I decided to be the best District Conservationist in the history of the world. No demand too great. No obstacle insurmountable. With a new staff, my major duty was to be a great supervisor. So, even though fieldwork was the responsibility of the staff, I figured the best way to be that great supervisor was to engage in as much of it as possible. I wanted to prove to them I didn't expect them to do anything I wouldn't.

I raced out of the starting blocks and sprinted towards a mountain of new goals. A mountain which grew higher and higher, while I took on more and more projects.

Meanwhile, while I was out in the field doing their work, the staff spent their days lounging in the air-conditioned office complaining about life. Worse, the paperwork involved with being a supervisor continued to pile up.

And on top of my mounting tasks, I wanted to learn all there was to know about farming and conservation. Using every moment I could spare, I devoured textbooks to learn about crops, cows, and everything rural.

Pretty soon life became a tornado, spinning wildly out of control. I was doing fieldwork during the day and working late into the evening trying to catch up on my paperwork.

In a crushing moment, it hit me: this wasn't the way I pictured my dream job.

My stress snowballed. Life's balance disappeared. No matter how hard I worked, I slipped further and further behind. The dreams of grandeur I had when I took the position dwindled... fading into oblivion.

Time off, even on weekends, became a pipe dream. I lost sleep worrying about the work accumulating on my desk and the countless unfinished tasks cluttering my mind.

Finally, after eight months in the position, I requested a meeting with my supervisor, George. Making the call to him consumed me with dread. It was the ultimate admission of defeat. But I realized it was time to fess up and let him know how far behind I was.

I felt dejected, burned out, and exasperated.

On the drive to George's office a week later, my mind played movies of George's rage and anger. I could already hear his disappointment. My pride would be bruised, my honor tarnished—even destroyed. I readied myself for the bitter pill I was about to swallow.

When I arrived, I feigned a smile at his assistant, and entered his office. I took a seat across from George and exhaled.

"I'm sorry George. I've worked so hard and poured my heart and soul into my job. But I'm feeling like a miserable failure. The more hours I put in, the more I get behind. I need help." I could barely look him in the eyes when I added, "I'm truly sorry to disappoint you."

The tourniquet in my stomach tightened as I readied myself for the worst. Then, to my surprise, George smiled.

He kicked back in his chair and said, "Relax. Enjoy yourself. Life's too short to waste with worry. There's one little word you need to learn. That word is no. You don't need to take on every project. You don't need to juggle every ball. You don't need to waste time with worry. You need to enjoy life and focus on all the good. You'll be far more productive with far less anguish."

At that moment, it felt like a two-ton weight was lifted from my shoulders. Then George reached into his desk drawer and pulled out a book, *How to Stop Worrying and Start Living* by Dale Carnegie. He handed it to me.

With a relaxed smile, George said, "Read this and learn to love your life."

I studied the book in my hands, feeling as if I'd been given a gift from heaven.

George continued, "Larry you are a darn good employee and supervisor. You make me proud. Keep up the great work and dedicated spirit and enjoy every moment."

The remaining weight on my shoulders lifted. A smile drifted back to my face and into my soul. I knew I'd just been handed one of those rare change-your-life-forever moments.

And then George dispensed some advice I'll never forget. He said, "A supervisor is someone who you look up to and respect, who wants the best for his people, and who guides with kindness. Be a fabulous supervisor and lead with a loving heart."

What a revelation! And delivered by one of the most amazing supervisors I've ever had.

I left the office a new man. I devoured the book. The words empowered me with a whole new perspective and respect for the rare gift of living a happy and fulfilled life.

From that day forward, when my mind would clutter with negative thoughts of worry and lead me down the path to despair, I became aware how hopelessness crowded out all the good. But positive thoughts made room for creativity, productivity, love, and happiness.

Now, after nearly thirty years, thanks to one man's wisdom and encouragement, there's an opening in my life for everything that is good and magnificent in this world. It's a treasure I cherish every day as I celebrate the magic in every moment!

~Larry Schardt

The Choice

Happiness is a conscious choice, not an automatic response.
~Mildred Barthel

I sat down on one of the logs that had been washed up by the sea. I loved to search them for the carved initials of kids in love. Not today though. I had too much on my mind. Bills to pay, the state of the economy and where it was headed, and the general strife in the world had left me sad and depressed. I came to the seaside hoping the crisp salty air would cheer me up.

Suddenly a spry elderly man appeared over the crest of a dune. A small white dog scampered over the rocks around his feet. I watched as he drew closer and closer and then to my surprise he came right over to where I was sitting and asked if he could join me. I nodded.

"How are you this fine day?" he asked with a smile, and I thought I could actually see the wisdom swirling behind his blue irises.

"I am okay," I replied with a sigh. I began wondering about him and his sudden curious presence.

"Well, it is my experience that when someone sighs after something they've said then it isn't always the full truth. In your face I can see that this is the case."

I produced a weak smile and told him he was pretty observant, and felt strangely compelled to tell him about how I was feeling and why. I was surprised how easy it was to speak with this stranger. It wasn't my nature at all. Perhaps it was his kind smile and his unthreatening demeanor that put me at ease. Whatever it was, this wonderful spirit and his frolicking dog had me laughing in no time.

"Thanks for turning my day around," I said to him.

"It was your choice to do so," he told me.

"What do you mean?" I asked.

"I will let you in on a little secret," he said in a low voice. "I wasn't always a happy person. I was more of a curmudgeon, angry at the world and what it had given me. My negativity pushed away all those who I cherished."

"What turned you around?" I asked. I had a hard time believing this man, with eyes that turned into happy upside-down crinkle-smiles every time he laughed, could be anything other than the pleasant man I saw before me.

"One day the thought hit me, I could go through life as I had been and continue a lonely existence, or I could make a conscious choice and turn it around. I could choose to be happy."

"Did it work?"

"Not at first. It was hard to change my lifestyle. I was an old man set in my ways, but I persevered. I learned to look around and see that I might not have control over what happened in my day, but I could control how I reacted to it. I think that might have been the whole key to my unhappiness, the feeling of being totally out of control of things."

I sat in silence and looked out over the beach and ocean while mulling over his words. Could it really be that easy? Could we just simply choose how we reacted to the unpleasant or negative things in our lives? I looked at him again, and knew it to be true, for here was the evidence before me.

"Don't take my word for it darlin'," he said with a wink. "The only way to be sure is to try it out for yourself." Then he gave me a smile and wave and started up the beach, with the dog bounding along the shore.

~Tracie Skarbo

Miracle Grow

Every problem has in it the seeds of its own solution.
If you don't have any problems, you don't get any seeds.
~Norman Vincent Peale

plastered on a Happy New Year smile as we rang the doorbell. It wasn't that I didn't like my husband's friends. It's just that they were so perfect. Everything about their girls—their sippy cups, ballerina outfits, and Veggie Tale videos—reminded me of the innocence my own daughter once displayed. But those dreams met reality when she moved out. Soon afterwards, Ashley was arrested for drug possession and later for a DUI. With all of the problems she faced, I couldn't help but wonder where I had failed.

As Keisha opened the door, the aroma of black-eyed peas and cornbread offered a warm holiday welcome. "I hope we're not interrupting," I said. "We just wanted to stop by to say hello."

"Not at all. Come in!" insisted Keisha as she gave us both a hug. "I'll get Anthony."

Anthony's 6'9" frame sauntered down the hallway.

"Hey big guy, Happy New Year!" bellowed my husband John as he embraced Anthony. "How's my brother from another mother?"

"Just fine," grinned Anthony, smiling at the familiar wisecrack.

Aside from the obvious height difference, anyone could tell by looking at Anthony's black skin and my husband's blond hair that they didn't belong at the same family reunion. But ever since their chance encounter in the office break room years ago that led to a life-changing Bible Study, they considered each other brothers for life.

"Have a seat you two lovebirds, but try to keep it G-rated. Our girls are still up," he joked as he nodded toward his daughters playing with their dolls by the fireplace.

A twinge of jealousy unleashed a backlog of emotion. I remembered when Ashley was their age. She loved loading up her Cabbage Patch dolls in her Cozy Coupe to go "gocey shopping." Now, even though she was old enough to drive a real car, her license was suspended due to her DUI charge.

Anthony's booming voice startled me. "Teresa, what are your hopes for the upcoming year?"

I shifted in my seat. There was no point in avoiding the obvious. He knew about my issues with Ashley, but he wouldn't understand. His girls were perfect. In fact, his whole family was perfect.

"Unity... in my family," I stammered. "What about you, Anthony?"

Anthony sighed deeply and paused before he answered. "The fruit for the upcoming year is in the soil of the previous year."

My forehead wrinkled. "The soil of the previous year?"

"Last year had its share of challenges, but even so, the hard times were beneficial."

This was news to me. From my vantage point, they lived in Christian Happy Hollow. They went to church faithfully, founded a thriving marriage ministry, followed the ways of Financial Peace University and home-schooled their girls, who quoted scripture at three years old and never disobeyed. All the bills were paid and life was grand. What kind of problems could he have?

"In order to prepare me for next year, God planted things in my life last year in anticipation of the coming season."

Anthony—ever the deep thinker—rarely gave answers that were understood without further investigation. I often teased him that his distinct "King James" accent was difficult to understand. "What kind of things?" I questioned.

"You know. Challenges... issues."

What kind of issues could he have faced? His family wore halos.

"Problems and difficulties…" Anthony continued, "those things are the riches in the dirt."

"Problems are riches? What do you mean by that?"

"If I were to mistake the riches for dirt, I would despise the very thing essential for my growth." Anthony was starting to sound like my mother and the time she bought manure for our garden.

I remember asking her in shock, "Why are you buying that?" I couldn't imagine why anyone would pay for recycled cow patties.

"It's fertilizer," Mom replied. "It makes the soil rich so that plants produce more fruit."

That made about as much sense to me as eating my vegetables, but Mom was right. Later that year, our garden was bursting at the seams.

As I thought about the loads of stinky fertilizer that I helped haul in my mother's red wheel barrel, I thought about my own stinky problems. I wanted unity in my relationship with my daughter more than anything else.

"I think I see what you mean, Anthony," I began. "As much as I hated the issues I faced last year, in retrospect, I can see how they have taught me to walk in patience and forgiveness."

"Aren't patience and forgiveness prerequisites for unity?" Anthony asked.

"How did you get so smart?" I asked half joking, half serious.

"I've been through a similar issue with my sister," Anthony revealed. "Heroin had such a grip on her that she lost everything she owned. It devastated our family and drove my parents insane. It wasn't until after she lost custody of her children that she made a serious effort to get clean."

I caught a glimpse of a family photo on the coffee table. I thought my issues were evidence of my failure, but this family that I mentally elevated had struggles too. Until then I thought the absence of problems is what made a family perfect, but Anthony's observations sowed new awareness in my heart. The struggles my daughter faced are not fatal. As long as I continue to cultivate patience and forgiveness my hopes for family unity are not far from reality. I wasn't really a failure after all. My insecurities and perceived failures are just doing their job—growing fruit in me.

~Teresa Brightwell

Coupon Bliss

Happiness consists more in conveniences of pleasure that occur every day than in great pieces of good fortune that happen but seldom.
~Benjamin Franklin

When I was twenty-something and single, I had no real responsibilities and no real concept of the value of a dollar. I was just happy to have my own apartment and to "have it match" as my grandmother used to say.

As time went on, I began to embrace the so-called "adult things" in life, like comparison shopping and balancing a checkbook. As more time passed and I became a wife and mother with real responsibilities, I realized how truly important it was to account for every penny and stretch my money to the fullest.

One day last week I found myself a little down. I used to enjoy going to the bookstore and hanging out for hours reading the newest Anne Rice novel, or reveling in the company of girlfriends in the local sports bar catching up on gossip. Now I get to sneak some free time in here or there when grandma or the sitter is available, and that's just fine, but I began to ask myself... if things like going to a bookstore or hanging out with friends brought me happiness, what makes me happy now?

The more I asked myself that question the more depressed I became. What makes me happy? I do love spending time with my husband and family. But what really brightens my day?

I ran to CVS after work before picking up the boys from day care.

I had a two-dollar coupon for diapers that I wanted to use before it expired. As I was checking out, the lady behind the counter pointed out that I had earned five dollars off my next household paper purchase. I politely smiled and made some appreciative remark.

I was about drive out of the parking lot when I remembered that I also needed paper towels. I debated whether or not to go back in or wait and make the trip to Walmart on some other dreadful Mommy day.

I decided that since I was already there and I had my new coupon, I might as well go ahead and get the paper towels. What was another five minutes? So I picked out what seemed to be the best deal—two dollars off with a CVS discount card. My afternoon was already getting a little better. I took the paper towels to the counter, and of course I heard "Back so soon!" I handed over my discount card for the two dollars off, my coupon for the five dollars off... already that was seven dollars off my twelve-roll pack of paper towels. I was feeling pretty darn good! Then just as I was reaching for my wallet, the lady behind the counter pulled out the big guns... she scanned in another coupon that someone ahead of me had left, and BAM another three dollars off. That came to a total of ten whole dollars off my twelve-roll pack of paper towels.

By the time I got into my car, I was so elated I could hardly contain myself. What was wrong with me? They were just paper towels! Then it hit me—in my new life as a busy wife and mother, my happiness comes from these little moments that occur from time to time, like coupon bliss.

~Megale Rivera

The Gift of Change

In all affairs it's a healthy thing now and then to hang a question mark on the things you have long taken for granted.
~Bertrand Russell

For years I was unhappy with most of the gifts I received for my birthday, Christmas or other occasions. I put a lot of thought into the gifts I gave to others, and it seemed to me that that they did not return the favor.

Didn't those closest to me know that I didn't enjoy reading romance novels? Or that gadgets for my car would go unused? And surely they should have figured out that if they wanted to get me a food gift it had to be chocolate! But no, the stream of gifts that I put in the back of my dresser drawer, gave away, or even sometimes threw away, continued.

I didn't speak up. I didn't want to hurt the feelings of those I loved and cared about, but my resentment began to grow. I felt like the most important people in my life didn't really know me, or maybe didn't care enough about me to think about my likes and dislikes.

One day I was unwrapping a birthday gift from my teenage son—a blouse more stylish than I felt comfortable wearing. My first thought when I peeled back the tissue paper and saw the blouse was that it was another candidate to hang in the back of my closet. But when I looked up at Jason's face and saw him smiling at me with anticipation, I finally got it. It was an epiphany that made me readjust the attitude of a lifetime in a moment.

"What do you think, Mom?" Jason asked, barely waiting for me to pull the blouse out of the box. "I thought it would look so nice on you."

"It's beautiful," I was able to say authentically as I hugged him. In that moment of clarity I realized that Jason saw me as someone who would be open to receiving and wearing something more elegant than my usual attire. He wanted to give me something special.

"Try it on — I want to see how it looks," Jason added.

"I know just the skirt to try it with," I said as I headed towards my closet.

When I re-entered the living room with the outfit on, Jason was waiting. "It looks just like I thought it would. It's pretty on you, Mom," Jason said.

I tried to stop the tears that were welling in the corner of my eyes. "Thank you, honey. It is a beautiful blouse. I can tell you put a lot of thought into picking it out."

"You're welcome Mom — glad you like it," Jason said, and he continued to smile as he gave me another quick hug before he walked away.

Jason probably wondered why I was so emotional over the gift. He had no way of knowing that he'd given me much more than a blouse.

I began to think back on gifts I'd rejected as a bad fit for me and grasped the fact that maybe the people who gave me the gifts saw something in me that I didn't see in myself. They might have thought I was more romantic, or adventurous, or saw me as a better cook than I gave myself credit for. I began to see myself as others saw me. That opened me up to change and growth.

In the years since I received Jason's present, I have rarely felt disappointed when a gift doesn't match my interests or desires. I go into holidays with no expectation of receiving anything, and then everything I receive becomes a blessing. The idea that someone thinks of me, and spends precious time, thought and money to purchase and wrap a gift is more than enough for me. It is amazing how much more pleasant each occasion is, and how much more I appreciate my family and friends since this insight.

There is definitely something special about receiving a gift that is perfectly suited for you. But I have found it is just as special to receive all gifts with an open mind and a grateful heart and spirit.

~Nancy Hatten

Tending Happiness

In order to have great happiness you have to have great pain
and unhappiness—otherwise how would you know when you're happy?
~Leslie Caron

I don't think I understood happiness until I experienced a tragedy. I know that sounds backwards, but it's true. Sometimes it takes a tragedy to make you realize that happiness can be found anywhere, and at any time. The trick is to stay open to the possibility.

My mother died of cancer at the age of fifty-five. The last two years of her life were filled with medical appointments, scan results, side effects, and the fear that she would not live to see her grandchildren grow up. Those years were also filled with holidays, birthday dinners, and last vacations together. We tried to stay positive, focusing on the moment and taking each day as it came. There was happiness, but it was tinged by sadness and the fear of an uncertain future. Happiness mixed with sorrow, which I was not used to. I had always thought happiness was a pure thing, like black and white. I was either happy or I was not. Now I know that happiness is more complicated than that, that you can experience happiness even when you are sad or worried. Happiness is often a mixed emotion. Perhaps it is only pure when you are a child. After all, when you are six, an ice cream cone can be enough.

The day before my mother died I sat beside her bed listening to her breathing. It sounded much more labored than usual. The hospice nurse stopped by during her rounds and, after checking Mom's vital signs, ushered us into the next room.

"She hasn't been talking to us," my father told her. "She doesn't respond to anything."

The nurse nodded her head, an apologetic look in her eyes.

"Your mother is slipping into a coma," she said. "She may only have forty-eight hours to live."

Forty-eight hours to live. My mother slept, unaware of the tension in the room. She did not hear the nurse giving my father instructions on how to administer anti-seizure pills. She did not hear us halfheartedly discuss what to do about lunch. Her breathing took on a rattling quality as the hours ticked by. We turned on the television to distract ourselves with the noise.

While I sat staring at the television but not really watching it, I noticed a small plant on the table next to Mom's bed. It was a tiny purple primrose plant, bought on impulse a few weeks ago. My heart ached to remember my four-year-old proudly carrying it into the house. The plant had been a nice focal point over the last weeks of our vigil, an early sign of spring and hope in the dead of winter. Now the plant was dead. The leaves were shriveled and dry and the flowers were crumbling. I mentally kicked myself for forgetting to water it.

To distract myself, I took the plant into the kitchen to throw it away. I planned to water the other houseplants while I was thinking of it. But I changed my mind as I held the plant over the trashcan. Instead I turned on the tap and warmed the water slightly before letting it run into the parched soil. Not really expecting much, I returned the plant to Mom's bedside.

As the day wore on, Mom grew gradually worse. The rest of us spent the afternoon beside her, flipping through old picture albums and remembering happier times. I hoped she could hear our memories, even though she seemed unaware of our presence. We made a pile of our favorite photos, planning to make them into a collage for the funeral. The somber atmosphere was punctuated by laughter, easing the tension even though it felt out of place. My sister held up a photo of my mother's perfectly manicured feet, facing a beautiful Caribbean beach. "Should we use this one?" she asked jokingly, and we all agreed that we should. By the time bedtime rolled around, we had amassed quite a collection of photos along with our memories.

My mother passed away early the next morning. We were all by her side. I hope that counted for something, although she gave no sign she knew we were there. She said no last words. The next few hours were surreal: part relief that the long ordeal was over, part despair, part fear of the future. But for some reason, I began to notice things that morning. I noticed that the day, although bitterly cold, was stunningly beautiful, with a clear blue sky and the sun reflecting off the snow. I called home and, though I had sad news, I noticed and appreciated the normal sounds of my children playing in the background. "Will you tell them?" I asked my husband, knowing I could not.

After hanging up the phone, I went to clear away some things from the bedside table. That's when I saw something that made my heart quicken. The primrose I had nearly thrown away the previous day was blooming. A tiny purple flower bud had formed and opened overnight from a plant seemingly devoid of all possibility. I placed the plant on a sunny windowsill and, for the first time in several weeks, I felt happy.

"It's a sign," I told my father, feeling somewhat corny as I said it. But even if the flower was not a sign from my mother, it was a sign that things would be okay. A sign that while the months and years ahead would certainly have their share of sorrow, there would be happiness and hope alongside. And rather than eliminate my happiness, the sadness would merely make it more complex. Happiness is rarely a pure emotion after all.

It's been over a year since my mother's death. I am slowly coming to accept that the happiness in my life will never be as pure as it was back when an ice cream cone was enough. I feel happy when I read to my toddler, when my five-year-old gives me a spontaneous hug, when Christmas is approaching. But there is always a tinge of something else: my toddler is growing up too quickly, my son will not always hug so readily, my mother will not be there to open gifts with us. Yet happiness can be found everywhere and anywhere, in the small things that make up daily living. I try to experience it as fully as I can, as often as I can. It is not easy. The tinge of sadness is always there.

The tiny purple primrose is long gone, but I think of it every day. I know now that primroses are like that. You can let them dry out and bring them back to life with a good watering. They can go dormant, seemingly dead, yet they will bloom again with a small amount of tending.

Happiness is like that too.

~Kimberly Misra

Find Your Happiness

Overcoming Adversity

*Even if happiness forgets you a little bit,
never completely forget about it.*

~Jacques Prévert

Happiness Through Forgiveness

Forgiveness does not change the past, but it does enlarge the future.
~Paul Boese

t was raining the day I found out. Not just a light sprinkle, but a heavy, foggy, cold February downpour. I had spent a lazy day at Color-Me-Mine painting a teddy bear with my friends. I was twelve years old. I was starting to fit in at school. I was happy. But little did I know that was all about to change.

I came home to my ten-year-old brother watching TV and playing a video game. Just past the television was a sliding glass door leading to our patio. My dad was standing outside on the phone with his back turned towards us.

"Dad's mad," my brother said, not even bothering to look up from his Game Boy. I was in such a good mood from spending the day with friends that I didn't even care to know why. I went into my bedroom and sat down at my computer, ready to spend the rest of my Saturday online. Not even two minutes later, my dad walked into the bedroom my brother and I shared, sat down, and said, "Nicole, we need to have a family meeting." He called for my brother to come into the bedroom, and as we waited for him, my mind raced, trying to think of anything I might have done to get in trouble. It was never a good sign when he called me Nicole. My brother finally shuffled in and sat down on the bed next to my father.

Without any warning at all, he looked at me and said, "Your mom's gone." I didn't understand what he meant. I didn't want to. Everything went silent. I could hear only my own breath echoing in my ears like a bad horror movie, and I watched my dad and my brother hold each other and cry.

"You're lying," I said, starting to laugh. Why was I laughing? I knew they weren't lying. My father was sitting in front of me bawling his eyes out—a grown man crying like a toddler. But I couldn't believe him. My mother was my best friend. He handed me his cell phone and told me to call my grandmother, and that she would tell me everything I wanted to know.

I ran outside and I stood in the rain and I listened as my grandma cried and told me that my mother, my role model, my favorite person in the world, had killed herself. I was devastated. I wanted to cry, but the tears just wouldn't come. They built themselves up in my chest forming a heavy anchor, but they would not come. I hung up the phone and walked inside. My brother was back at the television; my father was outside on the phone again. Everything looked normal. It didn't appear as if the world had just rolled over on its back. I returned to my bedroom, and did what any twelve-year-old girl would do in a situation like this: I updated my AIM status—"RIP Mom."

And finally, the next day, I woke up crying. I cried for two weeks straight. I didn't eat or go to school. I left the house once: for the funeral. I was guilty. I felt like I should have been a better daughter, gotten her a better birthday gift, done more chores around the house. I couldn't stand to look at myself. Suddenly, every little thing I used to do seemed like another cause of her suicide. She killed herself because I never did what she asked. She did it because I wasn't who she wanted me to be.

I beat myself up until there was nothing left to beat. I broke myself down so far that I could think of nothing else to do but hate myself. And that led to hating her. I hated her for leaving me. For making me feel worthless. For leaving me to take on the role of mother, of woman of the house. I was twelve years old. I needed her. How did she expect me to be raised by just my dad? Every girl needs her mother! She couldn't just leave when things got hard! Isn't the point of having children to be completely selfless and only think of them? I had endless thoughts, endless questions.

After two weeks, my father made me go back to school and promised me that everything would be fine. But he was wrong. Everyone knew what had happened. My friends could barely look at me. People I didn't even know pointed at me when I walked through the halls. I couldn't deal with the pain of everyone staring, asking questions I didn't know how to answer. So I turned away from my friends and spent all of my time alone. I was miserable.

My mother had gone from being my best friend to my worst enemy. This was all her fault. I hated her and I hated myself.

But the problem with hatred is that it eats you up. It burrows inside every little pore in your body. It drains you of all your energy. Living with hatred is an incredibly difficult thing to do. So I started working at forgiving. Because when it comes to forgiveness, sometimes it helps you more than the person you are forgiving. My mom will never know that I forgave her. I will never be able to go up to her, look her in the eye, and say, "I forgive you." But now, I can look myself in the mirror, and know that sometimes people are selfish. People are stupid and act without thinking. People are people and we all do things we regret, but if we are never forgiven and never forgive, we will never be able to move on in our own lives.

I took all the anger that I was feeling and I channeled it into forgiveness and understanding. Everyone deserves a second chance no matter how hard they have hurt you. I may never know the reason why she hurt me the way she did, but I don't need to. I have forgiven her, and because of that, I can be happy.

~Nicole Guiltinan

Don't Treat Me Differently

The only disability in life is a bad attitude.
~Scott Hamilton

I have always wanted people to see me as an average person, without any problems. I have, for the most part, been successful at that. However, I am not your normal twenty-three-year-old.

I have cerebral palsy. A mild form that is mostly unnoticeable. I have had it since birth. My mom said I had a small stroke either when I was born or in utero. This caused a hole in the right side of my brain, which affects functioning on the left side of my body. My parents did not know I had cerebral palsy until I was half a year old. They noticed I was favoring my right side more and rolling only to my right.

After doctors determined I had CP I was given physical and occupational therapy. I remember being three or four years old and in therapy, but I felt like I was just an average kid playing. I did not think I was different from any other kid because I did not look different.

The one noticeable quirk about me was I would have my left arm bent up and my hand in an awkward position. Actually, I was different from the other kids in therapy. I was one of the rare kids who could walk freely. Many children born with cerebral palsy are bound to wheelchairs or walkers. I was not.

I was able to go through mainstream school, but I had to be taken out of class to go to occupational therapy. That was when I felt different from the other kids.

In therapy I drew straight lines with both hands to improve my left hand. I threw a tennis ball against the wall and tried to catch it with my left hand. I did running exercises to keep me from dragging my left foot. I learned how to tie my shoes and zip my zippers. Those were everyday things that I was not able to do. Therapy helped me, but it also made me feel helpless and hopeless.

By the time I was in fourth or fifth grade I still could not tie my own shoes, I could not button my jeans without help or zip my coat without someone else doing for me. Because of this I had to wear sweatpants and Velcro shoes to school. I was picked on daily because I was finally different in a bad way. Bullies would pull down my pants or take my shoes and hide them. Others would mock my abnormal left hand, saying, "What are you, retarded?" I never remember crying about this or telling anyone because I didn't think anyone would care about kids bullying me.

I didn't tie my own shoes, button my own jeans, or zip my own coat until I was twelve. When I went into middle school, the therapy stopped, and the bullying also stopped because I grew to be bigger and stronger than the bullies. I had overcome a good part of my disability and could do things on my own. I could even pick up a pen with my left hand. This was a huge accomplishment considering the level of mobility on the left side of my body.

In gym class I was almost unaware of my disability. I could do everything other students could do, sometimes better. Sports became my outlet. That was my own personal therapy. I was excited. I played baseball for four years, and soccer for eight years.

My mentor in grade school was Chris Honness, my gym teacher and soccer coach for two years. He understood my disability and would help me do what I needed to be happy. When we did juggling in gym class he came up with an idea for me to just juggle with my right hand. He made gym class and sports fun for me. He made me into a good soccer player and significantly changed my life.

I also played basketball in camp and won two most valuable player awards. I did not try to play basketball in high school because the team would only take twelve players. I did not see myself making the roster. Neither I, nor others could really tell I was different when I played with the normal kids.

My freshman year of high school I had to try out for the soccer team—the first time I had to do this. I was not a star soccer player by any means, but to me I was the best. My position was goaltender, and there was already a proven starter for the junior varsity team and a quality backup. I did not make the cut. I understood; they asked me to stay with the team and be the manager. I thought I would have a strong chance of winning the starting job the next year, with only me and another unproven goalie in training camp. But I ended up being number twenty-six out of twenty-five players. I was enraged and thought they cut me because of my disability. I would never play soccer again. I lost my outlet, until I started paying more attention to professional sports. I knew then I wanted to be a sports writer or commentator.

I do not usually tell people that I have a disability because I do not want to be treated like that, and I do not consider this a disability. I want to be treated just like everyone else—equally. I do not always tell employers because I do not want to become their token disabled worker. I do not get benefits for this and I do not want them.

I graduated from high school and earned my associate's degree in communications and my bachelor's degree in journalism, something that doctors told my parents would never happen. I was not supposed to be able to walk, tie my own shoes, button my pants and zip my coats. I also am not supposed to look the same as everyone else, but I do and I am the same. I am just a unique person, like everyone else in our small world.

~Craig Wendell Learn

44

Believing Anna

If you don't like something change it;
if you can't change it, change the way you think about it.
~Mary Engelbreit

I used to feel like I was carrying a terrible secret, always afraid that if I said the wrong thing I'd give myself away and people would know. I say I'd give myself away because this disorder was a part of me and had always been, even though it hadn't surfaced until my third year in college. I had spent my childhood and adolescence blissfully unaware of my schizophrenia. Like some hideous monster, it had lurked within the dark maze of my mind, finally reaching the end of the labyrinth and manifesting itself just before my twentieth birthday.

For the longest time I feared having another breakdown and being sent back to the hospital. I had been a psych patient at several hospitals. Every time I was released from in-patient treatment, I vowed I would never go back. I would actively monitor my thoughts for signs that I was relapsing. As ridiculous as it sounded when my doctor would ask me these questions, I posed them seriously to myself: Was I having racing thoughts? Was I obsessing about numbers? Was I seeing or hearing things that others didn't? I asked myself these questions, foolishly believing that I could somehow outrun a monster that already had me as its prisoner.

My very first breakdown happened like anything truly awful does, without warning. I remember not sleeping for I don't know how many nights on end. I must have been acting strange because my friends noticed. Which is saying a lot, because I'm usually the quiet one who people overlook.

I remember having some pretty strange thoughts at the time, mostly about God and myself—I think my doctor called them "grandiose delusions." I had always been an imaginative person, it's true, but before my first breakdown I had always had a firm grip on reality. I honestly don't remember when I actually snapped, or if it can even be pinned down to one specific moment. I do know that I was experiencing what psychiatrists refer to as a manic phase. I had so much energy and so many thoughts racing inside my head that I couldn't sleep. I also know that these bouts of extreme energy gave way to some bizarre thought patterns.

I thought I was receiving messages from God. I thought that God had a special secret mission for me. I thought that the world had ended and God was coming for me. I thought that I was God. I can't explain how my brain created these ideas, or why I actually believed them. I was acting out a chemical imbalance. I was not in my right mind.

During this time, I hallucinated quite a bit. I can't decide which hallucinations scared me more, the ones I saw or the ones I heard. Familiar faces became sinister and warped, like frightening caricatures. Sometimes I saw bright flashes of light and other times I couldn't escape the shadows that only I could see. I heard strange clicking metallic animal voices, the likes of which reminded me of the sounds I heard when I was swimming underwater and the pool was being vacuumed. Only, I wasn't swimming and the sounds were all in my head.

It used to make me physically sick to talk or even think about things I had done under my delusions. For a long time, I tried so hard to pretend that everything was okay, that I was normal. I couldn't face what I had done.

I took a ride in a stranger's van. I walked the middle white line of the highway with cars swerving to avoid hitting me. I believed the voices in my head that told me, "God wants you to kill yourself." I didn't trust the kind faces of those I loved; I hit my father and pushed my best friend down. I threw water at nurses and went to court hearings in handcuffs. I did so many things I would never ordinarily do.

The ones who understood the nature of schizophrenia told me it wasn't my fault and that I shouldn't blame myself.

It was a hard line to swallow, though. I couldn't reconcile that with my long established ideology that I could overcome any obstacle if I wanted to, that my life was the product of my own actions and therefore of my own making. I didn't understand the nature of mental disorders nor did I understand people who suffered from them. I used to believe that people could overcome anything if they tried hard enough. I might have kept up this unrealistic notion had I not had another breakdown.

It was my third hospitalization and it was where I met Martin. Martin was a balding middle-aged man with bright blue eyes and a sad face. He had checked himself in because he was suffering from severe depression. He usually kept to himself and only came out of his room for meals and the occasional Group or Occupational Therapy session. Seeing him sitting by himself looking at his hospital tray with disinterest, I decided in a rare moment of bravery to join him.

"Gotta love this slop they call food," I said in an attempt at humor. He looked up at me and gave a feeble smile.

"Yeah," he mumbled.

I asked him how he was doing, expecting the usual (and often phony) "good" response. He was so close-mouthed in Group that I was surprised when he actually answered honestly.

He told me he was depressed and didn't know why. He said depression was a different kind of sadness, one that no amount of tears could alleviate. That it was an intense feeling of hopelessness and isolation, that it was a struggle to get out of bed in the morning, an immense burden to summon the will to go to work or to shower or even to eat. That there was this intensity of feeling and yet a powerful numbness at the same time, as if he was somehow still breathing but not really alive.

Out of candor, naïveté, or just plain stupidity, I asked him why didn't he just find something that made him happy and do that.

He stood up, anger in his piercing blue eyes, and said, "You just don't understand. This isn't something I can just will away!"

And that was when I finally understood. I couldn't just will my schizophrenia away. I had to recognize that my illness was beyond my control. I could manage it with therapy sessions and medication, but it would always be a part of me. I had to forgive myself for what I had done and face the memories I had blocked out for so long.

I began to talk to Martin and some of the other patients and I shared with them all that I had gone through. Talking to them, I remembered how to laugh again and cry again, I remembered how much I loved art and music, how I wanted to be a writer. I remembered who I used to be before my diagnosis. And I remembered who I could still be, in spite of it.

I began to paint again. I expressed my memories through brushstrokes, describing the frightening world I had lived in during each mental collapse. It was more cathartic than painting a pretty yellow birdhouse.

But I created happy things too; I made birthday cards with rainbow-maned unicorns for a male patient's young daughters and did a portrait sketch of a female patient named Darla. "You made me beautiful," she said when she saw it, and I told her she was. I enjoyed therapy and the colorful community it gave me. I laughed when a patient named John dubbed arts and crafts "Total BS" and elected to roll homemade cigarettes instead, saying the cigarettes would make him happier than a picture made of macaroni, but could he make a ceramic ashtray?

On my last day at Lakeview, a girl named Anna, who had jumped off a bridge, stopped me to say goodbye. "I'm glad I met you, Abby," she said. "I know that I'm going to be okay now."

Wondering how someone could be certain of something like that, I asked Anna how she knew.

She said, "Because you're going to be okay."

I made my way outside the hospital with my mom holding my hand for probably the first time since I was seven. I smiled at the brilliant summer sunshine, knowing I could believe what Anna had said.

~Abigail Hoeft

45

Battle Scars

Turn your wounds into wisdom.
~Oprah Winfrey

The trip had become almost routine. I had gone to the cardiologist more times in my life than I had been to the regular doctor. It was always the same. Sign in, wait; get stats done, wait; talk to the nurse, wait; get an EKG, wait; every other trip I would get an echocardiogram and then wait; and finally the doctor would come in and tell us there was nothing new and we would go to a movie. This had been the process many, many times during my twenty years, so this time shouldn't have been any different. In fact I had almost convinced my mom to postpone it, as the last thing I wanted to do on my spring break was see a doctor. I wanted to hang out with my friends and sleep late instead.

The wait wasn't long; not to brag or anything, but I am one of the doctor's favorite patients. Once when my dad wouldn't let me wear a bikini, the doctor wrote me a prescription for one. We went through the normal steps of talking and waiting. We did an echo, something I had done many times before. How was I supposed to know that this one would be a game changer? After the echo I went back in the patient room, and waited for the doctor. He came in and asked the basic questions and then after beating around the bush a bit he told us. My gradient had risen from the thirties to the high eighties and my thickness had widened as well. I was going to need a septal myomectomy. At twenty years old, when most girls my age were dating and going out with their friends, I was facing open-heart surgery.

I tried not to think about the surgery that much. I had other things on my plate. I was performing in a play in two days and I was quite nervous as lots of industry people were coming. The next few days passed in a blur. I performed my play, which went great, but then I was alone again with my thoughts. Time passed, I graduated from college, and then it was time for the surgery.

On the day of the surgery I was pretty calm until they came with the gurney. I saw it and broke down. It was the realization that they were coming for me, not someone else. I was the patient and that seemed so strange to me. The next thing I remember is the ICU. I woke up with a tube down my throat and my dad at my side. I was alive and it was over. A few days later I got to take a shower. As I slowly and painfully removed my gown I saw it for the first time in the mirror. Swollen and red, from my clavicle to the end of my sternum, was the scar. The surgery was over but it had left its mark, this "battle" scar would always be with me.

Most of the time I am proud of my scar. It saved my life. It reminds me that every breath could be your last, because we aren't promised tomorrow. Most of the time it motivates me to take advantage of the life that I have been given. But sometimes when I am home alone, standing in front of a mirror and it is staring back at me, I just feel damaged; sometimes I let the insecurities creep up and take over for a while. But when that happens I remember that everyone has scars. The only difference is that mine is physical and maybe that makes it more real. Which is a good thing, because the last thing I want to do is forget how blessed I am, how special God has made me.

The day has passed but the evidence of it is etched into my body forever. Some might call it ugly and that's okay, because the point isn't whether or not it's beautiful; the point is that it exists and if it didn't, I might not.

~Chelsey Colleen Hankins

46

Chicken Soup
for the *Soul*

Up in Flames

We must embrace pain and burn it as fuel for our journey.
~Kenji Miyazawa

Five years after my mother's death I realized that I was still hurt and angry. I hadn't dealt with the fact that my parents got separated when I was three years old, I hadn't dealt with the fact that my mother, my brother and I were abused physically and verbally for almost eight years by two of her boyfriends, and most of all, I hadn't dealt with the fact that my mother had died so horribly right in front of my eyes when I was only twelve years old.

"Jenn, write a letter and burn it!" Anne kept telling me over and over again. Anne was one of my mother's childhood friends. She stepped in after my mother's death and has been like a mother to me. She's the one I tell everything to, she's the one I cry with, she's the one I go to for advice, she's the one who knows me best and she's the one always encouraging me and letting me know how proud she is. She told me that burning a letter written to my past would help me get rid of some of my anger, sadness, confusion and stress. At first I really didn't think it would make much of a difference. I felt alone in the world. I was always sick and all I wanted to do was sleep. I was at my lowest point and writing a letter seemed like a waste of time. But, I always listened to Anne, because she always turned out to be right!

I wrote the letter one day after work. "Dear past..." I started. I wrote about my parents' separation and how that led us to having those two abusive boyfriends in our lives. Men who were alcoholics and treated us like dirt, men who I saw kicking, hitting and slapping my mother—men who didn't even deserve to live. And then I continued by writing about my mother's death and how much it hurt me, the fact that I had to see her die and how much I hated the fact that I had to live the rest of my life without a mom. I ended the letter by explaining how unhappy I was. It took all of my energy to write that letter, but four pages later, it was done.

I felt a bit relieved, but it really hadn't made a big difference; I still felt horrible. That's when Anne said: "Come on over and we'll burn the letter." So off to her place I went, crying my eyes out and feeling sick to my stomach. I was greeted with a hug and a chat and then we went outside and lit the letter on fire. As I watched it burn, I thought about all the horrible things I'd seen, heard and felt throughout my childhood. But most of all, I thought about my mother—the mother I lost, the mother I miss, the mother I love and the mother I'll cherish forever. I wanted to get rid of the horrible weight I carried around for all those years, and by burning the letter that's exactly what I was doing!

After the flame died out, I gave Anne the biggest hug ever, told her that I loved her and thanked her for being there. She gave me a box and told me to put a few pieces of the burned letter in it so that I could always look into it and say to myself: "It's over."

I randomly put some of the pieces in the box and when we went inside I discovered that the one word that wasn't burned on the pieces I had chosen was the word "mom." I felt like the happiest person in the world!

"I haven't seen a real smile on your face in such a long time!" said Anne.

This was proof that my mother was still with me and that she was proud of what I had just accomplished. It also reassured me that I can depend on Anne to be my mother now and that she won't ever let me down.

In order for me to be truly happy, I guess all I really needed was to get rid of that negative energy that had followed me around for so many years. And getting a sign from my mother helped me even more! Who knew that burning a letter would be such a life-changing experience? Thanks Mom and Anne, thanks for being a part of my life!

~Jennifer Gauthier

47

Not Your Average Joe

It takes courage to grow up and become who you really are.
~e.e. cummings

The burden of my secret was weighing me down. It was like a ticking time bomb, waiting to explode.

"Why don't you go hang yourself?"

"People like you should shoot themselves."

"You should be burned to death."

"God looks down on people like you."

It's hard to believe that by the age of sixteen I'd heard every single one of these phrases and hundreds more. Some came from the mouths of my peers, but what's even scarier is that some came from the mouths of adults, the people who we respect and look up to the most.

I had always been asked if I was gay. Most of the time people would just assume I was and tease me about it. I never came out and said I was, because I wasn't sure, and I was also afraid of the reaction I would get.

In middle school most of my days were spent observing how I was "supposed" to act and who I was "supposed" to like. I spent a lot of time arguing with myself as I tried to figure it out. By high school I had a clear understanding of who I was. It had finally clicked. I knew I was gay, it was something I would never be able to change, and I accepted that. I was not a mistake, and my confidence and acceptance of myself grew every day. I knew that my family loved me, my friends loved me, but most importantly, I loved myself.

I knew my very close friends wouldn't have a problem with my sexuality, so I decided to tell them first. I still had to do the biggest thing of all—tell my parents.

I have a dad who's as conservative as it gets, and a mom who, god bless her, is the complete opposite. I was raised in an open-minded household. This taught me to be myself, show emotion, and listen to both sides. I had an amazing family unit, which made it even harder to tell them because I didn't want to risk losing that. I knew when I told my friends, I could risk losing them and make new ones, but I couldn't make a new family. I waited half a year for the right time to tell them, but it didn't happen the way I planned.

It was a Saturday night and I had just gotten home from a friend's house. The news was on. Surprisingly, it was about gay people serving in the military. My parents asked me why I looked confused.

"Gay people can't serve in the military? What kind of crap is that?" I said.

"Yeah," my dad said, "it has been that way for a while."

The questions started, and then as usual, a debate erupted. I was very curious about this, not understanding why someone's sexuality should be a factor in determining whether or not they could serve their country. I had many questions and my dad was getting angry because I didn't think it was right.

"Why is this so important to you? Are you gay or something?" he asked red-faced.

My heart skipped a beat and time slowed. This was not how I had planned to tell them.

"Yes," I said firmly.

The room quieted. My dad started to say something but nothing came out. Eventually he took a deep breath and said, "Well, that's fine with me."

I was shocked and a little upset. It didn't sound sincere. I had heard all those horror stories about parents making their kids move out. I eventually walked out of the room, leaving my dad in there to grasp the situation, to look for my mom so I could tell her too. The words came out easier when I told her, probably in part because she had gay friends and was completely fine with them. She was shocked; she said she had no idea, but that she would love me until the day she died. My dad eventually came and hugged me. He said he was in shock but didn't want me to think he would ever not love me because of the person I loved. This put all my worries to rest, but I knew I still had a long road ahead of me.

The support that I had from my parents and my friends was unbelievably satisfying. I finally felt like I had nothing to hide, and I could be myself. My sexuality does not define me. I am not a stereo-type—I am a human being. My journey is not over, but the hard part is. Yes, I want to get married, and yes, it's to a person of the same sex, but why does that matter? Love is love. I'm truly happy with who I am.

Hi, my name is Ian and yes, I'm gay.

~Ian McCammon

Happiness Found

Writing is both mask and unveiling.
~E.B. White

I don't remember a lot about my childhood. I choose not to, no matter what my therapist says to the contrary. I believe there are some things that should be forgotten. The mind sometimes gives you selective amnesia for a reason.

For most of my twenties, people thought I was a strong confident woman who had all the answers. I was a fine actress. Judging by the way people treated me, I should have won an Oscar. Even though people came to me for advice all the time and I counseled people the best that I could, I didn't realize how people perceived me, until one day my younger sister-in-law said something that surprised me. She said that she wished she was as self-confident as I was.

Here was this really beautiful young woman, who was athletic and funny and seemed to have everything going for her, not only admitting to me that she felt like she didn't have any self-confidence, but that she thought that I did. How did that happen? When did that happen? So I took a step back and looked at my life.

I was twenty-seven years old. I had been married to an abusive man, but I divorced him, took my young son, and in time married an incredibly gorgeous man. I had a job as a manager at a beautiful apartment community with a staff of about ten people and various contractors that I had to oversee on a daily basis. I still couldn't believe that the really beautiful, nice man had married me. I wasn't sure why. Truthfully I didn't think it would last. Surely he would see the real me soon enough, although we had dated for a year before we married.

We were married about two years when he went to Seattle to visit my brother and his wife when he was on a vacation. The two of them got along great and seemed as if they could be real brothers. When he came back, he made a casual comment to me that shook my world.

He relayed to me that my brother had told him about the time I was a little girl and had to go live with our "hillbilly" cousins in East Texas. My husband had always thought I was sophisticated, so he thought it was funny that I had family like that.

I felt like I had been dropped from a thirty-story building. We didn't really talk about it, but soon memories started coming back to me. Nightmares and memories about that horrible time in my life. As the youngest of six children, I was sent away — alone — to live with those people. I never told anyone of the abuse and torture I suffered there. No one ever asked. My mother was hospitalized and the older kids were all in school, so my dad sent me to stay with his cousins. I was about four when they took me away, I don't know for how long. No one will tell me.

I began having problems at my job. And then panic attacks — this was before anyone really knew what that term meant. I thought I was going crazy and hid it the best I could.

Over the next ten years, I lost job after job. I got fired because of anxiety and panic attacks. Finally I had to tell my husband about them. I tried going to doctors. We lost our nice cars and then our home. I couldn't keep a job. I was worried to death that our children would suffer, that my husband would leave me. My physical health started to deteriorate.

I had always been a voracious reader. One day I decided to sit down and try writing for myself. It just came flowing out of me. I was in my forties and it had never occurred to me to try to write. Suddenly I felt a little better. This was fun — it felt great. I got other people to read some of my writing and they seemed to love it. So I wrote a whole manuscript. Even the people I thought would be my harshest critics said they loved it. It made me feel good about myself. It made me happy.

So now I've written three manuscripts and over 100 articles. I have found me again. My husband and I are about to have our twenty-fourth wedding anniversary. He still loves me. He knows the real me; I guess he always did. Our kids, now young men, love me tremendously. How happy can one girl be? Just ask me!

~KT Banks

Purple Candles

What a wonderful life I've had! I only wish I'd realized it sooner.
~Colette

Until recently, my life seemed extremely orderly. I was following an imaginary script, living out some unwritten play, doing exactly what everyone expected of me. I graduated high school. I went to college. I got my M.D. degree. Eventually, I got a job, got married, and had two kids. I was the good little girl, always doing the right thing.

Once I had my daughters, I left my job as a pediatrician and became a full-time mom. Being a mother was much harder than being a pediatrician, but the payoff was much more rewarding. As a mother, I got paid in kisses instead of cash. I fixed bruised egos instead of ear infections. I prescribed hugs and snuggling instead of amoxicillin. Life was certainly different when I wasn't a career woman, yet I wouldn't have traded it for anything.

As a mom, my life was also very orderly. I did exactly what everyone thought I was supposed to do. I volunteered at my girls' schools and signed them up for all sorts of fun and engaging activities, which led to hundreds (probably more like thousands) of extra miles on my car. We had play dates and went to playgrounds. We rode carousels and bicycles. We played in the pool and in the snow. Each day was filled with surprises, and each day was more exciting than the last.

On paper, I had the perfect life: great house, great kids, husband who loved me, a medical degree. What more could anyone want? My friends would tell me often that they wished they could do as much as I did in a day. I sometimes got teased about how incredibly clean my house always was. I even overheard a few people say that my marriage seemed perfect.

Yet, as a wise friend told me once, "When a house seems too clean, and a life seems too right, something is probably terribly wrong."

Suddenly, I hit thirty-five and my world simply fell apart. Somehow, I just couldn't hold it together any longer. I suppose that the stress of living up to what I thought everyone else's expectations were got to be much more than I could handle. At the time, I called it being overloaded. Yet, now I admit and even talk freely about the fact that it's actually called being depressed.

At first, I was just a little sad. I didn't enjoy life quite as much as I used to. But gradually, the sadness turned into despair, until one day, I just couldn't do my life anymore. I didn't want to get up in the morning. And, when I finally did, I counted the hours until I could go back to sleep. My once-spotless house was now piled high with trash, dishes, and long-overdue laundry. I'm not sure how or even what my family ate. I'm not sure who did the cooking; it certainly wasn't me. Not only didn't I cook, but I didn't eat. I lost ten pounds in two weeks. What I had once called my life now seemed like the beginning of my death.

The day my husband found me curled up on our bed crying hysterically, saying that I wanted to go to sleep and never wake up, turned out to be the best day of my life. Hitting rock bottom like that, having a complete and total meltdown, forced me into the hospital, and subsequently, into recovery.

Initially, I was extremely ashamed that I, the middle-class doctor and mother of two with the proverbial white picket fence life, ended up in a locked psychiatric ward and on antidepressant medication. That just wasn't supposed to happen to people like me.

People like me... What does that mean anyway?

My psychiatrist made me realize that depression is an illness, just like heart disease or diabetes, and it can happen to anyone. Depression doesn't care where your house is, what you do for a living, or how great your life was supposed to be. Illness doesn't discriminate.

Once I accepted the fact that I was actually sick and that I wasn't just crazy, I was able to start talking about my depression openly. Immediately, the shame I'd buried deep inside disappeared. Putting it out there, admitting to what I'd been going through, honestly, made everything seem okay. And, what I found as I began discussing my illness with more and more people was that depression was so much more common than I'd ever imagined. Suddenly, friends and acquaintances alike were sharing their own deeply personal stories with me. Sadly, many of them had, previously, been too embarrassed or ashamed to talk about their illnesses, just as I had been.

I quickly learned that talking about what I'd been going through, instead of keeping all of my emotions bottled up inside, actually helped my recovery be that much easier.

Several months into treatment, with therapy and the right medication, I finally began to feel like my old self for the first time in forever. But, recovery was a process, and a long one at that. There were days when I felt like I could really take on anything, and then there were days when I worried that I could easily be headed back to the hospital. Yet, overall, I was on an upswing from the day I hit bottom, and I knew that, soon, it would all be okay.

I was lucky because I got help. And through that help I learned how important it was for me to take some time each day, just for me. Having some personal time gives me the chance to relax and regroup, and honestly makes me a better wife and mom. My kids, over the years, have learned to give me alone time in my room when I need it to rest and unwind. That time, I've discovered, is priceless.

Right now, it's evening and my girls are asleep. I'm in my comfy chair, wearing my favorite pajamas, enjoying the glow of nine purple candles burning brightly on my kitchen counter. There's just something so relaxing about candles, and something so calming about purple. For me, this is therapy, and I'm happy.

Life is complicated, but it doesn't have to be overwhelming. I've finally taken the time to get myself in a very good place. As I watch the flames dance and flicker in my kitchen, choreographing a dance of their own, moving to a rhythm that only they can create, I feel that someday soon, I too will be that free.

~Sharon Dunski Vermont

Basket Case

Fear can keep us up all night long, but faith makes one fine pillow.
~Philip Gulley

With one house-shaking thud, my life shattered. My husband Jerry lay dead on the bathroom floor. The rest of the day was a blur of EMTs, doctors, teary-eyed friends and family who trickled in from out of town. I made it through the funeral and the holidays in a fog.

Then all went quiet. Everyone went back to their lives, yet I could never go back to mine. I longed for the blessed numbness of those first few weeks.

I tackled the laundry, hoping the whir of the machines would fill the silence. As I carried three weeks' worth of dirty clothes to the utility room in the house I could no longer afford, I tripped over the threshold where carpet met tile. The basket flew and the clothes tumbled, along with my brave façade.

I crouched on the floor, crying, as I gathered the strewn pieces of laundry. Each piece represented a burden I would have to carry alone — medical bills, legal papers, the for-sale sign in my front yard, the reality of Jerry's lost income. I picked up a blouse I had worn on my last unsuccessful job interview. Into the basket it went. A table napkin reminded me I must downsize to a one-bedroom apartment and sell half my furniture. I wiped my eyes with it.

Then I saw it. One lone sock of Jerry's, missed by good-intentioned family who'd bagged his clothes for charity. It screamed back at me that I must sell his truck as well as the power tools that crowded the makeshift workshop in the garage. More to add to my load. What should I do with his father's coin collection? The deer rifles? His grandfather's Stetson? The pile of wood he'd purchased for his next carpentry project and all the scraps from the last three?

Like my dirty clothes, the troubles piled up. I'd shuffled through each day as my basket of worries grew heavier and heavier. I felt overburdened with grief and stress. My back spasmed with pain. How could I possibly carry this load? To be placed in this situation was cruel and unfair.

I cried out loud, "God, why did you let Jerry die and leave me all this to handle myself?"

Then, for some reason, as I sat on the floor and hugged the toppled laundry basket, I remembered another basket long ago in the arms of a petite Hispanic woman.

I had been reading in the laundromat while my clothes spun in the commercial dryer. I looked up from my book. Through the window, I saw a small woman laboring to maneuver a heavy basket brimming with dirty clothes as she herded four small children towards the glass door. Two held bottles of laundry soap and bleach to their chests. In sympathy, I sprang to my feet and held the door open.

Her eyes widened. She froze to the spot, lips tight.

Not the reaction I expected. Had I offended her? Maybe she was used to doing things herself and didn't want help. Perhaps she thought I was trying to leave. Did she fear I'd be upset that she blocked my path or was she angry because I blocked hers? We didn't speak the same language, so I didn't know how to tell her I only wanted to help.

A man came over and whispered to me. "She doesn't understand. She doesn't know you. She isn't used to receiving help from strangers."

He reassured her in Spanish, then took the laundry basket and set it on the folding table. She gave me a weak smile and nod of her head, but wouldn't make eye contact. She gathered her brood like a mother hen and shuffled them inside. Though I'm not sure she saw my face, I smiled in return. I closed the door, fetched my dry clothes, and folded them into my basket. When I turned to leave, she looked up and nodded again. This time her eyes met mine and we exchanged smiles.

Our lives only crossed for a brief moment, yet now as a widow crouched on the floor with an overturned laundry basket, she greatly impacted mine. I too was burdened with a huge basket of things that stressed me. Anger and hurt weighed me down. Pride prevented me from asking for help.

Then it hit me. I envisioned God standing at the door, hand on the glass, ready to push it open for me. I made the decision to give God my laundry list of things to do each day. The heaviness in my soul lifted.

The next morning when I read the Bible passage in my daily devotional, I had to smile. Psalm 81, verses 5-6 said: "I hear in a language I had not known: 'I relieved your shoulder of the burden; your hands were freed from the basket...'"

~Julie B. Cosgrove

Making My Day

Hope is patience with the lamp lit.
~Tertullian

If life was a journey, then I, at age thirteen, had given up. On the outside, I was perfect. Talented, athletic, and prim, I was the girl who teachers counted on and parents asked their daughters to invite over. I befriended new students and cleaned my friends' rooms after sleepovers. I never said a word of gossip and had won countless "student of the month" awards.

Yet I was haunted by demons. I held a secret from the world, a secret I rarely let out. I was smart and calculating, and I never showed chinks in my armor. But my flawless demeanor is what eventually did me in.

Depression is difficult to describe to someone who isn't familiar with it. It shows itself in many ways: anger, emotional detachment, fatigue, loss of interest. Or it may simply be a crushing, unexplainable sense of failure. Simply put, it's not finding inner strength to live.

That's where I found myself at age thirteen. Hopeless. I was seeing a therapist after my mother had finally gotten tired of the fake smiles and black moods, but even with Kim's sensible advice and years of experience, something was deeply missing. I simply could not go on.

One dreary day in January, I leaned heavily against my school locker as the lunch bell rang. I had received a homework assignment from Kim the day before: to write a list of my best friends and why

I liked them. My problem with this task was that I couldn't think of people for my list. I had companions, but at that point in my life I couldn't bring myself to care much about anyone, including myself.

I slammed my locker and faced the throng of seventh graders on their way to lunch. I ran through them in my head, wondering who I could possibly include on my list. So many different faces passed, but none that I would die without. I sighed. It was official: I was going to flunk therapy.

"Hey," said a small voice to my right. I looked down and saw Luz, a girl in my grade. Luz was short and soft-spoken with something good to say about everybody. Her big eyes held a sweet soul that made her quite well liked. I had always had a fondness for Luz, but had never known her very well. Even so, looking at her accepting smile lifted my spirits a bit.

"Hey, Luz," I greeted. "How are you?"

"Great. Say, you got a haircut!"

I fingered my short hair, genuinely pleased that she had taken notice of me.

"Yeah," I murmured.

"You look really, really pretty," Luz exclaimed. "You're gorgeous!"

I blinked twice.

"Really?"

"Totally."

"Luz!" a voice called from down the hall.

"Got to go," Luz said. "Bye!"

She trotted down the hall.

"Gorgeous," I whispered to myself. "I'm gorgeous."

Watching Luz scamper down the school hallway, I had a bit of a revelation. I wasn't happy. In fact, I was clinically depressed. Each day was going to be a struggle, and ultimately I might lose. But seeing a person who was so good to the core shook me a bit. It reminded me, however briefly, of the happiness in the world. It gave me hope.

"Luz!" I yelled.

You see, happiness, at least for me, is slow to come and quick to leave. Life is a journey, but the pursuit of that precious thing we call happiness is more than a journey. It's a challenge that some, like Luz, seem to have already conquered. Like her name, Luz, which means light, she lit up the darkness for me.

As I opened my mouth, I took that light that Luz had unknowingly offered.

"Luz!" I called again.

My new friend turned. There was so much I wanted to say. Thank you. You're prettier than I could ever be, inside and out. God bless you.

What I said instead came straight from the heart.

"Luz, wait up. I'm coming with you."

~Monica Quijano

Find Your

Your
Happiness

The Joy of Giving

The best way to cheer yourself up is to try to cheer somebody else up.

~Mark Twain

A Deed a Day

Happiness is a by-product of an effort to make someone else happy.
~Gretta Brooker Palmer

I cast a warning glare and mouthed the words "Just a minute!" as my daughter tugged my hand. I was stirring chili with the other hand and balancing the phone between my shoulder and chin. The clothes dryer buzzer sounded as my husband walked in with our other daughter. The dog was scratching at the door, and we had about twenty minutes to eat before we had to take the girls to their next activity. My husband seemed a bit annoyed that dinner was not already on the table. The girls started arguing about who had to let the poor dog back into the house.

That night, I had a heavy heart thinking about how mindless my family's routines had become. We were becoming taskmasters who performed each day's activities as if we were on an assembly line. We had become absorbed in our own activities and not very considerate towards those around us. We needed to do something to bring back some meaning into our lives. It needed to be something that would refocus our own agendas and energize us toward the common good.

I purchased a journal, labeled it "Our Deed Diary" and held a family meeting. I told my husband and our daughters that I wanted us all to think about doing a kindness for others every day. It could be for each other or for people outside our home. The purpose was to reduce the focus on ourselves and brighten someone else's day in the process.

We talked about what a good deed would mean for this "project." We decided that a good deed was doing something nice for someone else that they were not expecting. It could be as simple as making a card for your teacher or going out of your way to give someone a compliment for something he or she did. We decided to record our deeds every day and discuss them over dinner. The girls seemed excited at the prospect of this new "game" we were playing. My husband rolled his eyes. I said a little prayer.

When I first conceived of this project, I thought that one deed a day was too easy. Let me tell you; it is harder than it seems. We all, of course, do things for others on a regular basis; but this had to be something above and beyond what we already do. Sending birthday cards to people that we already send cards to every year would not count. This had to be an unexpected effort on our parts.

We had a rough start. We were supposed to talk about our good deeds and write them in our Deed Diary at dinner every day. On some days, someone would forget to do a good deed, while on other days, we would forget to write our good deeds in the diary. After a few weeks though, I found myself waking up in the morning trying to decide what good deed I could do for someone that day. My daughters began to rush to me after school to tell me a good deed they had done for someone that day.

We have been doing good deeds for nearly a year now. I am happy to say that it is making a difference in our lives. Instead of always wondering what the day will bring for us, we think about what we can do for someone else. At dinner, we have an instant conversation starter, as we all share our stories.

I have expanded the deed experiment to my first grade classroom. I started out by having every student write a letter to someone in the school to thank him or her for something he or she does for us. It was most touching to observe the janitor, nurse, librarian, and other school staff hang our notes on their walls while beaming because they felt appreciated.

In my classroom, every student does not have to do a good deed every day, but our class, as a whole, tries to show at least three kindnesses to others each day. We record them and I am most boastful about how thoughtful the students are towards others. When a student spills his or her crayons, you wouldn't believe how many kids scurry over to try to help and clean them up! Just as with my family, keeping and sharing a Deed Diary changed our whole outlook on life.

Who would have thought that trying to do a simple kindness a day would be so rewarding? I feel my daughters and first grade students better understand the old saying that "it is better to give than to receive." They have felt that indescribable feeling of inner joy that you can only experience by giving to someone else from your heart. The best thing is that you feel so great about doing something for someone else, you don't even look for or expect anything in return. So, when someone does reciprocate, it is an enormous and positive bonus. When someone does something nice for me, I now think of it as, "What a great idea! I'll have to do that for someone too!"

~Shannon Anderson

It's What We Do

In about the same degree as you are helpful, you will be happy.
~Karl Reiland

I tried to fluff my pillow. Tried to roll over. Looked longingly at the book that lay on the chair across the room. But I couldn't fluff, roll, or retrieve. In fact, there wasn't much I could do. Since the disks in my back had bulged and protruded and extended to places they shouldn't, I'd been in bed. The MRI exposed a spine that looked like a zipper of uneven teeth. Even therapy wasn't an option.

"We'll fix you up," my neurosurgeon said, "after the birth of your baby."

But that was months away.

I placed my hand on my tummy and felt my third son move. Outside the birds were singing. Mowers hummed and the scent of fresh cut grass wafted through the open widow. I wished I could feel light, warm, hopeful with the promise of new summer. But I couldn't. Couldn't care for my young boys. Couldn't help them brush their teeth or make their favorite meals or fold their little T-shirts or push them in their swings. In fact, I couldn't stop thinking about all the things I couldn't do. Taking care of my family was what I did.

I cried. The ringing phone, muffled by a twist of pink cotton bed sheet, startled me. It was my husband, calling from work.

"Hey, Alice called. She'd like to come by the house this afternoon. To work out a meal calendar," he said. "I told her it would be fine."

"Sure," I said. Alice was an older lady from church. I was grateful for her willingness to help. But this was another reminder of what I couldn't do, and it broke my heart.

It wasn't long before Alice arrived. First I heard the front door open, then the soft, steady voice of my son's Sunday School teacher. "Shawnelle, it's Alice. May I come in?"

"Please," I called. "I'm upstairs. First door to the right."

The creaky stairs announced Alice's ascent. "How are you?" she asked. We talked while Alice gingerly perched on my bed. We chatted about my boys and my pregnancy and the weather and church.

"Well," she said after a bit, "many ladies have asked to prepare meals for you. I thought we should make a schedule, maybe every other night?" Alice's smile was warm.

"I don't know," I said. "That's so much. Too much." I was overwhelmed by the thought of my friends providing meals, every other day, indefinitely. I would feel guilty. Like a burden.

"Nonsense," she said. "I also know how the laundry piles up. We'll help with housekeeping, too."

I couldn't expect our friends to do our wash, an eternal knee-high hill of sweatshirts and socks. Much less wash the floors and do the dishes and deal with the upkeep of a house with a three-to-one ratio of men.

"Alice, we can't," I said. "Lonny can do the wash. The boys can help around the house. We'll manage."

"Well, I know that Lonny could manage the house. But he has other things to do. Like taking care of those boys. Taking care of you. Let us help your husband help you."

"It's too much," I said. "I'm not comfortable with all that."

"It's okay, dear. We're just sharing God's love." She was silent for a moment. Then she squeezed my hand. "Loving God. Loving each other. It's what we do."

I didn't know what to say.

"It's really that simple," Alice said. And she nodded her head to confirm the deal.

I remained uncomfortable, but I did relent. Alice and I talked details. And the very next evening, our friend Brenda delivered a hot meal at five o'clock sharp. And Mary, another friend, picked my boys up for classes at their school. Janet swept my floors and left with my hamper under her arm like it was the most natural thing in the world. Nancy cleaned my bathrooms. Karen delivered a yogurt and fruit every afternoon and stayed to listen and encourage and visit and pray.

My days were less lonely as my friends popped in and out. And to my surprise, they never, ever looked tired or frustrated or like they'd rather be somewhere else. And what I saw on each beautiful face surprised me.

Joy.

Plain, simple, unmistakable joy.

At first I was baffled. I'd read my Bible regularly for several years, and I knew that the Lord said that to love Him first and then to love others. But I had never experienced such an outpouring of care.

And a few months later, our household still intact due to the helpfulness of solid, strong, loving helpers, I emerged from the trauma a new woman. I had new strength, a new baby boy, and a healed back. But I also had a few other new things: new perspective, purpose, and pleasure.

When I had needed help, help was there. After I healed, I wanted to help someone else. Sometimes that meant a meal. Sometimes help with childcare. Sometimes it meant just listening to a sweet sister as she shared from deep places in her heart.

And a funny thing happened. The joy that my friends had shown when they'd taken care of me? I understood that now. I was no longer bewildered because that same joy had taken residence in my own heart. It grew stronger and stronger as I provided care, not just for my own family, but for other families, too.

"What are you doing, Mama?" my third baby boy asked one day, when he'd grown into a young man of two years old.

"I'm baking bread for the neighbor. Her knee is broken and is in a cast," I said.

"But why are you baking bread?" he asked.

I pulled a chair to the counter so he could stand, see, and help.

"Because it's sharing God's love with someone who needs it. He tells us to take care of others."

"Oh," he said. My little guy's eyes were wide. "I think I understand." Then he smiled. Ear-to-ear.

I smiled wide, too, reflecting the peace and purpose in my heart.

"Loving God, loving others," I said. "It's just what we do."

~Shawnelle Eliasen

A Friend in Need

In giving you are throwing a bridge across the chasm of your solitude.
~Antoine de Saint-Exupéry

I sat in the car, tears welling in my eyes. I did not want to push the garage door opener. I wanted to turn on the car engine and just fall asleep. Then I would go where my husband was and we would be together again. It had been several weeks and every morning I was leaving for work a full hour before I could even enter the building. The hardest part of the day was pushing the garage door opener when I returned.

Vern had died of bone cancer and life's purpose ended for me. No one needed me. My sons were on their own and I was alone. I wasn't sleeping well, had no memory of day-to-day activities, and eating? Well, let's just say everything I put in my mouth was wrong.

I was far too early to arrive at work so I stopped at a 24-hour market and picked up some bananas.

When I arrived at the parking lot, I saw one other car parked, in the handicapped space. It was Judy who worked in the clerical pool. Well, at least I had someone to visit with until it was time for her to start work.

I went directly to her cubicle and said good morning. She had a wide smile in spite of all her problems. Judy was tiny, several inches less than five feet. Besides losing a leg to bone cancer, she had two children still at home, a son with heart problems and a developmentally disabled daughter. Her ex-husband lived directly across the street from her and continually had her seeking the advice of an attorney. With all the negative karma in her life, it was no wonder she had developed bone cancer. But after her leg was amputated, she was still alive. And her fire, determination, and spirit made you sit up and take notice.

"Want a banana?" I asked her as I opened the bag.

"Oh wow!" she exclaimed. "I needed this potassium!"

We chatted a bit and she asked if I would stick her lunch in the fridge on my way back to my desk.

Several weeks later, I was still arriving early. Sometimes I would pick up a breakfast sandwich or a doughnut. But most often I brought a banana. One morning Judy was busy typing when I arrived.

"Are you working already? It's not even 6:30 yet!" I asked her.

"This is personal," she responded. "Kerri wants to go to summer camp and I don't have the money. Can you help me? I need to write a letter explaining why she needs a scholarship."

Judy was not a writer. She could fill out forms and perform clerical functions, but writing escaped her. I knew Judy's financial hardship and was happy to help her.

"Consider it done," I said.

Two weeks later Judy joyfully reported, "You did it! Kerri got the scholarship! She gets to go to summer camp."

Later Judy lamented that she was unable to find a dress for her son's garden wedding. She was extremely small and her prosthesis created a hip bulge. She was tired of wearing skirts and she really wanted a dress. But dresses large enough to go over the prosthesis were too large on top. And dresses that fit her on top were too small over the hip. Additionally, she was so tiny that she could almost wear a child's size.

"Why don't I make you a dress?" I volunteered. "You pick out the fabric and I'll fit it to you."

I had sewn for my whole family since I was thirteen years old and had fitted a sister with scoliosis. So I knew that fitting the hip would not be a problem.

Judy loved the dress. She brought in a photo of her son and herself (wearing that dress of course) and displayed it on her desk.

One morning Judy was crying when I arrived. The summer heat was wreaking havoc on her stump. She showed me the portion of her leg that was fit with a stocking and then slid into her prosthesis. It was so red that I thought it was bleeding. I knew how Judy felt about not wearing her "leg." She valued the limited independence it gave her even if she did need to balance near a wall while she was walking.

"Judy, take that thing off!" I advised her. "You can't put yourself through that. Just use your crutches or a wheelchair until your rash is gone. Are your crutches in your car? I'll go get them. I'll push your wheelchair. Or walk you to the ladies' room. Whatever you need, just call me and I'll help you. But you cannot wear this leg in the heat. You have blisters already."

It was not easy to convince her. We then had to lobby her insurance company for a re-fit on her prosthesis. I was now Judy's official letter writer. The insurance company eventually got her fitted with a child-size prosthesis. Although it fits her better, she has never been able to wear it in the summer.

In the meantime, my early morning hurdle was getting easier. I still missed my husband and cried buckets, but not every day. Judy's small requests for assistance were filling a gap in my life that I urgently needed. She needed me. We got another scholarship for Kerri to go to Hawaii. I put Judy's lunch in the fridge, brought things from her car, and took her shopping in her wheelchair. I pushed clothing racks out of the way in order to get the wheelchair through. My husband had been in a wheelchair too, so I knew what to do. I was Judy's cheerleader and she became mine.

In time I realized that in caring for Judy, my grief was easier to live with. I no longer felt that I was going to fall apart when I began each day. I was starting to look forward to the next day. It has been almost twenty years since I took Judy her first banana. We have gone through breast cancer, marriage, divorce, plastic surgery, the arrival of grandchildren and several family deaths. I truly don't know which of us needs the other more. But I do know that to overcome grief, I had to look outside myself and do something for someone else. Judy needed me and I needed her.

~Linda Burks Lohman

Always Something to Give

Do not let what you cannot do interfere with what you can do.
~John Wooden

"GIVE BLOOD!" A bold poster on Elena's office window, outside my apartment door, inspired me. However, the visiting Blood Bank refused my life-pulsing red. "Sorry," the Red Cross nurse explained after I'd filled out their form. "We can't take blood from anyone who's had acupuncture within the last six months."

It was February 14th, Valentine's Day. I longed to give something to someone. "If I can't give blood, then there's nothing I can give."

Unemployed for two months, I was filled with self-doubt. I'd been unfairly fired from my cashier's job at the local market. Hired with the clear understanding that I would work the 3-11 p.m. shift because I took morning classes at the community college, I felt betrayed when I was fired for refusing to work the 6 a.m. shift. Having survived paycheck to paycheck, I was alone and broke.

I needed to find a responsible job and rediscover my self-worth. I applied for restaurant work, telephone sales, house cleaning, babysitting.

Years ago, my grandmother had taught me, that when I give freely, with no ulterior motives or sense of obligation, I not only make others happy, I feel good too. And, by some magical process, my self-worth increases. Thus, despite being jobless, I searched for ways to give—library volunteer, in-home visitor, even storyteller at the day care center. Then I was told that I couldn't give my blood.

Sitting on my daybed, with nothing to give, I felt worthless. Through my tears, I glanced out the window at my thriving garden. I lived in a funky, one-story building, an odd rambling of rooms that had once been a rural clinic. Now, under that same roof, were two apartments and three businesses.

I slipped outside in search of solace among my green tomatoes and mini-zucchini. I stared at a calendula blossom, its brilliant orange petals expanding like the sun's rays. Suddenly inspired, I spoke out loud. "I can give flowers!" I raced around the building examining the border beds, which I'd inter-planted with flowers and vegetables. I picked daisies, alyssum, petunias and calendula.

At my kitchen sink, I arranged colorful bouquets, then washed up and put on lipstick. I scooped up my fragrant floral gifts and delivered them to neighbors, the beauty shop, the architect, and my landlady. Giving, especially something I'd grown and nurtured myself, lifted my spirits.

My apartment and the adjacent sales office shared a cement-slab porch. My porch neighbor, Elena imported and exported shoehorns of every size, color and material imaginable—metal, glass, plastic, wood, stone and bone.

"What's this long one for?" I picked up a twenty-four-inch ivory shoehorn.

"Long handles are for tall boots, cowboy boots and women's high-fashion boots," Elena explained.

"I never knew there were so many kinds or that shoehorns could be a business."

"You'd be surprised," she said. "A few are collectors' items." She picked up a long-handled, sterling silver shoehorn etched with an intricate image of a bullfighter. "This one is from Madrid." Then Elena grabbed a handful of colorful plastic shoehorns. "These are necessities. Some people can't bend over or have difficulty with their feet. Using a shoehorn makes an everyday task easy."

"Daily tasks easy? That's what I need. Do you have any shoehorns for the soul?"

Elena laughed.

The following week when I delivered my fresh flowers, Elena seemed depressed. Now, it was her turn to cry. Out poured the story of her alcoholic husband, the kids she could hardly support, and a diabetic mother. "I'm exhausted," she sobbed. "I used to find comfort in my religion. Now, I feel lost."

I put my arms around her and whispered. Her dark, tear-stained eyes implored. My stomach tightened. I wanted to help. After an awkward silence, I suggested, "Let's pray together. We could say the Our Father." Elena nodded. We held hands and found comfort in repeating the rote words of our childhoods.

My weekly flower delivery evolved into shared prayer with Elena. After an afternoon jog, I'd pop into her office. We'd hold hands, close our eyes and give thanks for all the good in our lives. We prayed for each other—a job for me, coping skills for her.

The tomatoes ripened and I had zucchini on the vine. Food! One evening while working in my garden, I met Elena's kids. The next week her husband stopped by and then her mother. Laughing and talking, we shared an unexpected camaraderie.

Then, one day the manager from the Rock and Mineral Shop called me. "We need a sales clerk at the store."

"I don't know anything about rocks."

"I'll teach you," he said. "I watched you cashiering at the market. You're great with people. That's what we're looking for."

Tourmaline, malachite, feldspar. Soon I was learning to recognize and appreciate the beauty of minerals. My enthusiasm for gemstones soared, along with my spirits and my sales commissions.

Meanwhile, I'd learned that Elena's husband had joined Alcoholics Anonymous, quit drinking and had moved home to Wisconsin where he found work as a computer programmer. Months later, after Elena and her kids moved there to join him, we lost touch. But whenever I think about her I remember Grandma's advice. "There's always something to give." Giving makes me happy.

~Shinan N. Barclay

New York City's Greatest Underground Secret

Don't judge a book by its cover.
~Proverb

I was four months pregnant, violently ill, and wished I was at home in bed. Unfortunately, I was at work in New York City. My home in Long Island was forty-five minutes away by train. I thought I had morning sickness. The company nurse set me straight.

"You have a forty-eight-hour virus. Go home and get some rest," she said.

I trudged downstairs and grabbed a cab to Penn Station where I could catch a train home. It was lunchtime and Penn Station was mobbed. Crowds of commuters and shoppers dashed to trains and subways. I shuffled out of their way and leaned up against the wall. My legs felt like rubber. Before I knew it, my knees buckled and I sank to the floor.

There I was, dressed in my sharpest pantsuit and long winter coat sitting on the floor of a train station. Some commuters stepped around me. Others tripped over my legs. Almost everybody looked at me in disgust. I couldn't blame them. I was a mess. I'm sure they were thinking that alcohol and drugs had done me in. I closed my eyes. Maybe I'd wake up and be home in bed.

I felt a tug at my sleeve and looked up. A toothless bag lady hovered over me. She had a ratty wool cap pulled over her hair. She smelled like a mixture of dirty clothes and rotten food. Not a good smell for someone who's pregnant. First I cringed; then I gagged.

"You don't look so good," she said.

I could have said the same thing about her. She waved over a fellow homeless lady and together they lifted me to my feet.

"You got to get out of the way," said the lead bag lady. "People stepping on you."

The two ladies stood on each side of me. One grabbed my handbag, the other my briefcase. I was too sick to panic. We staggered out of the lobby and headed down a flight of stairs. They led me through a maze of passageways. What had I gotten myself into?

Finally we stumbled into a dimly lit tunnel. A shopping cart filled with their worldly possessions sat to the side. For them, this was home, below Penn Station. The two escorted me to a wobbly wooden stool.

"Don't worry, you're safe here, honey," said the second bag lady.

Her kind smile showed me several missing and chipped teeth. She certainly wasn't worried about her appearance. Surprisingly, she seemed more concerned about how I felt.

The head bag lady disappeared for a moment. She returned with three cups of tea. I'm not much of a tea drinker, but this was by far the most delicious tea I had ever tasted.

"You lookin' better. Where you live?" she asked.

"Long Island," I said.

"We'll get you back to the trains, no problem. But first, you rest."

We chatted about the weather and family, as subways and trains overhead rattled the walls and ceiling. For a moment I felt like I was experiencing an Alice in Wonderland tea party moment with some major differences. While Alice fell down a rabbit hole into a fantasy world populated by outlandish creatures and conversations, I plunged into an underground tunnel populated by two unbelievably caring people.

After tea, my two saviors led me back to the Long Island Railroad concourse. They checked the departure boards, walked me to my train and waved goodbye. I hadn't felt this good all day.

After resting for two days, I headed back to work. It was rush hour and the subway was jammed. As I waited for my train to arrive, I stood back on the platform away from the crowd of commuters. I wasn't alone for long.

"How you feeling?" asked my bag lady friend. She wore the same ratty wool cap.

I smiled. I couldn't believe she found me down here in the subway.

"A little tired, but much better. Thanks again for your help."

"No problem. Today, you need a seat on the subway," she said. "No standing for you." She displayed a mischievous grin.

Subway commuters traditionally jockey for the best spot on the platform, which is where the train doors open. Once the doors open, the subway riders push and shove their way into the train and grab a seat, even while exiting commuters try to leave the train.

As my homeless friend approached the coveted spot on the platform, the commuters backed away. (It's an unwritten rule that commuters always keep their distance from bag ladies.) It was like the parting of the seas. She stood alone. She waved for me to join her. Heads turned as I walked over to her. My new friend put her arm around me. I forced myself to stifle a laugh.

"You gonna get a good seat this morning," she said with a wink.

I didn't doubt her for a moment. The train riders were furious. They had lost their coveted position… and there wasn't anything they could do about it. The train arrived; I scooted on board and grabbed a seat. My nomadic friend quickly stepped back from the tracks and angry riders swarmed the train.

The train doors closed and I waved goodbye to my wool-capped helper. I never saw her again. But for those special couple of days, we shared some laughs, some smiles and some tea. And I realized how lucky I was to receive the gift of kindness from two extraordinary strangers. Sometimes good fortune comes to us when we need it the most and least expect it.

~Maureen C. Bruschi

57

Chicken Soup for the Soul

Just One Loaf

We make a living by what we get, but we make a life by what we give.
~Winston Churchill

I was on the run again. It was Sunday morning, the busiest of my workweek. Mrs. Johnson needed some green yarn, Mrs. Craven needed a whole list of supplies. The nursery worker hadn't shown up yet, and several classes of adults would be upset if the coffee didn't get made! On top of that, I had two prayer requests to give the pastor before service began, and the pastor was nowhere to be found.

It was just an average Sunday in the life of a Children's Ministry Director. By the time the morning ended, I felt like I'd had a morning at the gym, instead of at the church. I wondered if my dry cleaning bill would be higher than my salary. The truth was, I loved every minute of it—all the details, all the running around to get what everyone needed, encouraging the volunteers, and, of course, working with the children. To see those "ah ha" moments when the kids understood a new Bible truth, to see them praising God in song, to pray with them to ask Jesus into their heart—those were the moments that made it all worthwhile, the reasons I didn't mind all the extra hours, nighttime meetings, or even doing menial work like cleaning up after events. In short, I loved my job.

Once a year, however, there was a not-so-happy event in the life of the church for me, a time when I felt disappointed, unappreciated, and ashamed for feeling that way. It rolled around every year in October — Pastor Appreciation. Each year the church would celebrate and thank the Senior Pastor, the Associate Pastor, even the Youth Pastor, but would not recognize me at all. They sent the pastors off on paid vacations, purchased symbolic gifts for them such as paintings or plaques, had receptions, and gave them gift certificates. Many members of the congregation sent cards or brought in small gifts or baked goods, or just came by the office to give them a hug.

I was glad for the pastors. I worked with them throughout the year and knew they were good, strong Christian workers, deserving of recognition. Yet I knew I worked just as hard as they, giving all I had to bring the good news to the children and families in my ministry. I didn't do the job for recognition or praise, and yet I couldn't help feeling slighted each time another year rolled around and I saw the huge piles of baked goods and cards on the pastors' desks. I prayed fervently for God to take away the need for human praise. I asked God to remind me constantly of the only praise I really needed, those wonderful words I hoped to hear on the day I would meet my maker, "Well done, thou good and faithful servant."

This particular year on Pastor Appreciation Sunday, I was guarding my heart against yet another disappointment, and trying to be happy for all the gifts the pastors were receiving. Out of the blue, one of the older ladies in the congregation came up to me with a brown paper bag in hand. She smiled sweetly and said, "I have something for you." My mind quickly thought of the possibilities. This lady was known for her cooking abilities. Maybe it was some delicious treat, or some fresh fruit from her garden. It didn't really matter, though, I was so happy to get anything at all in recognition of my hard work. All this went through my mind in a fraction of a second, and I said a quick prayer of thanks as I took the bag from the lady's outstretched hand.

"Thanks so much!" I said, smiling from ear to ear.

"I'm glad to do it," the lady said. "I know you've been collecting them."

Suddenly I got a sinking feeling in my stomach. I walked slowly into my office and opened the bag. Sure enough, it was full of toilet paper tubes. I had placed an announcement in the bulletin asking people to save them for an upcoming project. I sat down at my desk and shed a few tears, then poured out my heart to God, asking Him again to take away the desire for recognition, asking Him to help me be content knowing that my work was contributing to the salvation and spiritual growth of my students.

A peace came over me right then and there. I realized God had given me a job I loved, and even if I never received a single word of thanks, I was doing something of eternal value. As I stared at the bag of toilet paper rolls in my lap, it began to seem funny. Soon I started to laugh at myself, wondering how many more bags of empty rolls I would receive that day. God had taken away my sorrow and replaced it with laughter. The more I thought about it, the funnier it seemed and the more I laughed, and that is just how Delores found me.

Delores was a supporter of children's ministry, even though she had no children of her own. She had some health concerns, and teaching was not her gift, yet she supported the ministry in other ways, providing baked goods for special events, substituting in the nursery, and covering the ministry in prayer. Delores stuck her head in my office, and asked if she was interrupting. I pulled myself together and readied myself for whatever Delores needed.

"Come on in," I said.

Delores stepped into the office and pulled something from behind her back. It was a loaf of Delores's homemade cinnamon bread! It had a card attached. Delores said, "I just wanted to thank you for all you do for the kids." She put the bread on my desk and made a quick exit. I sat staring at the loaf of bread with my mouth hanging open. Just when God had given me peace and contentment without human praise, He sent some to me anyway!

Now I anticipate Pastor Appreciation each October, making sure all the pastors are properly thanked, and thanking God for allowing me to be His tool. I thank Him, too, for one very special lady named

Delores, and one loaf of bread, which, though eaten long ago, leaves a sweet taste in my mouth every October.

~Sarah Bergman

58

It Was Nothing

*To give and then not feel that one has given
is the very best of all ways of giving.*
~Max Beerbohm

My first lesson is at a meeting. As we settle around the table, I hear Meg, who is recovering from surgery, talking to Judith, the manager of our project. "Thank you so much for driving my daughters to all their dance and music lessons last week. I can't tell you how much that meant to me."

Judith checks her planner for the time of her next meeting. "Don't mention it," she says. "It was nothing."

I listen with awe, knowing how crammed Judith's schedule is, with her work, meetings, kids, and aging parents. Driving someone's children to lessons seems incredibly generous to me, bordering on the angelic.

The meeting is just beginning when Donna hurries into the room. "Sorry I'm late," Donna says, pulling out a chair. "I was hosting my semi-annual lunch for my friends who are over seventy. A few of the ladies lingered a long time."

I envision Donna, surrounded by white-haired ladies, each beautifully coifed and bejeweled.

"How many people came?" I ask.

"Eight. We have a lot of older people in our apartment building and they don't get out much, so I fix a fancy luncheon for them. The stories they have to tell are truly fascinating."

I think of my own neighborhood and realize that several of my neighbors don't get out much anymore. I never thought of inviting them over for a meal.

"That is so nice of you," I say, knowing how busy Donna is, how she doesn't really like to cook and clean.

"Oh," she says, waving her hand, "it was nothing."

Meanwhile, I am moving into a new house. Between unpacking and working, I feel fried and frazzled. That feeling lifts instantly when I come home from work and find two fledgling rosebushes on the front stoop. The note from Nick reads, "I know you like roses. Don't worry if you kill these. I have more." I pick up each plant and smile at the world. Roses are my favorite flowers and it is quite possible these magnificent plants will not survive under my care. Nick's note assuages my guilt. Despite the gathering dark, I plant the bushes and call Nick, spilling over with gratitude.

"Hey, it was nothing," Nick says. I hear the pleasure in his voice. He loved bringing me those plants. As a master gardener, he was sharing one of his great gifts.

I start thinking about this concept of "nothing," this serene and generous way of living. While I am in the middle of this pondering, Terri calls. She is giving an important speech and is very nervous.

"Can I practice in front of you?" she asks.

"Sure," I say. I know how terrifying public speaking can be.

Sunday afternoon, Terri stands in my living room and gives her speech. She sounds shy and uncertain. Her beginning is long and stumbling; her ending is abrupt. I have a few ideas.

"I think you could start with that great story you told in the middle," I tell her. "And you could look at me more often."

She tries the speech again, her voice stronger, her eye contact good. We discuss the opening story and she tries again. After the fifth try, I give her a rousing round of applause. "It's great," I tell her.

"I can't thank you enough," she says.

I smile and shake my head. "It was nothing," I say.

Then I stop — had it really been nothing or am I just saying that? I think about the afternoon. I was tired when we started, still worn down from working all day Saturday. Now, I feel alive and energetic. I feel confident, smart and talented! And looking at Terri, I can see she feels pretty good too.

"I was wrong," I tell Terri. "Helping you was really something to me."

And so, I learned that giving from the heart doesn't have to mean sacrifice and hard work. The trick is finding something we love to do and finding someone who needs that something. We can be generous to others and to ourselves at the same time! Once you get the hang of it, it's nothing. And it's really something.

~Deborah Shouse

Feeling Better, Bag by Bag

Those who bring sunshine to the lives of others cannot keep it from themselves.

~James Matthew Barrie

t was early April, and after a long, dreary Minnesota winter, sunshine and spring had arrived. I was happily married and three months pregnant. Yet there I sat, crying in the mall parking lot when I should have been doing errands.

A year earlier, twenty weeks into my first pregnancy, I'd been confined to the hospital on bed rest for eighteen days. It was a dark time, full of loneliness, anxiety, and above all, a paralyzing fear that my baby wasn't going to make it. Then, on Day 19, that fear was realized. Luke McKay was born. He lived only an hour.

Happiness returned over time—especially with the news that I was expecting twins. Still, as Luke's birthday approached, I was depressed. I hated remembering those weeks in the hospital. Like a black hole, they had sucked my power, my peace, even my faith. And while I'd done a lot of emotional work around the loss of my son, such as journaling, support groups, and counseling, it didn't seem that anything could heal the memories of that hospital stay.

So I sat in my car, sobbing. When I was done, I blew my nose and racked my brain. What could I do to feel better? That's when I thought of the care package.

In the hospital, one bright spot in the gloom had been a box sent by a college friend. It was full of little gifts—some useful, some silly—accompanied by a list of funny descriptions. About a jeweled hair clip: "A fashion must for every hospital patient." About a book of crossword puzzles: "For intellectual stimulation during TV commercials." And for a package of my favorite cookies: "To remind you of the days when we ate only the 'healthiest' of foods!"

Remembering how the box had raised my spirits, I decided to make my own care package for an expectant mother on bed rest. On the back of a napkin, I listed items to include. There had to be a hair clip. Some silly slippers, too. A package of the softest toilet tissue. And sweet-smelling hand soap; I'd always hated the medicinal odor of hospital soap.

After shopping my blues away, I went home, attached labels to each item, and packed it all in a gift bag. I also wrote a letter to the unknown recipient, sharing part of my story and offering my prayers for a healthy baby.

On April 19, the anniversary of Luke's birth, my husband Jory and I returned to the hospital. We walked through the lobby where I had checked in the year before. We visited the cafeteria where Jory had eaten supper the night Luke died. And we rode the elevator to the fourth floor, where I'd spent three of the hardest weeks of my life.

At the nurses' station, I hesitantly set the bag on the counter. "I brought this for one of your patients on bed rest," I said. "To cheer her up." The nurse looked inside and exclaimed over the contents. "I have just the patient in mind for this," she told me. "She's been here for thirty-one days." Thirty-one days! That's when I knew for certain the care package had been a good idea.

Five months later, my beautiful baby girls were born, and the following April, I was too busy (and sleep deprived) to think of care packages or hospital visits. But as my daughters grew, they learned about their big brother Luke, and it seemed natural to pair a visit to his grave with a stop at the hospital. I started assembling a care package every spring. Over time, I increased the number I delivered each year to three, then six. When the girls got old enough, they helped me pack them.

It has now been twelve years since Luke died, and at least fifty mothers-to-be have received one of my bed rest bags. I've received grateful notes from a few of them, but that's not why I do it. Packing those gift bags is a way of celebrating not being in the hospital. It's a way of celebrating my two living children. Most of all, it's a way of celebrating a reassuring truth, which I learned through the loss of my little boy: out of something bad can come something good. Doing something to encourage women who feel helpless—as I once did—has restored my sense of power and helped me to heal.

~Sara Matson

Finding My Mantra

The foolish man seeks happiness in the distance;
the wise grows it under his feet.
~James Openheim

As a writer I'm always looking for an edge. I've done yoga in Costa Rica, and walking meditations in Phnom Penn. I've even had needles stuck into the top of my head, an acupuncture move called One Hundred Meeting Places that is designed to unleash my inner muse. So when a doctor gave a lecture at a local hospital extolling the virtues of meditation as a way to increase mental acuity, productivity and creativity, I was all ears.

He led us in a seated meditation. We closed our eyes, breathed deeply and counted from one to ten. Despite the shuffle of feet and occasional sniffles, I found myself relaxing. After the lecture, I eagerly waited in line for my signed complimentary copy of the book. That night I sat down and read about the cutting-edge science behind his methods as well as compelling accounts of people for whom it had worked.

Then, on page 55, things took a different tack. There, instead of counting from one to ten, I was being asked to substitute a word. A mantra. One that was rooted in my personal belief system. And that's where I hit a wall. It's not that I don't have a personal belief system. I have many!

I was raised a Catholic. I loved the smell of smoking incense rising from the thurible our priest used to bless us congregants each

Easter. I fingered rosaries and lit Advent candles. I walked the Stations of the Cross.

Later I converted to Judaism. I liked the liberal politics of my reform temple. And ritual? I had ritual galore! I could light candles on Friday nights, inhale spices on Saturday evenings. There were prayers for waking up and prayers for going to sleep. Prayers before eating fruit, breaking bread or drinking wine. But how do you capture all that in a word: the religion that raised me and the one that called me? The incense, the candles, the Hebrew, the prayers. Wasn't that just ceremony anyway? Catholicism and Judaism, these were my religions. But were they my personal belief system?

The doctor's book had suggestions for mantras: "Jesus Loves Me" for Christians and "Shalom" for Jews. I tried. After all, I believe in peace. Who doesn't? But Shalom just didn't cut it for me. It was the easy way out.

I thought I had it when I thought of *ruach*, the Hebrew word for spirit. Aha! Breath. Wind. Spirit. Voilà! A mantra. But then I tried it. I found that meditative breathing doesn't happen easily when your mantra has that guttural "ch" sound in it. But it was also more than that. Ultimately, *ruach* just wasn't a personal belief system.

So I was back to square one. This time, instead of trying to come up with a word or phrase that captured my belief system, I tried going at it from the other end. I tried to figure out just what it was I believed in, and then tried to name it.

And this is the thing. I believe in family. I believe in us. In me, my husband, my sons. We are there for each other. My husband and I have taken turns as breadwinner and homemaker over the years. We have cared for our parents as they aged and passed on. When my youngest son was in a car accident a few years back, his older brother flew home from a semester in Mexico and literally slept on the floor beside him in the ICU. That's what I believe in.

This generational belief system manifested itself for me when my husband and I visited Vietnam earlier this year. It was Tet, the Chinese New Year. We watched folks readying their homes for the holidays. They strapped miniature orange trees and live chickens and pigs to the backs of their motor scooters. They placed fresh fruit and cups of water before the Buddhas in their homes. Our host family, too, placed their offerings before the gold-painted Buddahs. But then, our host Phi raised sticks of fragrant incense up to a faded photo of an elderly Asian couple above the mantelpiece.

"Before we pay tribute to the Buddha," Phi explained, "we must first honor our ancestors."

I froze. I took a breath. I remember thinking, "This is it. This is what I believe." Here, halfway around the globe, I had discovered it. My personal belief system. The hand of one generation giving to and caring for the next. The younger generation reaching back for that ancestral hand.

I watched with loving interest as Phi lit candles and bowed in front of his grandparents. I bowed, too, thinking of my own parents. Though they are gone, they come to me daily in the lessons they taught and the values they instilled. My father's work ethic. My mother's grace.

My father wore his heart on his sleeve. He loved my mother and acted as though he could hardly believe his luck that she loved him, too. My parents were role models for what a loving relationship looked like, sounded like and felt like.

My mother's lessons were more domestic but no less potent. She taught me how to square the corners of a flat sheet. That I could substitute a cup of whole milk with a teaspoon of vinegar in it for a cup of buttermilk in any recipe. How to save a fabric's nap by ironing on the wrong side of corduroy. These small household lessons keep my mother alive and with me daily as I live my own matriarchal role.

We ate the lunch our host family had prepared. Pumpkin soup, steamed rice, fried pork molded onto stalks of lemongrass, sliced dragon fruit for dessert. I ate quietly, absorbing the meaning of all I'd just seen. My husband knew I'd related deeply to the tableau inside. On the car ride back to our Hanoi hotel he summed it up. "Honey, I think you're Vietnamese."

But I was not Vietnamese. I was a Jewish-American woman in search of a mantra. A breathable phrase that captures everything I believe in. And on my next visit to our synagogue after our Asian adventure, I found it. It was right after the part of the service where we explicitly acknowledge our duty to teach our children our faith, to pass on the torch of religious tradition.

"These words which I command you this day you shall take to heart. You shall teach them diligently to your children."

And there it was. In Hebrew. My mantra. L'dor Va-dor. From generation to generation. My belief system, summed up and perfectly breathable to boot. L'dor. Breathe in. Va-dor. Breathe out. Inhaling one generation. Exhaling the next.

Now I happily meditate with my new mantra. Willing wisdom from my ancestors. Praying for insights to share with my sons. Oh, I still stick needles in my head from time to time, East meeting West in my constant quest for enhanced creativity. But at least now, I know what I believe in.

~Carolyn Roy-Bornstein

Find Your Happiness

Finding My Purpose

The purpose of life is not to be happy — but to matter, to be productive, to be useful, to have it make some difference that you have lived at all.

~Leo Rosten

I Don't Quit

Find a need and fill it.
~Ruth Stafford Peale

I had a special childhood fascination with high school reunions, idealizing what seemed a journey of transformation. Yet back at that tender age, I never imagined my ten-year high school reunion the way it actually played out.

"So what do you do, Leah?"

The question was asked hesitantly. You see, I spent my reunion sitting at a table, thin and pale, with a colorful bandana covering my bald head.

I'd spent most of high school struggling with chronic illness. An athlete and honors student, I caught a mysterious virus at fourteen, and my life changed forever. For almost three years I bounced between home tutoring and short-lived returns to school in an agonizing roller coaster fashion. It tested the patience of many fair-weather friends, it befuddled the doctors caring for me, and my so-called "wonder years" were spent incredibly lonely and heartbroken.

During the darkest of times my salvation came from the love of my family, my dog and my horse, who I sometimes only saw through a window. No doubt, my illness took a toll on each member of my family. Mom struggled to balance my needs with the needs of her husband and my younger sister, Mary. Mary struggled to identify with me as my life shrunk to the boundaries of a couch and a bed. And the burden of holding finances together while making sense of an emotionally charged house weighed heavy on Dad. Money for specialists and alternative treatments came from my parents' own pocket. Some things insurance just didn't cover.

"I don't want to be in this body anymore," I had told my mom.

One night Mom came home with a yellow journal and placed it in my hands. On the front was a poem entitled "Don't Quit." "I want you to read this because I think it will mean something to you," urged Mom. The poem was filled with inspirational words about overcoming challenges and it was perfect for me. After each and every stanza the refrain almost sang to me, "Don't Quit." I read it... and through tears understood.

Slowly over the next few days I began to write inside that journal. Writing had been my passion and somehow Mom knew the solace I'd find through my own scribbled words. In the passing weeks poems began to form between the lined pages and I began to make sense of the pain.

In the days before the Internet, support came in the form of pen pals, namely other teenagers suffering from chronic illness. Before I knew it, I had a slew of friends who understood me. I began compiling the poems we traded. Before I knew what I was doing, it became a literary newsletter. By year's end it was being sent out quarterly to a dozen kids just like me across the country... and by the second year it was being sent to England and Australia.

That newsletter became my salvation.

"Thank you Leah for making me see I'm not alone," wrote one of my pen pals.

Words like those made me realize I had the power to make a difference. I was not a victim of my circumstance. It may have not restored the loss of my high school social life, but it gave me a sense of purpose.

Miraculously, my health stabilized enough for college, where I enjoyed four years of a somewhat normal life. I had carefully hidden the "sick Leah" image. I didn't want to talk about being ill. Campus night movies, Division I basketball games and even research papers made me feel normal again. But I wasn't.

My entire college experience was punctuated by emergency room visits. Sometimes a weekend home turned into extended recuperation, and I had to hustle to catch up on my classes. "Not quitting" had become more than a mantra. It was the only way. Despite everything, I graduated on time with a degree in journalism.

Yet, just a few months after graduating, I was sitting across from my primary care doctor as he laid it on the line. My crushing fatigue, rapid weight loss and heart fluttering had returned. I'd lost my job as a reporter because of this. Now he had doubts about the true nature of my illness. This man had likely seen me more often than any other patient in his practice.

"I am going to refer you to my colleague who I deeply respect."

His colleague ended up being a psychiatrist, one brought in, I suppose, to verify I was suffering from some form of depression. I spent ten minutes on the couch of her in-home office, patting her two Newfoundlands, before she realized the battle I was waging was not with my mind. I should have felt vindicated, but there was still no resolution.

It was the word "cancer" at twenty-six that seemingly answered everything. It now seemed that the insidiously slow-growing and well-hidden monkey on my back was actually in my thyroid.

I barely had time to think before the radical surgery. I awoke from the lengthy operation surrounded by my family. I couldn't move my hands to dry the tears spilling out.

How does one even deal with the word cancer?

"Don't talk," my dad whispered. "They got it all. It's over."

But it wasn't. Sixteen months later it was beginning again—this time with a diagnosis of Hodgkin's lymphoma. I went home. I watched my hair fall out from chemotherapy. And then I went to that reunion. Friends had to reintroduce me to other classmates. Surely this wasn't the movie-of-the-week version of my high school reunion. It was the lowest I'd ever felt.

One night, particularly sleepless, I looked up at my old bookshelf. There in its yellow vinyl glory was the Don't Quit journal. As I leafed through it and re-read the inscribed poem I felt the inspiration come back to me.

From a long ago echo—a forgotten purpose. Again, I was not the only one. This time, with help from the Internet, it was easier to find those like me. Young adults with cancer are by no means a rare group. Rarer still is a person under thirty diagnosed in a timely manner.

It got me mad enough to do something about it. In sharing my story I found freedom. Today I fight on behalf of young people with cancer. I've been in remission for more than five years. I now help teenagers and young adults navigate illness. It feels right somehow.

I don't know that everything happens for a reason. However, I know at my next reunion when I am asked, "What do you do?" I'll say what I don't do.

I don't quit.

~Leah Shearer

Filling a Need

The purpose of life is a life of purpose.
~Robert Byrne

As I approached my fortieth birthday, I realized that my life was quite meaningless in the larger scheme of things: I had friends and a loving husband and yet something was missing. With no children, I felt that I hadn't done anything that would help mankind or change the world. I would have no legacy to leave.

I was watching TV one day and I saw Billy Graham speaking about prayer. He said that we should ask God for the "desires of our hearts." He explained that this is different than just asking for your wants and wishes. It is not like asking for a new red sports car. He was talking about the deepest and truest desires of your heart.

My desire was to be someone who mattered. I wanted to make a difference in the lives of people and in the lives of animals. After all, dogs had always been a large part of my life, from the time when I was a little girl growing up in central Oklahoma. I thought that my "purpose" would somehow include my love of singing, writing, travel, and of course, working with animals.

Then, something happened that shook my entire core. The "love of my life" dog, my Nicholas, was diagnosed with terminal cancer. He died thirteen months later. I became quite concerned for Bear, our remaining Cockapoo, who was six years old. Bear had been Nicholas's shadow and now that Nick was gone, Bear wouldn't even eat. Our vet suggested that we get another dog to see if that would encourage Bear to eat.

I found an online ad for a Bichon Frise and when we arrived at the place it was a nightmare, like one of those puppy mills you read about or see on the television news. I decided to delay my search for my "purpose" as I needed to tell the world about the horror I had discovered right in my own backyard.

I had even a bigger fight ahead of me than Nicholas's cancer. This was a fight that would take years. I did research and then I spread the word on the Internet. People began to listen and we formed a small group of Bichon Frise lovers called Small Paws Rescue.

I started out sending the latest news on our rescue efforts to about twenty-five people. Within a few months we had grown to a group of several hundred. Some had Bichons and some had other breeds of dogs.

I felt bad about the delay in finding my "purpose in life," but after all, I was now on a mission.

A few years passed and my rescue stories were being read by more than six thousand people in twenty-eight different countries. National media outlets began asking me to do interviews and to film episodes for Animal Planet.

It took me a while to realize that I had not only found my purpose in life, but each of the desires of my heart had been included as well.

Yes, losing Nicholas was part of this journey. If I hadn't lost Nick, I wouldn't have found myself involved in this magnificent obsession called Small Paws Rescue, along with some of the finest people anywhere. Now my days are filled with helping people and animals. I travel this beautiful country attending Small Paws Rescue functions.

Because of this awesome and wonderful gift to me, in the past thirteen years, Small Paws Rescue has rescued more than 8,000 Bichons and has made a difference in the lives of thousands of people, too.

I've been made whole and complete, and what more could any person ever ask? The sheer joy of doing what I do overflows from every pore of my body, and I can never repay this wonderful gift that has given my life purpose.

You too can find your purpose in life, and the desires of your heart. And look behind you. You may even be followed by a few thousand small, white, fluffy dogs.

~Robin Pressnall

Finding Me

Know, first, who you are; and then adorn yourself accordingly.
~Epictetus

I've been a lot of different people in my life. Not very many of them were really me.

Because I was such an insecure child, I became both a straight-A student and a sullen argumentative "hippie" to impress my parents and my peers at the same time. It was a pretty big task. All that skipping school to be with the cool kids made for some very long nights of make-up work to keep up my straight A's. I did it, though. I'm sure there are still teachers out there who think I was the perfect student, and students that think I was the perfect radical. The real me was neither of those things.

Once I started dating, things got even worse. Like a chameleon in a rapidly changing environment, my personality would transform to fit whatever man I happened to be dating at the time. In the span of a couple of years, I went from being an overzealous religious fanatic while dating a good Catholic man, to a bar-hopping, beer-drinking groupie when I dated a local musician. Other versions of "me" included the reluctant beach bunny who suffered through the humiliation of displaying my skinny, scrawny bikinied body at the beach to be with my surfing boyfriend. Or the hermit who quit my job and moved away from my family to try to find the right place where my unsociable boyfriend-du-jour could feel comfortable in isolation. Then I was the New Ager, who ate tofu and bean sprouts and thought I was actually going to pass out and die while I tried to reach enlightenment by sitting through the searing heat of a sweat lodge. I tried not to think about the sweaty naked guy sitting right next to me with his sweaty naked bottom on the sweaty, naked ground.

I've worn high heels and hot pants and push-up bras and dressed like Madonna and dressed like the Madonna and all just to please somebody else. I was not me for so long that I eventually began to forget who the real me was. And the really sad thing was that I thought I had to do those things to fit in and be accepted. And the even sadder thing is, that when you do that, you either have to choose to not be yourself for the rest of your life, or you need to face the inevitable place in any relationship where you do decide to be yourself, and your mate or friends are sitting there wondering what in the heck happened to the girl they fell in love with.

I was actually over forty before I realized what a mistake I was making with my life. I went to a guy's house for a date and he didn't like the way I was dressed and he actually took me by the hand and led me to the store to have me buy different clothes that he approved of. It's funny how we sometimes need Life to give us a little slap in the face like that to make us realize what we are doing to ourselves. The guy might have even loved me for myself if I had given him the chance. But it was easier for me to become myself again while I was by myself again, so I left him at the store and went home and began the difficult process of trying to find "me" inside all the layers that I had put around myself to please others.

I'm still working on the process of being comfortable being me. Writing helps. Oddly enough, although I'm sometimes reluctant to show the real me to individuals, it isn't that difficult for me to write my innermost thoughts and deep secrets and life experiences and have them published in newspapers and magazines for the whole world to read. So that's what I do. I write about life and the things I have learned that have helped me to find my way and I hope that some of the things I've learned in life help other people to find their own way, too.

Because it really seems like once I began to live my life my own way, then everything I always wanted in life and asked for in life began to come to me. It's almost like Fate was looking for me all the time with a big sack full of goodies. It just didn't recognize me in those high heels and hot pants.

~Betsy S. Franz

64

A Ride on a Carousel

Happiness is like a butterfly which, when pursued, is always beyond our grasp, but, if you will sit down quietly, may alight upon you.
~Nathaniel Hawthorne

One year when I was in my thirties I found myself alone on a carousel horse in the middle of December wondering what I was supposed to do with my life. The carousel ride was a lot like my life—it kept going and going but never got anywhere. I went up and down on the horse as I experienced ups and downs in my life, but my place in the world never really changed. I was always behind someone else and never seemed to make a difference. I wanted to make a difference. I wanted to help people but I didn't know how.

I spent some time visiting the rest of the amusement park and looking at the Christmas decorations. I found myself smiling at the children around me on the train ride, all of us braving the cold while we drove through fields of twinkling lights. I laughed at the street performers telling jokes and I applauded the theater cast for putting on a great Christmas show. I scared myself a little on a few rides and when I got cold I enjoyed a cup of hot chocolate and some popcorn. I didn't mind at all that I was alone because there were so many people around me having a good time.

And I was having a good time too. I loved being at amusement parks in any season. There is just something about them that still makes me excited even though I've visited our local park at least five hundred times in my lifetime. I still feel like a kid when I walk up to the gate.

I was thinking about how much I had enjoyed my evening as I sat on a bench finishing my hot chocolate. A couple stopped in front me trying to read a park map. It was dark and the maps have small print so they were having trouble. They had a young girl with them, about three years old, who was dancing around a lot but not saying anything so I guessed this was a bathroom emergency. I excused myself for interrupting them and asked if they needed to find a restroom. They looked relieved and said yes — and soon.

I turned them around and pointed to the closest bathroom. It was only a few yards away but if you had never seen the park in the daytime you wouldn't know it was there at night. They thanked me, and the woman and the little girl quickly ran to the bathroom. The man asked me how I knew they were looking for a restroom and I explained that I had a daughter also and I knew the "potty" dance when I saw it. Because of her I knew where every bathroom in the park was.

The woman and the little girl came out and joined the man and thanked me again for my help. I had saved their evening since they didn't have a change of clothing with them for their daughter and if she had had an accident they would have had to go home and miss seeing Santa. I pointed the way to Santa's workshop for them and they left smiling, with the little girl running ahead.

I know how bad it would have been if they had had to leave. I still remember how hard it was to scrape up the money to bring my daughter to the park when she was young and how important it was that we had a good time since we could only go once a year. We were lucky that as she got older we could afford season passes so she and I were able to become regulars at the park.

That night on that cold bench, with an empty hot chocolate cup, I finally figured out how I could make a difference. I could do what I did for that little girl's family for a whole lot of other families by sharing what I had learned about amusement parks. I could help them save money and time, plus tell them how to have a great day while they were there.

I walked through the park watching the people and thinking of all the things I knew that I could share. Some of it was simple advice such as drink lots of water and find the bathrooms on the map early in your trip before you have an emergency. But I also knew some other things that took some time to figure out, such as where to find the best milkshakes, who serves a kid's meal that is big enough for an adult and when are the lines for the coasters the shortest. Knowing all those little things can add up to one big thing—a fun day out with the family.

That December evening my life changed. I began to share my travel tips with others so they could have more fun with their families at amusement parks and other places in our state. I began traveling to more and more amusement parks to find their hidden joys and the pitfalls parents might encounter. I shared what I found on a website I started for families planning trips. These days I spend my time doing something I feel makes a difference—helping families create great memories.

Now when I ride the carousel I don't feel like I'm going in circles. I feel like I have a whole new life filled with purpose. As my painted pony spins around and around I smell the popcorn, I hear the people screaming on the roller coaster and I tap my toes to the melody of the Wurlitzer organ while I think of my next travel tip for my readers.

I am still riding in a circle but now I am going somewhere.

~Shawn Marie Mann

65

Too Dumb to Be a Nurse

Though no one can go back and make a brand new start, anyone can start
from now and make a brand new ending.
~Author Unknown

When I was eight we moved to a house a block from Saint Vincent's Hospital in Erie, Pennsylvania. Always a rover, it wasn't long before I had checked out all the different nooks and crannies around the building. One entryway caught my attention because at certain times of the day the nurses came and went through that door.

After a while my curiosity got the best of me. I was no longer content to watch the nurses arrive for work—I wanted to see them at work. Before long I was roving the upper hallways and watching my Nightingales in action, despite the sign in all the hallways that read, "No Children Under Age 14 Permitted to Visit."

By the time I reached junior high I was sure I wanted to be a nurse. If you didn't study Latin, you couldn't be a nurse, so I enrolled. Many Latin words were familiar to me and I thought it would be pretty easy. The hard part turned out to be the usage and creating sentences with the words that seemed so easy to pronounce. Several weeks into the course my teacher came to me, without tact or gentleness, saying,

"I think you should withdraw from this course. It seems to be too hard for you and you are slowing the rest of the class down."

Teachers and other adults should be careful when trampling on young people's dreams. That was the day I learned I wasn't smart enough to become a nurse. With shame and humiliation, I handed in my Latin textbook and switched to study hall for that period for the rest of the year. Throughout high school I never again took a math or science course that wasn't required for graduation. I left those courses to the smart kids.

After high school the years raced by. I married, had children. Most women didn't work outside their home and if I did become acquainted with a woman who worked, she usually was a nurse. The conversation would go like this:

"Do you work?"

"Yes. I'm a nurse."

"Oh. I wanted to be a nurse, but I'm not smart enough."

"Oh I doubt that."

"No, really. I couldn't even learn Latin."

Then one day my husband John came home from work with news that would change my life in a major way.

"Carol, Mav died this afternoon." I looked at my husband with disbelief.

"What!" Mav was young and healthy. "How?"

"He was a passenger in a car that came over the crest of a hill that was obscuring a truck parked half on the highway. They couldn't see the truck until they were right on it and had no time to swerve, and well..." his voice trailed off.

Mav and John had been friends since they were in their early twenties. John was devastated by this tragedy. As the days passed he was unusually quiet. Finally one evening he said, "Carol, Jackie has never worked and now she's alone with four children. Unless Mav had great insurance, I don't know how she will manage. I've been thinking—if anything happens to me, I want you to be able to take care of yourself and the children. Why don't you think about what you'd like to do and get the training you'll need to do it?"

I couldn't believe what I was hearing. For months before Mav's death I had been having the most unusual experience, but hadn't shared it with John since it was spiritual and at that time he was skeptical about matters of faith. Many times a day a verse from the New Testament book of James would come to my mind: "Is any among you sick?"

Then one evening, while I sat reading, I suddenly saw myself, vividly, on what seemed like an internal movie screen. I was walking down the hall in a hospital dressed as a nurse. I entered a room with two female patients and walked to the bed nearest the window. I knew the patient had had a stroke and I was checking on her. After I watched her for a couple of moments and was certain she was sleeping comfortably, I turned and walked back to the nurses' station where I picked up a chart.

The combination of these two occurrences started me thinking that God was calling me to become a nurse. His calling didn't diminish my belief that I wasn't intelligent enough. But He gave me the determination to try because that was what I believed He wanted.

I began looking at nursing programs. I was certain that I would never be able to become an R.N., but maybe I could become a Licensed Vocational Nurse, as their courses weren't as difficult. I signed up for the entrance exam.

The day of the exam I entered a large room full of people also wanting to enter LVN training. I imagined every one of them would do well on the test and would go on to become an LVN except me.

One day not long after I opened our mailbox to find a letter from the school. I wanted so badly to open it, but with my lack of confidence, I laid it on the kitchen counter saying, "I'm not in the mood for a rejection letter today."

Letters like that call to you, though. With every trip through the kitchen, I saw it. Finally I forced myself to open it, thinking, "Let's get this over with."

"Dear Carol," I read. "We are pleased to notify you that you successfully passed the entrance exam for Licensed Vocational Nurse.

We are saving a seat for you in our next class provided we hear from you within one month."

Twenty-five hopeful LVNs started in my class on that September day. To my surprise, for the next eighteen months I earned the highest grades in the class and eventually graduated as valedictorian. With this success under my belt, a year later I challenged an R.N. program and was exempted from the first year of studies. At the end of the three-year course I finished fifth out of a class that started with forty students.

An insensitive teacher once stole my dream. It took an act of God to get it back, but there is a saying that whom God calls, He also equips. If I were a motivational speaker I would urge my listeners to adopt this mind-set: If you have a dream, exhaust every effort and every avenue necessary to reach it. I've worked thirty years now as a nurse and I've never been more certain that this is what I was meant to be.

~Carol A. Gibson

66

Hugs, Hope, and Peanut Butter

You cannot always have happiness, but you can always give happiness.
~Author Unknown

I n 1998, my connective tissue disease attacked my eyes. For several weeks I could see nothing but white fog. Even after my vision was restored, I couldn't return to work. Because of scarred corneas, I would forever view the world as if looking through a dirty window. Distinguishing details was difficult. I found myself unable to enjoy hobbies, without a worthwhile job, and sinking into depression. Sitting alone at home all day, I felt useless. My self-esteem plummeted as I was thrown into the world of disability.

To ease my boredom, I joined a prayer group. There I met a woman who told me a sad story about her grandson, Michael, who had an inoperable brain tumor. He was just two years old, the same age as my grandson, who was recovering from severe burns. I could relate to this grandma's emotions. I understood how helpless you feel when a child you love is suffering and you can't take his pain away.

Through the prayer group, I also met a mom desperate for emotional support. "My daughter has brain cancer," she told me. "I feel so alone and scared. Family and friends have deserted us."

I wondered how caring people could do that to a sick child and her mother, during their time of greatest need. "They don't know what to say," she explained. "Seeing my little girl's bald head and pale skin makes them uncomfortable. They can't stand to see her suffering."

This heartbroken mother was searching for someone who cared enough to help her through this ordeal. She said, "I feel like running into the street screaming, 'My child is sick! Won't somebody do something?'"

At that moment, I decided to be that somebody. I couldn't do a lot, but I could do something.

Because I understood pain, fear, frustration, and isolation, I could relate to families affected by illness. And, because I was "retired," I had the time to invest in making a difference for these families.

I sent the children cheery cards and small gifts. I called and e-mailed the parents to encourage them. I created a monthly newsletter for families of ill children and I started a chat group where parents could find support. I created a website specifically for stories about kids who needed cheer. Visitors to the site could read children's stories, pray for them, and brighten their lives through programs like providing balloon bouquets, birthday parties, or Christmas gifts for children in hospitals.

My disability, which had seemed at first to be an ending, became an asset leading to an exciting new beginning. The temporary pause, as my life train switched tracks, propelled me into a new passion and purpose.

Another surprise came when parents told me that my small efforts were having a huge impact on their families. They were encouraged by knowing people cared about what they were going through. They were building strong friendships through the chat group.

Moms were grateful that their kids now had more to look forward to than needles, pain, and hospitals. One boy told his mother, "I can't believe so many people care about me!" His dad said, "Your group provides an invaluable gift that no other organization can."

Over the years, I've added hundreds of children to the website. Now in its twelfth year as a nonprofit charity, Hugs and Hope has one simple goal: to put a little more joy into the lives of sick kids and their families.

A mother told me about her six-year-old son who was unable to see, walk, or speak. The mail he received was the highlight of each day. He would lie on the couch eagerly awaiting the arrival of the mail. When his mom brought it into the house, he would clap and giggle with excitement. "He sleeps with those cards under his pillow," she said.

Over 3,000 volunteer "hug givers" and "hope builders" not only send hundreds of cheery cards each month; they also provide the rare gift of friendship, a listening ear, and much needed moral support to parents through the "parent pals" program.

Children like Nathan and his little brother PJ have benefited from being part of the Hugs and Hope group. They suffered from the fatal Batten's Disease, and their parents needed $100,000 for medical treatments. As a result of volunteers contacting television producers, the boys were featured on the show *48 Hours*.

After his bone marrow transplant, ten-year-old Zack had been in isolation for months. Hugs and Hope volunteers arranged for his favorite singer, Kid Rock, to call the boy and send him his own autographed guitar. Zack's smile is something I won't forget—especially since we were able to deliver the surprise just weeks before his death. It's heartwarming to make a child's last days happier.

Although disability closed some doors for me, a huge window opened. I'm not depressed these days, because I stay busy creating smiles—and some of them are my own. You see, I've learned that no matter what your abilities—or lack of them—there is always something you can do. And when you focus on that, amazing things can happen. I've even become a published writer—something I never dreamed of doing! My book is illustrated by—you guessed it—"cancer kids."

When The Hugs and Hope Club began, I was helping one little boy named Michael. Now hundreds of hurting families are part of the circle of love. I want them to learn, as I did, that no one has to face struggles alone. I've discovered that joy and hope are sticky—like peanut butter. When you spread them around, you're bound to get some on yourself.

~Marsha Jordan

67

Listening to My Heart

Wherever you go, go with all your heart.
~Confucius

The fall of my senior year of college I was an emotional wreck. When I looked ahead to my bright, shining future all I saw was a cubicle with my name on it. This was not the future I wanted, but to me it seemed as though the major forces in my life (mostly my family, friends and the college career center) were forcing me in that direction. Without ever stopping to ponder what I actually wanted to do with my life after graduation, I had begun applying for positions at Fortune 500 companies because that's what I "should be" doing. In the busy hustle of college life I had forgotten that I had a choice, and the inner turmoil that resulted was crushing me.

Luckily, I was given the opportunity to travel to a conference focused on finding "the life worth living." The conference centered on living with purpose and spiritual direction. I was placed in a group of fifteen total strangers, but that was where I found my direction.

During one session we were asked to read an article called the "Cup of Trembling," and then to individually reflect on what fears were holding us back from following our dreams. When it was my turn to share I heard things coming out of my mouth that I didn't even know I had been thinking. I shared my fear of the nine-to-five desk job and the lack of direction that I felt looking past graduation. I shared my fear of living in poverty, and the fear of leaving the nest and beginning my own life.

This group of random people listened to me pour out the contents of my soul and then they probed me for more information. They genuinely wanted to help me straighten myself out so that my future matched what my heart was saying. They asked me to put aside all of the barriers and excuses I made for myself, and to reflect on what I would most like to do.

I explained that I wanted to serve others, to go somewhere and be in a program like the Peace Corps, where I could dedicate my life to something that would make a difference in other people's lives. Speaking the words out loud made me realize that if this was my goal I had the power to make it my reality.

I felt renewed and ambitious. I returned home with a new perspective and a fresh energy. The sadness and anxiety was replaced with a sense of purpose. I researched the Peace Corps, and started discussing my decision, but I didn't tell my parents until I was reasonably sure that it was the direction I wanted to take. I was a little apprehensive about their reactions. I envisioned the conversation taking a variety of directions. I felt they would see my decision as irresponsible. I feared they would think that now was the time in my life to grow up and to start earning money to pay back my student loans or that I was somehow trying to back away from my responsibilities as a young adult. How on earth could I go so far away and expect that they would take care of things for me while I was gone? I was worried they would take my decision personally. I remembered back to high school when it was time to choose a college. My mother felt that four hours was too far away. How would she feel about her only child moving across the world?

I told my father first. I was nervous and afraid, but I knew that my father would embrace my ambitions more easily than my mother. After I told him, I felt the immediate flood of release: it was as though telling him made it real and now it had been decided that this is what would happen just by speaking the words. He responded by helping me find out more and explore my options. Overall, he seemed supportive and a little excited.

My mom was less enthused by my new ambition. She made it clear that although this wasn't the direction she had hoped I would take, she didn't think it was a bad decision and she still loves me. That was enough for me, so I endured the lengthy application process. I wasn't sure how it would all turn out; I prayed about it and asked God to place me where I would be most useful. During my interview I didn't express any preferences for location, but I did mention that I would like to learn French or Spanish. My recruiter's eyes lit up as she explained that she would like to find me a business assignment in French-speaking West Africa.

And here I am one week away from leaving the familiar comfort of everything I have known for the past twenty-one years. One week away from turning my life upside down. One week away from moving to Africa to serve as a Peace Corps volunteer for two years in Mali, a country I had previously never even heard of.

Sometimes life takes you places you never expected to go. The call to follow one's own heart is not always a voice of reason. This is what I must remind myself every time I ask the real questions weighing on my mind: What on earth am I thinking? How am I ever going to survive? Am I tough enough to face the challenges ahead? Will I actually do any good? Wow, am I prepared for this?

As my parents will surely attest, no, I am not prepared for this. I have lived a pampered life so far, and this will most certainly be one of the hardest times of my life. However, I feel deep in my soul that God would not call me to service if it weren't something we could get through together.

~Danielle M. Dryke

68

You Go Girl!

It's not that successful people are givers; it is that givers are successful people.
~Patti Thor

I believed that I was well on my way to fulfilling all I had been placed on this Earth to accomplish, or so I thought until 2003. I was a wife and mother as well as a woman who had used her professional training as a medical rehabilitation counselor in both remunerable and volunteer activities. I had chosen my field as a teen, influenced by my desire to work with patients and families who had suffered serious illness or injury. I was a happy woman, content with my personal and very private life path.

My life had been directed since I was a little girl. In 1953, at the age of six, my twin brother Frankie and I had contracted polio in an epidemic that had devastated our suburb of DeWitt, New York. Frankie had died sixty-one hours after admission to City Hospital; two of our friends had eventually succumbed to complications. I was temporarily paralyzed but had eventually made a complete recovery.

My parents had always told me, "Janice, God wanted you to live for a reason." I was comfortable with that philosophical and religious concept and thus chose a medical-allied field as a profession. You see, I knew what it was like to suffer the loss of a loved one. I knew what it was like to suffer physical pain. Learning to walk again was tough. Learning to accept Frankie's death was tougher still.

I like to call it my "wake-up call," the short note and magazine that changed everything for me. A college friend and grad school roommate sent me a note in March of 2003. The note was simple: "Jan, now you have to tell your story." The magazine she had sent was *The Rotarian*, the official magazine of Rotary International. I couldn't believe what I was reading. For years, I had read nothing of polio. Like most people in the Western world, I thought we were done with polio—how wrong I was!

That night, I sat down with my husband Dave (an orthopedic surgeon who had trained under one of my polio docs) and told him that I had to do something. We settled on a book project. What else could a private person like me do?

For the next four years, I was glued to my laptop as I researched and wrote about the disease that I had hated for so long. I had always believed that Dave was the lucky one, marrying a girl who could never be jealous of his profession and its demands because she knew what it was like to be on the patient end of things. But, now I was looking at our life from a different vantage point. Perhaps there really are no coincidences in life... I could have never written my book without the constant support of my husband and our son Kevin. More importantly, I needed Dave to make sense of the mound of medical information that I needed to include in the book.

There were other things that seemed beyond chance as well: Without my friend's note, I might have remained unaware of polio's continued presence or of the enormous contributions of the Global Polio Eradication Initiative. Moreover, I had family and friends who supported me in this project, adding insight into the various ways that polio had changed all of our lives. Their recollections reinforced the rehabilitation philosophy that I had embraced since my time at Seton Hill and the University of Pittsburgh: illness affects many beyond the nuclear family. Similarly, my new endeavor came at a critical time for the public health community and at an opportune time in my personal life. 2003 found me well adjusted to my "empty nest" status, but without a new passion to sink my teeth into.

My book was published in 2007 with a second edition released in 2008—I was on a roll! Many people told me that I should expect a call from a famous TV person. That sounded perfectly plausible:

I was confident that anyone who read my book would fall in love with Frankie, and thus appreciate the importance of preventing other children, just like Frankie, from contracting polio. Frankie would be famous and his story would be told around the world. I must admit I've always had a vivid imagination, a personality trait that helped to sustain me during fifteen-hour writing and editing blocks while providing a never-ending series of apologies for forgetting to make dinner. I had also found the perfect excuse to do some serious shopping. After all, I had to be ready for my "TV gigs."

Well, needless to say, I'm still waiting for that phone call, but something much better has happened. After speaking to an immunization coalition in the Erie-Niagara County region of New York State, I began to be asked to speak to other groups far beyond my home turf. I had no idea how powerful word-of-mouth recommendations could be. Today, my life is full with speaking engagements to a diverse group of individuals and organizations in both the United States and Canada.

As I reflect upon the last few years, I'm struck by the realization that our life's mission has many twists and turns. We have to be ever ready to listen to the cues, sometimes subtle, sometimes obvious, and to be willing to "connect the dots" so to speak. Happiness doesn't mean that we escape sadness and disappointment. It means that we take what life has given us and turn the ups and downs into something bigger than ourselves.

In 2011, I feel that I'm right where I'm supposed to be, speaking out about a disease that I know all too well. I look forward to the day that I'm no longer asked to speak in public because we will have successfully eradicated polio… I look forward to a new path along this life journey of mine. Where will it lead me? Happiness is all about staying vigilant to the possibilities!

In the meantime, I like to think that Frankie is cheering his birth partner on with a resounding, "You go girl!"

~Janice Flood Nichols

69

Reclaiming Myself

The value of identity of course is that so often with it comes purpose.
~Richard Grant

Before my two daughters were born, I was a very different person. I worked full-time, had a downtown office with a view, and regularly traveled to New York, Los Angeles, even Guam.

My life was full and exciting, and I didn't want it to change just because I became a mother. So after my first child came along, I continued to work. I trusted our caregiver, but soon began to realize how close my daughter was becoming with her. Instead of me.

I wanted to have a second child, and I wanted to have time to bond with them both while they were young. So I left my job to become a stay-at-home mom, raising my first daughter and having a second. Financially, it was a stretch, but with some lifestyle changes, my husband and I made it possible.

I envisioned a new life filled with walks to the park, creative activities with my kids, and gab sessions over coffee with fellow at-home moms. Instead, my days quickly began to blend together and my head became foggy from a lack of sleep. I found myself wearing the same baggy sweatpants and T-shirts every day, stopped wearing make-up, and only read books that rhymed. Then along came Take Our Daughters to Work Day. Where could I possibly take mine, I wondered—the laundry room?

Now, I don't mean to imply that a mother has to work for

validation—being a parent is the most rewarding and fulfilling job in the world. But that realization underscored a growing concern I had. By giving up so much of what I had previously enjoyed, what kind of example was I setting?

Even though I had graduated from college, and gone on to earn an MBA, my daughters didn't know that side of me. To them, I was the one who hosted play dates, baked cookies, and folded endless piles of laundry. Sure, in the life of a preschooler, these are important duties, and I was good at them. But as my girls matured, would cooking, cleaning and carpooling be all I represented to them? Should it be?

After three years of being a full-time at-home mom, I decided the time had come to find the path back to myself.

First, I needed to clear the "brain fog," so I signed up for a night class in writing for children. Because my husband often didn't get home until after dinner, I hired a babysitter to watch the girls for the two hours I was in class. Leaving the house once a week with a notebook and sharpened pencils was invigorating, a feeling I'd long forgotten.

A few months later, I joined a health club. While the girls were in preschool, I headed to the gym for my twice-weekly yoga class or a walk on the treadmill. It was just a couple of times a week, but it really made a difference.

Soon after, I joined a book club and dug out my library card. The club's members were mothers, just like me, but we discussed books, not our children. It felt great to talk about life, literature and writing. For that hour, I was more than "Mom."

These small changes resulted in some big benefits. I ditched the baggy sweatpants and dug out some of the nicer clothes I hadn't worn in a long time. To my surprise, they fit. I continued writing stories for children, joined a writers' group, and started sending out my manuscripts. A little over a year later, I had a contract from a major publisher for my first children's book!

I realized that although I enjoyed the responsibility (and the gift) of motherhood, I didn't need to give myself entirely over to the job in order to do it well. In fact, as they grew older, it became increasingly important for my daughters to see me as an individual, taking care of myself and pursuing my own interests. They would always be my first priority, but there was no need to neglect my own needs in the process.

My girls, now in their early teens, are bright, independent and caring young women. They know that I'm always there for them, but they've also come to see me as an individual, and I hope I've helped them see all the possibilities they have to look forward to in life. Spending more time with myself has allowed me to give more to my children.

~Ruth Spiro

My Detour to Destiny

Act as if what you do makes a difference. It does.
~William James

Growing up as a pastor's kid, my parents always said God had a great plan for my life. And I believed it. I always imagined myself living in a lavish four-story home with a white picket fence and a red BMW parked in the driveway. Sure, they were lofty dreams, but why not dream big? After all, I was on my way. I had a successful sales career, a wonderful husband, and a beautiful baby.

Yet inside, I felt unfulfilled. Like something was missing. What could possibly bring me the happiness and fulfillment I longed for?

Like all new parents, my husband and I looked forward to watching our little boy grow and develop. But Jayden's growth lagged behind. Each well-baby checkup reminded us of another milestone missed. Finally, at two and a half, we took Jayden for diagnostic testing. That's when we learned the truth.

"Your son has autism."

My mind began to race. Autism. I'd heard of the word, but what exactly was it? I turned to my husband and said, "Take me to a bookstore."

As I sat on our basement floor, piles of books and papers

scattered all around me, I began to read the painful truth. Book after book contained the same frightening phrases. "Children affected by autism may never speak... prepare yourself for institutions... life-long disabilities... financial devastation... eighty percent divorce rate." I began to weep.

My son would never go to a regular school. Never attend college. Never get married or have children. Forget about my picket fence, what about his? I grieved the death of my little boy's future.

After two heart-wrenching days of darkness and depression, I picked up another book, *Applied Behavior Analysis*. I flipped through the pages, and a small bit of hope began to rise up within me. "Lovaas' 1987 UCLA study showed a forty-seven percent recovery rate." Hope grew into excitement. That would be us.

But through that window of hope, I faced many closed doors. I made phone call after phone call, searching for anyone who could help Jayden. Every call ended with the same disappointing news.

"Sorry, we can't provide that therapy. It's too expensive."

At $1,000 per day for an in-home consultation, how could anyone afford it? Not only was applied behavior analysis (ABA) costly, it was time consuming. All of the books I read strongly recommended forty hours a week of therapy. The obstacles seemed impossible, but I didn't care. This was my child, and he needed help. I would not give up without a fight.

I became obsessed with learning everything I could about ABA. I studied manuals, read textbooks, searched the Internet. I soon realized that if Jayden was going to receive this therapy, I would have to be the one to provide it.

I seized every opportunity. A local autism expert did some training for an area school district. I convinced her to allow me to come into her home and observe. Then I learned of Dr. Vincent Carbone, a well-respected autism specialist from New York. When Dr. Carbone conducted an ABA workshop, I drove to Chicago. I prayed that this man could teach me how to teach my son. And he did.

We turned our basement into a therapy room, and I spent all my days working with Jayden. I taught him new skills by breaking them down into the smallest of tasks. Sometimes I presented a task hundreds of times before Jayden would master it. Once Jayden accomplished a small skill, we celebrated, and promptly moved on to more complicated ones.

I joined a local support group and met other families affected by autism. As they searched for hope, I shared my experiences. They became interested.

"Can I come to your home and see what you're doing?"

"Can you assess my child with the assessment you used for Jayden?"

Well, sure. Why not? I certainly didn't feel qualified, but there was nothing else offered in the area. If they were willing, I was willing.

Before long, a few children from the support group joined our humble classroom in the basement. I trained a couple of college students to help, and together we celebrated as the children made small steps of progress.

But while the children learned, I learned an important lesson as well.

I learned that I loved teaching children with autism. I loved getting down on the floor and playing with them. I loved connecting with a little boy who flapped his arms or rocked back and forth. I felt excited when I made him smile or taught him to speak. Every little milestone was huge, and I felt the same joy when another child conquered a skill as I did with my own son.

I began to see a completely different destiny for myself. It was a future filled with helping children and families affected by autism. I wanted to save parents the agony I went through to find services for my child. Then God opened a door.

Our church decided to convert an old high school building into a community center. I knew just who to call: the church pastor. "Hi Dad, it's me." I smiled. "How about letting me open an autism center?"

Today the Quad Cities Autism Center is going strong, and provides children and families hope for a brighter future.

God did not allow me to fall through the cracks by giving me a child with autism. Somehow, that was part of the journey I was meant to be on. He didn't take me out of the situation, but He certainly has carried me through it.

It's amazing how life has evolved since those couple of nights when I sat on the floor weeping in despair. I feel more fulfilled today than I ever did on my journey for financial success. I don't live in a four-story home, or drive a BMW, but I have something even better. I have an indescribable joy and an excitement for the future. White picket fences and luxury cars are great, but I'd rather fulfill my destiny any day.

~Michelle L. Smyth

Find Your Happiness

Chapter 8

Simple Pleasures

Pleasure is spread through the earth
In stray gifts to be claimed by whoever shall find.

~William Wordsworth

The Small Things

Why not learn to enjoy the little things — there are so many of them.
~Author Unknown

I dated Dan for two and a half years, through the end of high school and my first year into college. Like any other naïve teenager in love, I hadn't anticipated that someday we'd break up, so when this happened just before my sophomore year of college I was devastated. I clung to my feelings for him, and tried masochistically to maintain a friendship with him through the semester that followed. It hurt worse than I could have imagined seeing him go out with other girls and pretending to be happy for him. As I sank further and further into a solitary depression, my friends could see that I was turning into an entirely different person. Weeks turned into months, summer turned into fall, and as the air chilled and the last leaves fell I began to seriously consider transferring to another city where I couldn't torture myself anymore.

On one of my particularly down afternoons — one of those gray days in early winter where even nature itself seems to be in low spirits — I met up with my good friend Jon for lunch. We sat in the dimly lit second-floor common room, eating sandwiches from the nearby Wisemiller's deli (a student favorite, affectionately nicknamed Wisey's). I unloaded my troubles on him, and, like the patient and caring person he is, he listened sympathetically and gave me a shoulder to cry on. He also gave me what I later realized is some of the best advice I've ever gotten:

"Do something each day that makes you smile, no matter how tiny or how dumb that thing is."

"I'm going to need an example," I said.

"When I feel down, I call and place a pickup order at Wisey's. When they ask me what name the order is under, I say 'Pants.'"

"…Pants?"

"Yep. There's usually a pause on the other end of the line, and then they ask me to repeat. By the time I pick up the order and announce myself as 'Pants,' I can't stop smiling."

I'm fully aware of how odd and insignificant this may sound, but it worked where nothing else had. The next day around lunchtime I called and placed the order. I hadn't even said the word "Pants" before I felt a huge and genuine grin spread across my face for the first time in months. I'm still not even sure why this works so well, but it was definitely worth it to take the time out of my day to do something silly, solely for the purpose of making myself smile.

This quickly became my go-to tactic when I needed a quick grin. I changed it up a bit, sometimes ordering as Harry Potter or other fictional characters, and slowly started to get over Dan and climb out of the slump I had fallen into. I began to find other small pick-me-ups to add into my daily life: letting myself eat Spaghetti-O's out of the can for dinner, watching the sun set over the city from the benches on the rooftop of my dorm building, keeping a baggie of peanuts in my coat pocket for feeding the squirrels…

The best advice I can give to anyone who needs that extra boost on an off day is simply to find your own version of "Pants." Do something tiny, something silly, something relaxing, something pointless… most importantly, do something every day that makes you smile.

~Michelle Vanderwist

The No-Share Zone

Don't wreck a sublime chocolate experience by feeling guilty.
~Lora Brody

I am a disciplined person, especially when it comes to food. I watch what I eat. I regularly consume admirable quantities of fruits and vegetables. I strictly monitor my intake of sweets, resisting that deep craving to sink into the blissful blur of sugary extremes. I do not keep cookies, candy or cakes in the house. I rarely allow myself to order dessert in a restaurant. If I must have chocolate, I make sure I have to walk to the store (preferably through rain or snow) to get my candy fix.

But my discipline disappears when it comes to the Personal Box of Chocolates.

When such a gift comes into my life, I abandon all pretense of sensible eating and sink into that rare environment that many adults silently yearn for—the No-Share Zone.

This is what happened when a dear friend handed me a wrapped birthday present.

"Don't leave this sitting out in the heat," she said and I knew it contained chocolate. That night, I tore into the wrappings, then reverently removed the plastic that protected a small Whitman's Sampler.

I eased off the lid and smiled when I saw eight pieces of cozily cradled candies.

That small box of chocolate transported me to that mystical Zone, where politeness yielded to the primal and I embraced a supremely selfish, divinely decadent indulgence of the highest order. I was home alone. I was going to eat what I wanted, how I wanted, and I was not going to consider any other human being in the process.

Lavishly, I bit into two chocolates, the caramel and the coconut. I loved the insolence of only partially eating each one.

Then I reviewed the remaining chocolates, thinking about the order I might sample them in. I had no thoughts of calories or restraint—I had only the pure joy of possession.

Normally, of course, I loved to share. Had someone been around, I might have pleasantly offered her a chocolate. Had my friend given me a larger box, I would have saved it for a party or meeting. But she wisely fulfilled the secret wish of the chocolate-obsessed: permission to graze, glory, gorge and revel in sweet sensation.

When I was growing up, the Whitman box came into our household once a year, a symbol of romance from my father to my mother. My mother, normally a very sharing person, kept tight rein on the Sampler. Her face looked almost pained as she offered my brother and me one chocolate each. I remember studying the map of those chocolates more carefully that I ever studied any atlas. Nuts, chews, creams, caramels—making the right choice was crucial. After that one luscious candy, the box would disappear, hidden somewhere in my mother's bedroom.

At the time I thought my mother was selfish and unfair. But now, I understood and applauded her. Like so many moms, I realized how much she had to share, all day, every day. I imagined how utterly luxurious she must have felt, surveying her box of chocolates, sampling, tasting, and savoring, without worry that anyone would interfere.

Like my mother before me, my candy box allowed me to simply care for myself. The bliss of the No-Share Zone, that lovely luxury of not worrying about even one other person, renewed and delighted me.

My small Sampler was an invitation to be frivolous and beautifully indulgent. I took a bite of a nut bar and let the flavors flow through my mouth. For this moment, I was feeding only myself and that made the chocolate even sweeter.

~Deborah Shouse

Treasure Hunting

What a bargain grandchildren are! I give them my loose change, and they give me a million dollars' worth of pleasure.
~Gene Perret

When I was a little girl, I used to walk with my grandmother up a quiet, poorly paved road that intersected the street on which she and my grandfather lived. We would stroll, hand in hand, moving at the equal pace of small child and elderly woman. The sun would be shining; the birds would be singing. I remember hearing the familiar call of "Bob White! Bob White!" Sometimes, butterflies would flutter in the grasses along the roadside, and the occasional car would rumble carefully past us. Grandma and I would chat about this and that, or we'd just walk in silence, enjoying the outdoors and each other's company. Yet, for me, these times were not just a chance to get some exercise and be with my grandmother, though both were important. These walks were treasure hunts.

More often than not, mixed with the gravel and dust at the road's edge, would be money. Not lots of it—a penny here, a nickel there. Sometimes, on really lucky days, I'd find a dime or even a quarter, but mostly pennies. Shining in the dirt, little copper and silver circles that I'd leap on, proudly show Grandma, and joyfully stuff into my pockets.

Some days, I wouldn't find anything. "Maybe next time," my grandmother would say. Other days, I'd come back from our walk with more than twenty-five cents to put in my piggy bank, or to buy penny candy—a genuine treat for a six-year-old. Looking back now, it wasn't even the money that was such a big deal; it was the joy of discovery. It was the anticipation and the hope, the delight of finding something small left and forgotten along the side of the road that I could keep for myself. It made me feel so lucky, and so special. That simple act of finding spare change brought me happiness, and it's a memory that has always been precious to me.

Yet, it wasn't until years later, when I was in my late twenties, that that simple memory came to mean so much more to me than simply a child's happiness. It was my mother who told me the secret, who revealed a truth I had never suspected but one that brought a whole new depth to my experience.

"Remember when you used to walk with Grandma up Cummings Road?" she started the conversation. All those years, she confessed, my grandfather used to drive up and down the walking route, dropping change for me to find.

I was amazed. He never told me himself, and it seems like he had never planned to. I remembered how he'd smile when I'd return from a walk and dig my find out of my pocket to show him, but I'd always thought he was just happy for my luck. I'd never imagined that he was the one responsible for it.

My grandfather was a gruff man, a World War II veteran who loved deeply, but usually guarded his emotions, especially his affection. He wasn't a man who hugged me often as a child, but I had never doubted his love for me. He pushed me on the swings, held me up to cross the monkey bars, bought me root beer Popsicles, and shared a million other joyful moments. Now, I knew, he had given me joy in ways I hadn't even connected to him.

Now, every once in a while, when I take a walk down the street, or even across a parking lot, I drop a penny or two, or maybe even a nickel or a dime, and watch it plink onto the pavement. I imagine some small child finding it, delighted at the discovery. They'll never know someone put it there on purpose for them to find. But that's part of the joy. Thanks, Grandpa.

~Laurie Leal

The Returning Light

If we shall take the good we find, asking no questions,
we shall have heaping measures.
~Ralph Waldo Emerson

Every year, as soon as Halloween is over, our son Matthew waits for the lights. He's been doing it for more than a dozen years. As the days grow shorter and the nights longer, as the temperatures drop and the leaves fall, he waits for the lights. He knows that they will come.

The neighbors across the street always put up a beautiful and brilliant (and tasteful) light display for the holidays and Matthew loves to wait for them to be turned on, which usually happens right after Thanksgiving. But he begins his vigil a month before their arrival. And then, each day between Thanksgiving and until the lights are turned off after the new year, he waits, excitedly, from mid-afternoon on. Each day he'll stand by the front windows or walk back and forth between the windows and the front door, in energetic and coiled anticipation, laser-focused, undeterred, intent on the moment of their nightly illumination.

And when each evening's moment comes, you don't have to be right with him when that moment occurs. You know it no matter where you are in the house. The effervescent squealing. The rhythmic clapping. The dancing around the house, the steps staccato, loud, repeated. It's pure joy. Pure delight on his face! And it happens every single night.

He waits for the lights. During the darkest days of the year. He stands and he waits. Transfixed by those lights brightening the dim, winter sky.

For all his limitations, in the world's view—his severe mental disabilities, his autism, his two-year-old mind in a twenty-three-year-old body, his inability to speak—Matthew knows something very profound, that light will shine in the darkness, that no matter how dark, how long the wait, eventually, and without fail, those lights will shine again. No matter how many seasons of the year without them, there will come a season when those lights will shine again. They always do.

Life brings its own seasons of darkness. Desperate, at times. Lonely. Painful. Full of fear. But despite those seasons, a new season can come and the light can be seen again. Whatever darkness I find within and around me, I look to my son, and remember that a light can pierce that darkness and can begin to bring beauty and joy again.

In that I find my hope and my happiness.

~Michael D. Gingerich

Everyday Miracles

Why, who makes much of a miracle?
As to me I know of nothing else but miracles.
~Walt Whitman

Six a.m. Already I'm going over my daily to-do list in my mind. The garage door rumbles open, then closes again, telling me my husband has left for work.

I knock on my youngest son's bedroom door. An adolescent groan emerges from the shape under the covers.

Downstairs, I open the back door, flip on the patio light and let the dog out. He hesitates for a moment, then clambers on his short legs down the snow-coated steps. I watch him scramble over the snowdrifts into the dark backyard to do what needs to be done. I know just how you feel, old buddy, I think.

Next I unload last night's dishes from the dishwasher. But wait—no sounds from upstairs. "I don't hear the shower yet!" I shout, tired of my own voice, tired of the words I've repeated just about every morning since before this child was born.

Same old same old.

Sometimes it feels as if I've been waking kids up for school for a lifetime. Actually about twenty-two years. And because my three sons are widely spaced in age, I still have three and a half more years until my youngest graduates from high school.

Thunk.

Good. He's up. Next I have to throw some salt on the driveway, warm up the car and scrape the ice off the windshield. And the dog is barking to come in. But first, I check the yellow sticky notes I've posted all over the kitchen to remind my middle-aged brain of all the humdrum errands I'm supposed to do this humdrum day: "Get gas," "Go to ATM," "DON'T FORGET: Bananas, eggs, bread, something for dinner?"

My son and I run through our usual morning drama, me playing the part of the cuckoo clock ("It's 6:25! We've got five minutes!") and my son moving as if in slow motion ("I'm coming!"). Somehow by 6:32, we're in the minivan. I back the car down the driveway, headlights glaring into the gray mist, to meet the carpool.

But this morning, something is different.

It happens three-quarters of the way to the house where the carpool meets. The fog hovers over the piles of snow left by the snowplows. Suddenly I don't recognize the street signs. Was that shopping center always there?

I'm lost.

"Wake up, Mom! You missed the turn!"

"I did?"

"I can't believe it! You're going to make me late!"

"Wait a minute," I look around, panicky, trying to get my bearings. Everything looks wrong. I'm really lost.

Leaning over, my son points the way. "Turn here, Mom. And now there. See? Here we are."

I pull up to the house, relieved to be on time (well, almost).

"Sorry, buddy," I say to my son.

"You gotta pay attention, Mom!" he scolds, as if he's the grown-up.

I drive home in the haze, pull the car into the driveway—and stop. Inside the house, there's a computer and a wall full of sticky notes waiting for me, but I sit still, staring at the crust of dirty snow that has petrified on the flowerbeds. After all these years my brain has turned to mush.

But this is something else. My son is right—I was half asleep.

Like a robot, I'd been going through the motions I've gone through every day for years, and didn't even notice where I was.

This is exactly what I promised myself I'd never do, on that spring day twenty-six years before. I was eight months pregnant with my first child. I knelt in the soil of my garden, planting pansies, my cheeks flushed with sweat, fresh air, and the possibilities of life. A friend passed by and, seeing me hauling my pregnant self into a standing position, she called out, "Hey! I bet you'll be happy when the pregnancy is over."

"Oh no," I blurted out, "I'm happy right now!" Even as I said it, I realized it was true. I didn't want to hurry time. I wanted to hold onto it and savor it like the first bite of dessert.

As the seasons flowed, I heard these words in many voices, "I'll be happy when the baby sleeps through the night!" "I'll be happy when we move into the new house." "I wish the winter was over!" "I can't wait until the kids go back to school!"

"Don't wish it away," I whispered to myself, over and over. I taught my kids this lesson along with their bedtime stories. Happiness isn't something out there, beyond the next obstacle, like "happily ever after" in a storybook. Happiness is right here, right now.

And yet, this morning in the carpool, I forgot. I wasn't paying attention. I'd done the same things every day, until they became rote, invisible, just items on a to-do list to check off in my mind.

Shaking my head, I resist the memory of me in all my ditziness, circling the neighborhood, lost, five minutes from home on our way to a place where we go every morning. My son's voice echoes in my mind, "You're going to make me late!"

I'm going to make him late? Suddenly the whole situation strikes me as so funny that I laugh out loud. What a ridiculous little comedy of errors we've just performed! I sit in my car, laughing to myself.

As I laugh, I glance to one side. The sun is rising. Its warm rays burn away the fog, smearing the sky with purple light. I sit where I am and watch the dawn unfold—an everyday miracle I could easily have missed.

What else did I almost miss today? So many things I take for granted: our health, our home, the seasons, the dependable sound of my husband leaving for work, the comedy of our little dog climbing the snowdrifts, the thunk of our son's feet landing next to his bed, his sulky teenage presence in the passenger seat of my car. Each of these things has happened many mornings before—but they won't go on forever. Even tomorrow they won't be quite the same. Suddenly I ache with love and longing for the blessed details of the life I already lead.

In the flowerbed in front of me, a tiny green crocus reaches up to pierce the crust of snow, as if to sniff for the slightest hint of spring. I make an imaginary sticky note and stick it on my brain: "DON'T FORGET: Happiness is here and now." And with that simple change, I embrace the everyday miracles unfolding all around me. All I have to do is stop and take notice.

~Faith Paulsen

A Remodeled View

Anywhere is paradise; it's up to you.
~Author Unknown

I was totally frustrated with the house I lived in. The structure was a "real fixer-upper" and was rumored to have been built as a high school Industrial Arts project. Plumbers, electricians and carpenters often remark at some aspect of the building: "Hmmm... never seen something like this." Worn and rustic looking when I first purchased it, the fifteen years since had weathered it even more. Comparing my rundown dwelling with a remodeled or nicely decorated home, I would whine, "if only I had a new house like this" or "if only I had money to remodel." It seemed impossible that I would ever have the funds or ability to live in a modern or refurbished house.

Then this winter, my friend George, having some time off between his house-painting jobs, volunteered to do some work on my house. He found leftover cans of paint in my basement and other random materials around. Every day when I came home from work I would discover holes patched and walls repainted. A broken light fixture would be fixed or a new one added, gaping spaces would be filled with planks and wooden panels stained or shellacked.

Catching his enthusiasm, I found myself cleaning out the closet in my bedroom and carrying bags of clothing and items I didn't use anymore to be given to the Salvation Army. I started seeing areas in various rooms that needed de-cluttering, and when I tackled them nicely decorated spaces appeared. We improved many of the rooms, but the one that was the most transformed was the downstairs bathroom.

That room, just big enough for a tub, sink, and toilet and small freestanding cabinet, was unsightly. The paint on the wooden floor was worn, and the walls, a non-descript pale color, were covered with scratches and scrapes. An ugly broken light fixture that was not hooked up to any working electricity hung down from the ceiling looking like something from a haunted house movie.

George asked me why we never used the downstairs tub and shower. Did the tub have a crack or did the water not work? I didn't remember. I didn't know why my family only took showers and baths in the upstairs bathroom. But somehow I had gotten in the habit of storing recyclables and bags in the downstairs tub when I didn't know where else to put them. It was a clutter nightmare.

Envisioning a new look for the room, George sanded and repainted the floor a cheerful red and patched the walls, coating them a gentle yellow. He removed the broken light fixture and re-plastered the ceiling, creating designer effects with a sponge. Inspired by these improvements, I rolled up my sleeves and removed all the bags, boxes, and recyclables (and other mystery items) from the bathtub and scrubbed it clean. I turned on the tap, and clear clean water ran from the faucet, hot and cold! I replaced the showerhead and added a new bathmat, shower curtain and bath rug. A black-framed set of nature photographs, and a black-framed mirror graced the walls.

I decided to finally try the shower in my "new" but "original" bathroom. After I stepped into the tub and turned on the water, I looked around at the refreshingly unfamiliar setting and it felt like I was away on a trip to a delightful resort or spa. When my shower ended, I pulled the curtain back and stepped into the cheerful bathroom feeling appreciation and delight.

My charming home had been here all along... it just needed the help of a benevolent friend, a little elbow grease and a fresh coat of paint. I only had to see it. And now I wonder: what other areas of my life could use a renewed look, what dormant blessings could be revived by a new perspective?

~Donna Paulson

A Perfect Ten

If we all did the things we are capable of doing,
we would literally astound ourselves.
~Thomas Alva Edison

At 303 pounds, my size 32 frame was beyond fun-size... I was fat. Three kids into an eleven-year marriage to a happily obese man, I still identified more with the fairytale princesses than the old queens. My husband loved me, I loved him, and we loved to eat. And we did. Ice cream sundaes, endless enchiladas, bottomless pasta bowls, cheesecakes; we were not choosy. Food was our passion.

And it was intimate. We truly enjoyed food... the chopping and preparation, the cooking of it, the succulent aromas that lingered in our home, the taste of it, the sharing of it with friends and family; food was a central part of who we were. Bread from scratch to share with new neighbors, homemade chocolate chip cookies to wish a friend a speedy recovery, fudge for Brent's co-workers at Christmas and the occasional cupcake "just because." Food was our bond. It was like a drug that the Feds just hadn't caught onto yet. People needed food, and we were the go-to neighborhood pusher.

Our lifestyle was interrupted annually with the preparation for my husband's summer trips. Around March he would enter a whirlwind of getting into good enough shape to lead kids on hikes and adventures. He did not have to look good in a swimsuit, but he had to be able to trek a five-mile trail with a group of eager teens without dying along the way.

A couple of years ago this health "kick" turned out to be more than a temporary occupation for us. We set a treadmill in front of the TV, and rather than enjoying a hot fudge sundae with Redi-Whip and caramel sauce at night, we took turns walking, then jogging, and eventually running while our favorite shows entertained us. Several months in, we invested in an elliptical so we could exercise together and hold each other accountable.

And we started rewarding our successes with a new dress here and new pants there. Before I knew it, the weight was melting off and two years later, I am 140 pounds lighter.

As people started noticing the changes, they were in awe that we did this without diet pills, a diet plan, a gym membership, or surgery. We did it with good old-fashioned calorie counting and exercise. And we did it with three kids six years old and younger hanging off our arms and doing jumping jacks beside us. We taught the importance of fitness and healthy food choices along the way and having a seven-year-old daughter that can now do more push-ups than me thrills me.

After posting my latest success on Facebook one day, a friend and I had the following text conversation:

Her: Hey skinny minnie I've got a pair of Lee jeans, size 9/10 medium length. Wanna try them on for keeps?

Me: Ha! Can't fit yet but I'll get there!! Thanks!!

Her: I bet you could they're stretch fit. Lemme know!

Me: I would love to take them if you don't want them. If I can't wear them now... I'll get there. Funny... I don't see myself as a size 10 at all.

Her: They're yours. And they will fit. If not now, then soon!! I'll drop them by.

Five minutes later, a knock announced her arrival and my two underwear-clad superheroes-in-training stopped wrestling long enough to follow me to the door. As soon as she left, I slipped them on, buttoned them, zipped them, and ran out to the curb doing a victory dance that would make even the Dallas Cowboys cheerleaders proud.

I was a size 10!

I was always the girl with a cute freckly face and a good personality... now I was a size 10 full of self-confidence and joy. For the first time in my life, my outside matched my inside.

But the joy was not in the scale or in the jeans; the true joy, the true happiness was about accomplishing such a huge task on my own terms. It did not take a death sentence from the doctor, forking over thousands for a surgery, or selling my firstborn to a gym... I did this. Just me. This was my victory, and no one could steal it.

And I did it without giving up my passion for food. Now instead of sharing homemade bread, I make hummus. Instead of fresh chocolate chip cookies, my kids get smoothies to die for. Company gets homemade fajitas and pico de gallo that dances the salsa on the tongue. I gift flavor, not fat.

When a person cuts their weight by the measure of another adult human in just eighteen months, you feel invincible, empowered, and truly in charge of your life. I love sharing that strength and sense of accomplishment with others who are struggling beneath the bondage of food.

Happiness isn't in the numbers; it is in finding the will to set a goal and achieve it. No matter how small or big that goal may be.

~Jamie Anne Richardson

78

Pockets of Happiness

Ice cream is happiness condensed.
~Jessi Lane Adams

As parents we spend a good part of our time making preparations for our children. From lunches and sleepovers, to soccer games and Halloween costumes. Then SATs and junior proms, to road tests and senior proms.

My most recent preparation was for my older daughter's freshman year of college. As I found myself cramming a semester's worth of necessities into plastic bins and cardboard boxes, I thought about the emotional disconnect I was beginning to feel as I arranged to ship my firstborn off.

Here I was, preparing her to leave the security of home, but how was I preparing to see her go? The answer, as it turned out, was not found in a dusty old parental handbook, it was one I would have to discover on my own.

During the three-and-one-half-hour drive west on Route 80 toward Lewisburg, Pennsylvania, my mind stayed busy taking inventory of my emotions. The repetitive interstate mile markers and merging traffic rekindled a very familiar feel, and might just as well have been a summer drive to Disney. But now the green and yellow Playskool talking piano was replaced by the tapping keys of a laptop, and the sing-along Mickey radio is an iPod crammed with a wide selection of songs: music to her, audio graffiti to me. I would occasionally glance at my daughter as she bobbed her head to the music being delivered through thin white wires. There was a time not so long ago, I thought, when she was happy just listening to me.

Slightly more than halfway through our journey, somewhere between the Delaware Water Gap tollbooths that separate New Jersey and Pennsylvania, I pulled into a Luvs gas station, to do what all weary travelers do. Fill up and rest.

There I was, leaning against a packed car, squeezing the gas pump handle, watching the dollars fly by, and thinking about college tuition. I walked into the convenience store and purchased a bottle of water. I unscrewed the cap and began to sip as I walked out the double glass doors.

Lost in thought, I vaguely felt the figure of a young man brush past me. Normally he would have gone completely unnoticed had it not been for the package he had cradled in his right arm. There draped over his shoulder, was a little girl perhaps five or six, in a white summer dress with red trim, softly sobbing and whimpering just enough for sensitive ears to hear. The kind of cry a little one utters when she's overtired, or when she's fallen on her hands, and receives the slightest of scrapes and pebble marks from an unforgiving sidewalk.

I watched them through the glass doors, never really seeing the young father's face. He sat his little girl on the counter while she attempted to catch her breath through quivering lips. And then with what almost appeared to be a sleight of hand, he quickly produced an ice cream pop and like a skilled magician with a pass of a wand, suddenly, tears were dried, a frown was a smile, and curls were bouncing with joy.

The young father then placed his hands under his daughter's arms and lifted her up off the counter and onto the floor. She clutched her father with one hand and with the other, gripped the ice cream as her tiny bites splintered the hard chocolate coating. I watched her small sneakers with Velcro straps skip happily back through the doors.

It was during that interlude that I realized what had been relentlessly gnawing at me. I was simply losing control. Not the control of curfews, or decisions, or the company she kept, but mostly, her happiness.

I thought back to when she was young and under my protective wings, her happiness my responsibility. A few extra hours granted at the beach, with a pail and shovel. A piggyback ride, a trip to the schoolyard playground, a Beanie Baby unexpectedly dropped in her hand, or ice cream to make everything all better.

Now she was going to have to find it on her own. And to find it, she was going to have to sift through the human wreckage of heartaches, letdowns and disappointments; the very thing I tried to shield her from when she was young. There will be break-ups with boyfriends along the way, and promising doors of opportunity will be slammed in her face.

My magic wand was gone.

While driving the final remaining miles, I decided that when it was time to say goodbye, I would perform one last fatherly task. I had planned to remind her of the crime of wasted potential. About overcoming her fears, and safeguarding against predatory frat boys. About how proud a blue-collar father with nothing more than an equivalency diploma tacked up on the wall is seeing his older daughter entering a university like Bucknell. About how happiness comes in pockets, and how she should keep hers full.

I had my little speech all meticulously rehearsed and fine tuned, and attempted to deliver it to her during a final farewell embrace in front of the dorm.

But as I gave her a hug and began to whisper those tidbits of parental wisdom in her ear, the only words I was able to squeeze past the lump in my throat was a sad, little "I love you." And for that, I received a pat on my back and her assurance that everything would be fine.

"It's college Dad, not rehab," she said, sounding confident and suddenly full of knowledge. And at that moment, like the many that life grants us, I knew it was time to go. I left her in a group of other nervously excited freshmen, and prepared myself for a very quiet and very long ride home.

A few weeks later, during one of the summer's last remaining nights, while I began to adjust to a slightly quieter house, I opened the front door to put out the recyclables.

"Hey Dad," my remaining daughter said, catching me halfway out the door. "How about some Carvel?"

"Not tonight, honey, I'm beat," I wearily replied, releasing the screen door. "I'm putting out the trash, locking the cars and then I just want to relax."

But before the screen door could make its final stutter step closed, I turned back and yelled past the living room, "What flavor?"

And there it was, etched on her face, that unmistakable look called happiness.

~Patrick Sepe

79

Authentic Happiness

*Those who can laugh without cause have either found the true meaning of
happiness or have gone stark raving mad.*

~Norm Papernick

I came home eager to share what I'd learned at my class on authentic happiness. My ninety-year-old father sat at the table waiting for his beer. My husband sat at the other end folding over his newspaper to examine the Sudoku.

"Dad," I said. "Guess the one thing in life that makes people the most happy?"

He pursed his lips. He glanced longingly at the beer I carried to him and then pushing himself slightly away from the table, he said, "A bowel movement?"

I rolled my eyes.

My husband peered up from his calculations, suppressed a chuckle, and stared at his father-in-law. "At your age, that's about right," he concurred.

Dad laughed.

"Seriously, Dad, what do happy people feel that unhappy folks don't?" I persisted.

I saw his mind clicking away. "No more bathroom humor," I cautioned. A few minutes later, after I'd forgotten about our conversation and was busy with cleaning the table, Dad spoke.

"Empathy!" he announced.

"That's a good guess," I replied.

"Consideration for others," offered my hubby.

"You're on the right track," I prodded.

"I give up," said Dad, and he took a swig of Warsteiner.

I carried the knockwursts to the table.

"I like bauernwurst better," said Dad. "You got these at the grocery store, didn't you?"

"In the deli section," I replied.

"You need to go to a German butcher," Dad said.

"There aren't any around here. Remember, you now live with us in Carolina."

"No exotic food, huh?"

"That's right. Now be grateful for the knockwurst," I advised.

We all bit in and the juicy sausages tasted good. "I'm thankful I found these," I said.

They munched away. "I appreciate good food, don't you?" I queried.

"I do," said Dad.

"Okay, now, if you've been listening to me, I've given you clues. What is the number one thing that makes people kinder to each other and makes them do more 'good' in the world than unhappy folks do?" The two bookends, my dad and husband, stared at each other like stone gargoyles on Notre Dame. Dad shrugged.

"Gratitude!" I announced. "Happy folks recite their blessings and know how they occurred and savor the moments in life; they are mindful of the present. They thank people for favors and they thank their God for being blessed with life."

"I still like your father's answer," replied my spouse.

I thought about all the things and people and institutions I am grateful for. I studied my husband, now in conference with my aged dad as they huddled over the crossword puzzle, and my husband said to the old guy and patted him on the back: "Good job! How in the world did you know that word, 'olio'?"

"I'm a warehouse of worthless knowledge," my stooped old dad answered.

And, I smile. I feel grateful for these men, the moment, and the merriment of mirth.

~Erika Hoffman

80

Sometimes Bliss Is a Place

You can fall in love at first sight with a place as with a person.
~Alec Waugh

I've always been something of a wanderer. I've lived in a lot of different places, most of them interesting... but none of them permanent. Of course, unlike other sensible wanderers, I've also accumulated artifacts of my interesting homes, mostly in the form of books.

Books, as even the most casual observer would agree, make moving around a little more of a daunting proposition. Well, that's true, at least for normal, sane people. Not for me, however, which says something about my sanity: I accumulate books the way other people accumulate postcards, and I've always been undaunted by my library. The inevitable result is that I know more about packing and carrying cartons of books than do most moving professionals. Put them in storage? Surely you're not serious! My books are my friends, creased and underlined and marked up, read and re-read and quoted and shared. Where I go, they go.

So I spent years moving about and happily experiencing various lives and loves and accumulating wisdom, experience... and more books. And while every place I lived touched me in some way, I always left when it felt like it was time to leave.

Minor digression: the English author Phil Rickman, one of my favorite people in the world, writes amazing suspense novels that are guaranteed to keep you up late at night—I highly recommend them—but one of the things that's the most noticeable in his books is their venues. The landscape, the place, is as much a character in his stories as are any of the people.

I love reading about the places he describes, about those remote places he makes accessible to me, and I've always felt instantly connected to the places he writes about; but at the end of the day I couldn't particularly relate to them. And so I packed my Phil Rickman books with the rest of my library and moved again. And again.

And then I went to spend a winter in Provincetown, Massachusetts.

Provincetown is truly land's end—it's at the tip of Cape Cod, and it feels like the tip of the world. It's the first place that the Pilgrims landed, well before Plymouth, and the last place one reaches before the Atlantic Ocean... beyond it, there's nothing but waves and whales before Portugal. It's not a place that people come by accident; no one "happened" to stop there as they were passing through, because it's not a place that's on the way anywhere else.

People, I learned, go to Provincetown deliberately: to heal, to find love, to find peace, to find themselves. People go there to live and they go there to die. But no one is there accidentally.

Provincetown is at the edge of land, the edge of the sea, the edge of the world. And there I went, thinking that I was going to a quiet place to spend the winter, an isolated wild place to write. Nothing more than that.

Almost magically, my first morning there, I innocently tuned my stereo to the local community radio station and heard Dave Carter's song "Gentle Arms of Eden" and after that I went down to walk out on the pier and by the harbor and... well, the reality is that something happened.

Perhaps I merged the lyrics of the song I'd just heard—words that talked about this being my home, my only home, sacred ground that I'd be walking on—and perhaps I integrated Phil Rickman's sense of place, which so permeated my consciousness, but suddenly I was enveloped by an incredible warmth, an amazing sense of being exactly where I should be. And—this was new for me—not just "where I should be right now," but, rather, "where I should be. Period."

As the days passed, the feeling intensified, and with it a sense of wellbeing that I had never experienced before. This was where I belonged, where I fit in, just like a missing piece to a puzzle.

I got involved in the community, met people, made friends. I walked the beach in the vilest weather, my coat wrapped tightly around me, the sand stinging my face, and I never felt so alive. I sat in my aerie and wrote and wrote and wrote... finishing the novel I'd originally gone there to write, and letting more projects flow and fall into place... a short story, an article, essays, poems... it was as though the place had unlocked everything that was real and vital and creative inside me.

And after months and months of living there—after years and years of wandering—I finally put down roots and bought a house. An old sea captain's house, built in 1835, where I finally built the library of my dreams, floor-to-ceiling shelves filled with my friends, filled with stories and tales and information that fed my life and imagination.

And as I settled in, suddenly I understood Phil Rickman's portrayal of place as a character in a story, for I felt that I was entering into a relationship with this place. Every day I woke up and was immediately aware of where I was, enjoying the sun shining through my windows and illuminating the myriad spines of books on my shelves, and realizing that within ten minutes I could be walking on a beach on the ocean side of the Cape.

And I fell in love.

So many people attach their bliss to falling in love with a person. That is the fairytale mentality of western civilization, but that's not what happened to me: I became happy once I fell in love with this place.

The world—the wide world that I'd spent most of my life

exploring—suddenly became focused on one place. All my life, I'd been looking for something, and I never knew what it was... and then, suddenly, I seemed to have found it, without ever having articulated—even to myself—what I was looking for.

And yet I finally found happiness in this place. Every morning I wake up and smile, because I live in paradise and get to spend my day doing exactly what I love doing. I start my days early, with a walk on the beach where I watch the sun rise, no matter what the weather is: I love the ocean in the calm summer months as well as in the wild winter ones. The sun up, I go back to my wonderful house where I eat and drink and start writing. In summer months, I watch the bees from my hives fly out on their mission to pollinate the vineyard next to where I live; in winter, I look out over undisturbed snow and stillness and beauty. And no matter what the season, it all encompasses me in its embrace: this is where I belong. As those long-ago words from Dave Carter's song told me, this is sacred ground.

I've found my happiness, my bliss. I was raised to believe that I would find it in another person, and that has not happened; but I have found it in a place, my home, my very being.

And that's not such a bad thing after all.

~Jeannette de Beauvoir

Find Your Happiness

Making the Best of It

To be interested in the changing seasons is a happier state of mind than to be hopelessly in love with spring.

~George Santayana

From Illness Comes Strength

We acquire the strength we have overcome.
~Ralph Waldo Emerson

It seemed unbelievable that anyone could have been both a nursing student and a patient at the same time. That is the truth I struggled with every day as I attended my B.S. in Nursing program at Georgetown University from 1999-2002, while also suffering through my second major relapse with Crohn's disease. Living with a chronic illness, while also attempting to make my dreams come true, was a frustrating experience. I was able to comfort my patients, yet I could not comfort myself. I could relieve the pain of others, yet I could not find pain relief myself. Still, I know I was a better nursing student for having been a patient. I often knew what my patients were going through, because I had lived through it, too.

As a student nurse, I reassured my patients that they would be okay, but I knew all too well about unpredictable tomorrows. In my blue and white nursing student uniform, I stood at the bedside of a fellow student with Crohn's disease who had taken the semester off to care for his health. Three hours later, I lay in a blue and white hospital gown on an exam table in my doctor's office, trying to ignore the searing pain that was shooting through me as my abdomen was palpated by my gastroenterologist.

I was diagnosed with Crohn's at the age of eleven, and the carefree laugh I had as a little girl got lost somewhere between my prednisone chipmunk cheeks, my IV feeding line, and the scars marking my abdominal surgeries. When I started working with pediatric patients in nursing school, I would hear them laugh, and the lost little girl inside me prayed they would never have to endure what I did as a child, that they would never lose their innocent giggles to their illnesses, as I had.

I spent my teenage years pretending the Crohn's did not exist, a façade I was able to maintain long enough to move to Boston and attend journalism school. But when the tests confirmed the Crohn's was back and my first remission had ended, I had to leave that life. It was then that I finally allowed myself to think about what having Crohn's really meant.

There are defining moments in life that some of us are lucky enough to realize early on. My moment arrived unexpectedly, in 1998, after a particularly invasive exam from a new doctor in Massachusetts who acted as if we were old friends, although we were strangers. I walked out of the exam room feeling as if my body had once again turned on me in some cruel, ironic joke. I wanted to cry, but there was no one to lean on. My family and friends were hours away. I tried to be brave, but a nurse I had never met before took one look at me and saw right through me. She invited me to sit down with her, and wrapped her arms around me. She gave me the only hug I would have that day and whispered to me, "It's okay to cry here," and so I did.

That was my defining moment, when I found not only solace and comfort in that nurse's embrace, but a *purpose* in the embrace of nursing. Suddenly I knew, without a doubt, my life's purpose was to become a nurse and help other sick children the way so many nurses and doctors had helped me. Less than a year later, by the end of 1999, I was well into my first clinical rotation as a student nurse at Georgetown University, working towards a BSN and focusing my clinical studies on pediatric gastroenterology. I also worked part-time at two different children's hospitals. Oh, and in 2000, I had two abdominal surgeries without having to take a semester off from school.

Every day, I showed the world that it was possible to be both a nursing student and a patient. My days began much like everyone else's, but somewhere between brushing my teeth and going to class, my life changed. I swallowed a handful of pills and skipped breakfast out of fear that I'd need to go to the bathroom while stuck in rush hour traffic. And yes, my days continued to be unique, more like those of my patients than those of my fellow nursing students, as I made trips to numerous doctors, picked up more pills at the pharmacy, planned my meals around my meds, and tried to make time to rest between classes.

By juggling those two identities every day, I learned something about being a patient that I never knew before: *from illness comes strength*. And I learned something about being a nurse, too, in nursing school—that there is nothing more important than real nursing care. Still, there were days during my nursing school clinicals, and at my jobs, that I wondered if perhaps I cared too much for my sick little patients, days when I had to take a deep breath to compose myself before entering their rooms. Despite my concern that I would respond too emotionally to every sick child I worked with, I returned to my pediatric clinicals and my jobs week after week, certain that my presence in these children's lives would make it all worthwhile, no matter how emotionally painful it was for me to work with them at the time. A five-year-old boy newly diagnosed with Crohn's disease proved me right. His mother feared they would always be in and out of the hospital, but I shared with her the fact that I also had inflammatory bowel disease and that this had not stopped me from realizing my dreams. The greatest gift I was able to give this family was proof that life after such a diagnosis does go on.

In 2001, I underwent more tests, which unfortunately showed that the remission I had been in since my second bowel resection in 2000 was now over. In spite of my active Crohn's disease (or maybe because of it), and my determination to succeed, I finished my junior year of nursing school with honors. But I do not simply mean good grades. I mean that I finished the year having touched the lives of dozens of patients and their families in ways I would not have had I not been ill, as well.

Due to my Crohn's flare-up in 2001, I had to take a semester off from nursing school. But I knew that I would never let Crohn's beat me... it might knock me out once in a while, but I would always be the ultimate winner in this battle. And, although I did not "officially graduate" with my class in May of 2002, the nursing school faculty urged me to come to graduation anyway, in cap and gown, to wear my Sigma Theta Tau nursing honor society rope proudly. At first I did not want to go, and I could not understand why they would want me to. It turned out they needed me there because I was being presented with three awards! I won an award for The Most Publishable Scholarly Paper, I won a Dean's Recognition award for superior service to the school, and I was given an honorable mention in a speech; they spoke of my journalism background, my writing and editing, how I'd been published, and how I made their school a better and more respected and famous place. I was stunned! And, in the end, despite the surgeries, hospitalizations and Crohn's flare-ups I had experienced while in nursing school, I graduated from Georgetown University *magna cum laude* in December of 2002, and my first nursing job was at the #1 hospital in the country, Johns Hopkins. So, you see, no matter what obstacles life throws at you, the key is to take them in stride, to never give up. But really, in my experience, the most important thing is to have faith in yourself.

To this day I lead a double life, just as I did in nursing school ten years ago, and because there is no cure for Crohn's disease, I always will live the life of both a patient and a nurse, but I am living it for myself and for my patients... and in honor of the nurse who cried with me that day when I otherwise would have cried alone.

~Tracey Miller Offutt

82

Seeing My Purpose

Great minds have purposes, others have wishes.
~Washington Irving

My friend ran to me in the parking lot, gripped my arm and shook it with excitement. "You won't believe what I just read," she said. "There's a doctor in California with a procedure to restore some sight for people like you."

People like me? I'm blind, that's true. And, to my joy, I am surrounded with friends who look out for me and hope to help out. But I wonder why most assume that the highest priority is to see again? The truth is I have so many other things at the top of my "want" list.

My friend tapped my hand. "After all these years, don't you at least want to try?"

"Okay," I said, "I'll check my schedule."

We both laughed.

That night, in the silence of my room, a thought fluttered in. What had changed in me? Years ago when I lost my sight completely and my sons were three, five, and seven, I would have done anything for a cure. In fact, desperate and anxious, I did that very thing—tried every supplement, experimental trial, vitamin, diet, and anything anyone suggested. All for nothing.

But now, after twenty-five years of living in physical darkness, my life is brighter than ever. The change began one day, many years ago, when my sons were in school and my husband was at work. I had put the last cereal bowl in the dishwasher. And as it sometimes happened, without warning, my blindness reminded me of the life change I never wanted. I took sips from the cup of self-pity, swallowing gulps of "poor me" and wondering what my future would hold. Then, the doorbell rang. I groped for the hallway wall to follow it to the front door. "Yes?" I asked.

"Hey Janet, it's Mary," the voice said.

She came in and we chatted. But the great thing was that she brought an idea with her. "Did you ever think about working as an interpreter?" she said. "You speak Spanish. Go for it."

Her idea prompted me to make a phone call. And the interpreting company I contacted invited me to take a test. Thank goodness it was oral.

"We're so impressed with the results," the receptionist said the next day, "that we want to send you on your first assignment tomorrow. It's in the Immigration and Naturalization Court."

I gave a silent gasp.

That was the beginning. That was when I began to focus on possibilities where my blindness wouldn't get in the way. The view of my world had changed. Blindness didn't have to label me as unproductive. On the contrary, the lack of sight enhanced my ability to retain information and render a quicker and more accurate interpretation.

The letters from judges and attorneys, praising me for my work, rewarded me for the hours and hours I'd spent studying, memorizing, and practicing.

Blindness? Not a handicap anymore. Instead, it became a handy tool to sharpen my creativity. Not only in the courtroom, but at home, in my relationships and in the way I viewed myself.

So often, while cooking on the stove, I'd burned myself, and frustration seared each time. But now, with a different and renewed outlook, I quickly grab a wooden spoon to reach for the hot pots. When placing items in the pantry, I put one rubber band around cans of fruit, two rubber bands around cans of soup, etc. I do the same with boxes.

When doing the laundry I place one staple on the label of my oldest son's shirt, two on my middle son's and leave the youngest son's shirt as is. Then, when folding the laundry, I can easily know which shirt belongs to whom.

Following recipes was difficult, but when they were my own, the task was easier.

While my sons romp in the kitchen, I grab two potholders and lift the casserole dish. Then, with slow, careful steps, I head for the table. "Look out, hot stuff coming."

I lift the lid. "Guys, you need to try at least a little bit," I say. "Mom fixed a new recipe."

I ask my husband to purchase healthy ingredients so I can try my own recipes. Some are popular and others become my lunch for days.

"Sit here," my husband said as he guided me to the computer chair. "Press some keys and listen. It repeats what you're typing."

The software he installed on our computer read the screen. And through a robotic voice, I heard what I keyed in—words, phrases, and paragraphs of any length. And with additional key commands, I navigated through various applications.

A new world had opened up for me!

With the same passion I used to care for my sons, I learned how to use this new technology with ease. I began to write.

The words I strung together ended up as journaling at first. Then, the stories I wrote seemed to inspire others. I wrote some more and the longer pieces became chapters. And with insights, humor, and fun stories, my first book was created.

"I felt like I was freed from a cage," a reader wrote. "Your story helped me to find my own freedom."

One day I got a phone call from a state agency. "Would you consider coming to our group and giving an inspirational talk?"

I did. And that was the beginning of my speaking ministry. Now I give presentations to crowded churches and impart insights to professional groups. And while at home, I teach ladies' Sunday school.

So, should I follow through with my friend's suggestion to go for that procedure to potentially regain some sight?

I'll have to remember what my passion has become — not to see again, but to look for ways to inspire others. I use my energy to find ways to put a bit of encouragement into the lives of those who have physical sight but are blind to their potential.

When I travel across the country and abroad, my white cane and I meet folks who always want to know, "Were you born blind?"

I smile. That's my clue to begin my story, to start the dialogue and ask them questions. Most often, their lives seem dark like mine used to be. And delight fills me when I bring a little brightness to their day by pointing out that "seeing" our troubles with the eyes of sadness blinds us from seeing what life could be.

Years ago, I wondered what had happened to happiness. Then I realized I held it in my heart. What happened to joy? I choose it each day. And what happened to purpose? I live it each moment.

And what happened to my hunger for a cure? I changed it for the passion to help heal others from defeat and discouragement.

~Janet Perez Eckles

83

Here I Stand

May men rise on stepping-stones of their dead selves to higher things.
~Lord Alfred Tennyson

I sat staring at the pink stick. It can't be true. I looked at the directions again and back to the stick. It's true. Oh no. I am pregnant. What will my friends say? What will my boyfriend say? Worst of all what will my mom say?

There I stood nineteen and pregnant.

I quickly married my boyfriend of two years. We began to play house. We filled our apartment with baby gear and decorative couch pillows. We purchased throw rugs and lasagna pans as if that were what a typical nineteen-year-old girl and twenty-one-year-old boy would do. We were mature, we were going to have a baby, and we would be together forever.

Everyone told me we would never make it. We were too young. We were babies having babies. I spent four years trying to prove them wrong. But they weren't wrong.

There I stood, twenty-three and a single mom.

I was angry more than hurt. I was still so young I didn't feel the pain of a failed marriage. I felt the pain of "I told you so." I was furious. I didn't want to be another statistic. I wasn't going to be a young single mom who couldn't afford to feed her child or an unsuccessful single mom who wasted her life.

There I stood in my empty apartment. No furniture, no money, and only macaroni and cheese in the bare cupboards. There I stood with only one thing on my mind. I was not going to accept this fate.

I watched my son running around the empty living room like an airplane. He smiled and laughed at all the freedom he had.

I ran and got some paper. I sat on the floor and wrote out a list. A list of all I wanted from life. My list ranged from getting a couch to starting my own business. I wrote down everything. And then, I put it in a drawer and played airplane with my son. We both discovered freedom in the hollow living room that first night in our new apartment.

Two years passed. I was twenty-five. I had an apartment full of furniture. The cupboards were full of food. I was making it. I occasionally would pull out my, now tattered, list and check things off. I surprisingly had more things checked off than I thought I would after such a short time.

As I looked at my list I realized only the biggest of dreams and goals were left. I wanted to buy a new car. I wanted a condo. I wanted to own my own business. I wanted to give my son a better life. I wanted the most out of life.

I pulled out another piece of paper. It was time to make a new list. The new list consisted of stepping stones to get me to the bigger dreams. If I was going to own my own business I had better make some goals to get me there. Step by step. Things I could do, to grow, to rise up.

There I stood at the age of twenty-nine. I had gone from the receptionist in the accounting department to the accounting manager of a small business. My income had doubled. It was only then I made the attempt at getting my dream condo. I was shocked, and still am to this day, to know I did get that condo. I purchased it myself, with my own money, without anyone's help.

It was at that moment I realized anything is possible.

At the age of thirty-four, I started my own business. Anything is possible.

Here I stand. My son is now grown. He has moved out to build his own life. I have since remarried. I still have my own business. I would consider my life a success. Not because of the business. Not because of the material things. But because of the will; the will I have to keep going. To keep growing. To never give in to what others believed was my fate.

My fate is in my hands and I can do anything.

~Diana DeAndrea-Kohn

84

Listening to My Inner Passion

Most folks are about as happy as they make up their minds to be.
~Abraham Lincoln

It was my forty-fourth birthday and I was feeling down. I was sitting cross-legged on the pontoon boat on Christie Lake, watching a water skier zip by. Tears were falling down my cheeks. I felt old... fat... and washed up. Were the best years of my life over?

I thought back to some happier times and drifted all the way back to my teen years. I learned to water ski on my bare feet and spent three summers barefooting with the guys on the lake. Barefoot water skiing was my passion, and every time I was out on the water, I was happy.

One day, when I was nineteen, I turned to cross the wake, caught a toe and fell. I slammed sideways into the water. In an instant, I went from hard of hearing to deaf. When I climbed into the boat, I was engulfed in an eerie silence. My friends' lips moved, but I couldn't hear them.

The next several months were tough ones as I learned to adjust to this new change in my life. I started college at Northern Illinois University and I lived on a floor with other deaf and hard of hearing students. I was extremely uncomfortable at first. Hands flew back and forth in American Sign Language, and I found myself a foreigner in this strange, new land.

During the day, I struggled in my classes and discovered that it was next to impossible to lip-read a professor walking on stage. At night, I cried myself to sleep as I battled tinnitus, a horrible roaring sound in my head. There were times I was in despair—I couldn't understand what was being said in my classes and I couldn't understand the American Sign Language that zipped back and forth at parties. I cried my frustration out in the shower as well.

One morning, I woke up and had an epiphany: I could continue to struggle and mourn the loss of hearing, or I could learn to become the best possible deaf person I could be. I put my hair in a ponytail, slapped on my hearing aid and marched myself to the disability office. It was the first time that I went out in public with my hearing aid perched for all to see. I returned the useless FM system and I requested sign language interpreters for all of my classes.

That was the day that becoming deaf turned into a blessing: I unwrapped a passion for living life as a deaf person and I found happiness in that acceptance.

Life became busy and full. I got married and had three deaf and hard of hearing children. I worked as a sales manager and a writer and served on the board of a non-profit organization. I started to lose myself in the process. I had stopped barefooting a few years after becoming deaf. Over the years, I stopped exercising and the weight began to pile on. So by the time my forty-fourth birthday rolled around, I missed the very thing that I truly enjoyed: water skiing on my bare feet. I figured I was too old and too overweight to ever do it again.

A few months after my birthday, my husband sent me a link to a *Today* show segment that featured a sixty-six-year-old woman barefooting on the water. In the video, Judy Myers was carrying a few extra pounds, but there she was, skimming the water with her bare feet. What's more, she learned to barefoot when she was fifty-three. Surely, at forty-four, I wasn't too old to get back on the water again?

I was so inspired by her, that I reached out to her on Facebook and told her my story.

"Come to the World Barefoot Center in Florida and we'll get you barefooting again," she suggested. So I flew to Winter Haven and met with Judy and the two-time World Barefoot Champion, Keith St. Onge. On my first try, I placed my feet on the water and went barefooting again. I had a million-dollar smile on my face.

I unwrapped my long-buried passion that day and found incredible happiness as a result. Along the way, I met women barefooters from all over and they quickly became my new friends. In an unexpected bonus, Keith helped me to change my eating habits and the weight began to come off. At the end of the year, I accomplished something that I could never have imagined as a teen: I learned to barefoot backwards.

The sport that brought me both happiness and sadness was now filling me with happiness again. I also learned something valuable from meeting Judy and getting back on the water again: the best years of life are still ahead.

~Karen Griffard Putz

85

How I Talked My Way to Happiness

Isn't it cool when the days that are supposed to feel good, actually do?
~Jim Carrey

I stutter. I stammer. I have a speech impediment. Whatever you want to call it, it's part of me, and helped make me who I am today.

And I had been challenged with it for what felt like forever.

I had spent years hiding from people and shying away from speaking, especially public speaking. Speaking and reading aloud in class as a kid, whether it was answering questions in front of the class, reading aloud from a novel, or even worse—oral presentations—were all sheer torture. I sweated, quaked, and cried myself through school, the teasing from kids compounding it all. Although I had been taught many different techniques through different speech therapy sessions, no one ever taught me how to cope with it. Not only with the stutter itself and with other peoples' attitudes, but also how to sort out and manage my tumultuous feelings, and nurture my fragile self-esteem.

As an adult, unfortunately, those feelings of shame, embarrassment, and avoidance of situations never went away. I shied away from jobs that would have me constantly talking. Jobs requiring much talking on the phone were a definite "no." Service industry/retail jobs proved equally stressing. The looks and reactions from customers when I was having a "bad day" while I struggled to say a word, never mind a sentence, had my face flaming in embarrassment and sweat trickling down my neck. Even as an adult, I felt like I was always back on the playground.

But then, eventually, I learned to be thankful for it.

But how can that be? How can I be grateful for something that gave me a lifetime of heartache and grief? In turning it into something positive that I could be thankful for, I was able to realize if it weren't for my speech impediment, I wouldn't be who I am today.

Without my stutter, and all the emotions and experiences accompanying it, I wouldn't be as compassionate, patient, and understanding of other people with challenges. I wouldn't be as tough, or as sensitive, as I am. I often wonder who I would be—what type of person I would be—if I didn't have the fortune of stuttering.

It wasn't until I was able to be grateful for my stutter, and able to accept it, that I was then able to move on with my life—and be happy. I spent years fighting it, resisting the acceptance of this challenge, and letting it control my life. I let it get in the way of my own happiness and peace. But as soon as I let it go, I relaxed, and in doing so, I took control of it, often forgetting about it—finally. Being able to turn it into something positive and constructive in my life, and be thankful for it, was a great release. It was the first step towards my happiness.

I had this epiphany in my early thirties, and with that big four-oh milestone just around the corner as I write this, I am still happy, still grateful.

I sometimes wish I knew then what I know now. If I did, I wouldn't have wasted away years of being miserable, quaking in fear, and shying away from opportunities. But all the wishing in the world won't change things. I am happy now, and I don't intend to let anything change that.

Those "bad days" with my stutter are just single moments in a whole lifetime, and I don't let them get me down. I have a whole future of good days, of being happy and grateful, ahead of me. Gone are those years of crying and shame. Ahead are the years of happiness, gratitude, and being—me.

~Lisa McManus Lange

86

A New Best Friend

Cheerfulness is what greases the axles of the world.
Don't go through life creaking.
~H.W. Byles

Thirty years ago I'd wake up all too often engulfed in raw, jagged emotions. My life was so full of unhappiness and yet I was only thirty. I hated my job, I couldn't get out of debt, I didn't care much for a lot of the people I called friends, and half my family had just died in a car accident.

The only ray of sunshine on a dark horizon was my relationship with Tom, and as much as I loved him, I needed more than love to lift me out of my depression.

As I sat home, my leg in a cast after I broke my ankle, smoking a pack of cigarettes a day and watching repeats of old TV shows, I wondered how I'd ever gotten to this point. "I need to change my entire life," I said to Tom over dinner.

"Why?"

I stared at him. "Can't you see I'm in a rut so deep that if it rains I'm going to drown?"

He nodded. "That is an awfully extreme way of looking at it, but yes, you have been sad since the accident."

Sad? I wanted to scream, sad is how you feel when you lose a contest or your puppy runs away. This is so much more than sad. "I'm despondent!"

He nodded. "What can we do about it? Want to go away for the weekend?"

I always wanted to go away, but this time I knew that leaving wasn't the answer. I couldn't run away from myself. "We can go to the shore after I get the cast off in two weeks but for now, whatever my problem is, I have to figure it out myself."

The two weeks came and went and I was cast-free and back to work but still unhappy. As the months passed, I got a grip on my mourning and was able to accept the deaths of my brother and sister-in-law.

When summer arrived I had two and a half months off. Away from the teaching job I hated more than anything, I decided to take stock of my life. Sure I'd had some really harsh breaks, starting most recently with my broken ankle. It had been my own fault playing kickball with my students in three-inch heels and I was stuck with a bum ankle that wasn't healing well. I was still missing my family members who were gone. My pay was so low I was broke and in debt, never quite able to pay off my credit cards. Most of all I hated my life and I guess that meant I wasn't too fond of myself.

But there was also some good in my life. Tom was always there for me. He loved me and supported me even though I was such a downer to be around. I was lucky to have a job and although the pay was considerably less than the other area school districts, it still paid for my car and apartment and my occasional trips to the shore. I still had my parents, my sister and my nephew.

"If I'm ever going to be happy, it will be up to me," I said to myself in total disgust. "I'm going to change my life because no one is going to charge up on that white steed and do it for me."

Yes, the job made me unhappy, but I was just going to have to deal with that. It was only a job. It didn't have to come home at night and I really did enjoy working with my students. I forced myself to detach from the problems of a corrupt urban school district and inept administration. With Tom's help, I stopped constantly talking about the events that were so disruptive to my existence.

Slowly, I began relating the things that happened at work as humorous stories. Sure, I embellished a bit here and there, but I started making the people around me laugh, including my students and co-workers. Then I started laughing as well, looking forward to the evenings to share my day with Tom. I began writing stories, in the beginning thinly veiled tales from work, but soon I didn't need that any more. I had found a way to tolerate and even sort of enjoy going into work every day. As time went on, I married Tom, left the horrid job and had my own children who supplied me with so many stories, I just had to keep writing and actually ended up penning a column about my family for nine years.

As I changed my life, cleared out the people who weren't good for me to have around and tried to surround myself with real friends and things that made me happy, I also changed myself. It was a long, difficult process but throughout it all, I learned how to be happier, even though bad things still happen in life. Best of all, I really learned to like myself in the process.

Life is a series of bad and good, but it can be easier when you face it with a good friend you can always depend upon, especially if that good friend is yourself.

~Dina A. Leacock

Peter Pan

Nothing splendid has ever been achieved except by those who dared believe that something inside of them was superior to circumstance.
~Bruce Barton

"**G**ood news," the oncologist had said. "The cancer is only in the right breast." Bad news: it had broken through the chest wall. Stage III. "Have you considered having both breasts removed," the surgeon asked, "as a prophylaxis?"

The plastic surgeon—young, enthusiastic—could undoubtedly conjure a silk purse out of a sow's ear, or a woman's breast out of plastic and saline and a chunk of her belly. A nip here, a tuck there, a little tattoo work and eureka—a breast almost as good as new. He commented that women like big breasts. I retorted that men like women to have big breasts.

Today was Friday. Everything was arranged for surgery on Tuesday: a right breast mastectomy and pedicle flap reconstruction. Clutching my armful of medical brochures, we proceeded home. Dinner out that evening was sprinkled with laughter and remote from the shadow of my cancer.

I was unbelievably despondent.

I trusted my doctors, but I didn't trust myself. My husband admired my body. I was proud of it, lean, strong and whole. Now a fourth of my torso would be hacked away and then stitched back together, scarred, disfigured. I had the weekend to come to grips with my decisions, their decisions, somebody's decisions.

I needed time alone. My husband said he loved me; he had not married me for my breasts. Thus assured of his affection, I began my journey into self.

I am analytical and logical. However, this time I wasn't comfortable with either the process or the outcome. I had only one guideline: be true to yourself. But who was I?

I closed my eyes and took a mental inventory of my body, small, slim but not unfeminine, my muscles, lumpy, honed by wilderness camping in the Minnesota Boundary Waters Canoe Area. Only a part of me was sick. I knew I had to be as healthy and strong as possible, as soon as possible. Based on the size and location of my tumor, mastectomy was the best, only, choice.

But should I have reconstruction? Surgery would take twice as long, recovery would take weeks to months longer, more tissue, muscles, areas of my body would be weakened by the extensive surgery required to move tissue from my abdomen to my chest. I would have two breasts made of my own flesh, pulsing, alive. Were they necessary to be who I am?

The heat of the radiator at my feet washed over me. I was back in the BWCA.

My first trek in—a day's journey—just the two of us, portaging packs and canoe or paddling for hours, stopping only to drink from the pristine water of the lakes, or swimming, naked, in the frigid water. I had clambered onto a boulder to dry off. My towel was warm. The rocks radiated heat into my feet through my legs, torso, chest, to meet the glow of the sun beating down on my face. Clean, warm, pure, aligned—and it had nothing to do with breasts.

Returning to the present, I hugged myself. "Yes, that's me."

I had discovered a vast secret. I felt exhilarated, alive with my discovery. I had found myself. I was happy, very happy.

Dared I say no to my doctors? How would my two daughters—young women now—view their breast-less mother, my sexuality and their own? I squeezed back the tears. "To thine own self be true."

I had to tell my husband.

"I'm not having reconstruction of any kind. No implant, no balloons, no pedicle flap." Chill bumps danced along my arms. "It's hardly mentioned in the literature, but I can use an external prosthesis after the mastectomy heals."

I waited.

His eyes glistened. "Good."

I flooded him with my logic, my discovery, the importance of the BWCA trek. "I have to tell the doctors." I cringed.

The following day, Monday, I insisted on speaking to the surgeon and on being present when he rewrote my surgical orders, sans reconstruction, and destroyed the original ones. When he had finished, he said, "You've made a difficult—and appropriate—choice."

The surgeon's assistant, who had piloted me through my appointments that whirlwind Friday, called me aside. "I've thought a lot about you. With your body type and your active lifestyle, I don't think you…"

I cut her off. "No reconstruction—of any sort. The surgeon changed my orders."

She hugged me. My tears resurfaced—tears of happiness, reassurance that I was being true to myself. "Good for you," she said. "I'll break the news to Plastics."

The surgery left me with a Peter Pan profile, appropriate for who I am. I tolerated the surgery well and was home two days later. My first visitor was a volunteer from the American Cancer Society. Among her gifts was an ultra-lightweight breast prosthesis to wear while my chest healed. I thanked her politely and solemnly as she left, but when my two grown daughters arrived, the three of us laughed; the prosthesis could have been easily divided among the three of us and still have some to spare.

My husband's affection for me and his admiration for my body remained as strong and apparent after my surgery as before. Gardening became an important and enjoyable part of our lives. We were amused by the story of the "potato lady," who liked to garden in the nude. The potato lady's husband could always tell when she was in the garden because both lanes of traffic slowed as cars passed their house.

A few months after my surgery, on a warm, sunny spring day, my husband and I were working in the garden. He took off his sweatshirt. I said I couldn't strip any further as I had little else on underneath. His dark eyes twinkled as he impishly said, "You could stop traffic—like the potato lady." I laughed, embarrassed, remembering my disfigured body. He sensed my discomfort and said gently, "Well, maybe just one lane of traffic!"

I don't regret my Peter Pan body. I am happy being healthy and strong. I have returned to the wilderness many times and have immersed myself in the wonders of the ocean, things I might never have done if I had not first discovered the magic of who I am.

~C.M. Downie

No Longer Waiting for Godot

The man who acquires the ability to take full possession of his own mind may take possession of anything else to which he is justly entitled.
~Andrew Carnegie

t was the morning after Boxing Day. The sounds and smells of my kitchen rose up to my bedroom where I lay, motionless, trying to will my body to shift and stir. I wanted to call out to my husband that I was unwell, but my voice barely reached the end of my bed. My entire body as well as my brain felt like they were filled with heaviness. I began to wonder if I was having a stroke. It was at that moment that my husband came into the room.

"Aren't you getting up, hon? It's almost 9 o'clock! Breakfast is ready."

"I can't."

"What do you mean, you can't?"

"I can't move."

It pained me to see the familiar look of concern and distress in my husband's eyes as he processed the situation. My health had been on a progressive decline for many years, and although I had done test after test and had visited the ER as well as my doctor multiple times, no one was able to explain my symptoms, their causes, my progressive failure to improve, let alone provide me with any type of solution or treatment. The words "Mystery Lady" are not the ones you want to hear from the mouths of medical specialists! When I began the round of ER visits and medical specialists, I had lost thirty pounds, was basically bedridden and could not concentrate for more than a few minutes at a time without breaking into a sweat or uncontrollable shaking. I suffered from severe insomnia and had chronic pain. I was lost in a confused state of undiagnosed illness.

That particular December morning was worse than all the other mornings over the years. I was literally weighed down by a fatigue so extreme, I barely felt alive. My husband called an ambulance.

Ten hours later, I came back home from the hospital with a diagnosis. The doctor on call that day put all the pieces of my health puzzle together, pinpointed some of the chronic, overlapping symptoms and bluntly hit me with her conclusion. "You have chronic fatigue syndrome (CFS). It is untreatable and incurable. We don't know the cause of this illness but it could be from a virus. Based on your medical history of the last five years, you have probably had CFS for a while now, which explains why you've been waxing and waning. There isn't anything that Western medicine can do for you. We can prescribe antidepressants to help you deal with the situation and sleep better but that's about it. Sorry."

Sorry? I cried for a few days, more of a whimper really, since my energy was so low. I didn't know how I was going to travel on the road to recovery, but I felt that I was now at a crossroads. By telling me that Western medicine did not have the tools to help me improve, the ER doctor, unbeknownst to her, put me on a quest for health through an energizing path—that of mind, body and soul.

So began my exploration of Eastern philosophies, particularly Buddhist psychology. I learned that although life circumstances may disturb our happiness, joy itself is an internal state. This wisdom of the heart keeps us standing through storms of despair and winds of uncertainty. I taught myself to remember that no matter what my particular life or health challenges were at the moment, joy lived inside me. I also became more acutely aware of my responsibility to navigate through any barriers that could block me from experiencing a deeper sense of contentment and purpose. At first, it seemed impossible to feel joy when so much of my body was in pain and my energy unbearably low. But even when joy is sitting on the edge of our life, it doesn't mean that it isn't there! I simply needed to bring it off the edge, back into my heart. I found a meditation coach and slowly began to trust myself to think, sense, feel and behave my way into a path of light.

After a few months of practicing meditation on a daily basis, I realized that this ritual was giving my body and my soul room to breathe. These moments of silence became a way for me to cultivate present-mindedness and to widen my gratitude. Through the practice of meditating, I was making deposits in my spirit bank. As I broke out of old patterns and embraced new ways of being, I was reminded of the characters in the Samuel Beckett play, *Waiting for Godot*. In this play, Vladimir and Estragon wait endlessly and in vain for someone named Godot to arrive. They do not know who Godot is or what he can do, but still, they mindlessly wait for him every day. However, Godot never shows up and, at the end of the play, we are left with the impression that the two characters will wait forever for nothing. I realized that illness has a potential to become a leading character in our lives, and as such, can maintain a state of endless waiting—waiting for life to get better, waiting for energy to return, waiting for illness to leave our bodies, waiting for solutions.

The clarity of mind attained through daily meditation provided me with the confidence to stop waiting. I symbolically replaced one letter of the word "waiting" to transform it into "wanting." Every day, I filled my mind with the energy of wanting. I named what I wanted: more stable health, a gentler life balance, a stronger spiritual self, a grateful heart, and joy. I wanted whole-hearted, deep-seated, far-reaching joy in every cell of my being. Meditation became one of the healing building blocks that allowed me to enter my peace of mind though the experience of connecting my breath to my life right here, right now. A quieter mind prepared my body for restoration. I deeply understood that illness could be a time of repair and reweaving of all the levels of self.

Illness is a teacher and meditation is a learning journey. To bring back balance to a disharmonious state of a mind, body or life is challenging but meditation nonetheless offers an immediate sense of comfort. Meditation is like cracking a window open to let in fresh air and sunlight. In that moment of living fully in the present, there is a sense of relief. We are no longer waiting for anything or anybody. We are simply enjoying, and sometimes, that is enough to be happy.

~Jeannine Ouellette

The Girls on the Bus

There are many wonderful things that will never be done
if you do not do them.
~Charles D. Gill

A s I backed my car out of Mom's driveway, I asked her a question. "Have you taken the senior bus yet?" I held my breath as I waited for her answer.

Mom adjusted her seatbelt and stared straight ahead. Emphasizing each word, she said, "Oh-yes-I-did."

There was an uncomfortable silence.

Finally, I asked, "How was it?" I said the words as cheerfully as I could manage, even though I sensed the answer was not going to be positive.

"Well," she said, once again with emphasis, "I called the Senior Center and made the arrangements for the bus to take me to the grocery store. When they came to the house the next morning, I climbed on and looked down the aisle. And what do you think I saw? I'll tell you what." She clenched her hands. "I saw about thirteen depressing little old ladies and one depressing old man."

Something clutched my stomach, and I didn't know if it was sympathy for her plight, fear that she'd refuse to use this helpful transportation, or anger that she maligned what she needed desperately.

More silence. It didn't take a genius to figure out that in her own mind she thought that now she was one of them. My dad had recently passed away after six weeks in the hospital. He had been in a coma after surgery for an aortic aneurysm that burst while he was having an MRI. The long hours of waiting and hoping all those weeks had taken a toll on my mother and the rest of the family, too.

Mom had seemed to wear down a little more each day as she watched and waited in the hospital, but she got through the many decisions each time another crisis arose and finally agreed to disconnect life support. Then, surrounded by her children, their spouses and her grandchildren, she reigned graciously at the visitation and funeral.

When the family left to go back to their own lives, she was suddenly alone and frightened. For fifty-seven years, my dad had walked by her side. He had always told her, "Don't worry about it. I'll take care of it."

Dad took an early retirement twenty years before his death. These were years my parents were always together. Mom never learned to drive, so Dad chauffeured her everywhere, on errands to the grocery store, to get her hair cut, or whatever she needed. Now, her wheels were gone, as one grandchild so aptly described her situation.

I spent the week after the funeral helping Mom with paperwork and other chores, and I contacted the local Senior Center to inquire about transportation for her. I teased her, saying she could now see her tax dollars at work and get some real benefit from them. She agreed, although reluctantly, that she'd need to use the senior bus since I lived an hour and a half away.

Now, as we drove to the shopping center, I thought about what courage it had taken for her to call that first time and then to ride the bus with other seniors. As I wove in and out of traffic, Mom changed the subject. We didn't discuss the bus again that day.

The following weeks when I came to visit, she would mention the bus and often end by saying, "No one ever talks on that bus. They all sit there staring into space and looking sad." Her mouth turned downward, and she heaved a great sigh.

I thought to myself that surely couldn't last too long, not with my mother on board. Mom grew up in a small coal-mining town in Iowa where she knew everyone. She often waited for her father at the mine at the end of his shift and chattered constantly on the long walk home. Even as an adult, living in a large metropolitan area, she chatted to clerks in the stores or the mailman walking down the street as if she'd known them forever. I couldn't imagine her sitting silently on the bus, but her life had changed so drastically, and she wasn't the same person anymore. I so hoped to see a spark of life in her on one of my visits, but how to bring it about escaped me.

I worried needlessly, for after several more weeks went by, I noticed that many of Mom's sentences began with "The girls on the bus told me…" After hearing the same phrase on several visits, I dared to hope.

One day, as she made tea for us, I asked, "So, they talk to you now?"

She smiled and there was a sparkle in her eye, the first real sign of life I'd seen in her for many months. She poured the steaming tea into my cup and picked up a cookie before she answered. "I decided one day that it was silly, all of us sitting there saying nothing. So I climbed on the bus one morning and greeted them all. Then I remarked on what a nice day it was. I think I scared them at first. It took a few tries, but little by little they began to respond. And now we have some good conversations, and it makes everyone's life a little nicer."

She slid the plate of homemade cookies to my side of the table, and in my great relief, I ate several.

My mother had little formal education and had done very little on her own while Dad was alive. Nevertheless, she held the key to open the hearts of the other lonely people on that bus. A smile and a friendly word or two was all it took. She sowed tiny seeds of happiness for herself and the girls on the bus.

~Nancy Julien Kopp

The Palm Tree

He conquers who endures.
~Persius

The children and I raced each other out to the patio to take a break from home-schooling while the late-morning heat was still bearable. Our rough-hewn outdoor furniture faced an inlet of Lake Victoria, about 150 yards away, past native grasses and a communal garden plot. On one side was a tall, picturesque snag, its man-sized trunk shiny with smoothly peeled bark, the branches high and irregular. Close to the water's edge was a lovely palm tree, shapely and symmetrical. It was the centerpiece of our lake view, a symbol of beauty, creating a postcard panorama.

Visual beauty was important for nourishing and refreshing my soul because of the primitive nature of our living situation. Our compound had been scraped from the jungle just a year before, and the red earth surrounding our house had a bare, scarred look. I planted starts of purple verbena, neon-bright cannas, and poinsettias outside our house to beautify the dull mud-brick walls. We decorated the interior of our enclosed pit latrine (a hundred-yard trek from the house) with "Far Side" cartoons and samples of the children's penmanship lessons.

Our small village had only sporadic electricity and no running water, and we were reluctantly becoming very familiar with kerosene lamps and plastic water cans. We became expert at getting clean with a one-gallon plastic "camping" shower bag. Our daughters managed to keep their long hair well groomed, in spite of shampooing with tepid water in a red plastic bucket. It was the absolute height of luxury when we took our semi-monthly trip to the Lake Victoria Hotel in Entebbe, a bouncy twelve miles away. We gladly paid the fee for a long hot shower and a swim in the sparkling pool.

Life on the shore of Lake Victoria was both a pleasure and a frustration. We enjoyed the rhythmic sound of the oars of the local fishermen leaving the shore just before daylight, and appreciated buying fresh tilapia or Nile perch for dinner when they returned with their catch. During the rainy season, we saw spectacular electrical storms across the lake, and once even witnessed the awesome but scary approach of a tornado as it advanced on the surface of the lake and passed directly over our house. A major frustration was not being able to swim in the lake, as it was a breeding ground for a nasty tropical parasite. We could only wistfully imagine the pleasure of cooling our overheated bodies by sinking into the refreshing water. The nightly arrival of malaria-bearing mosquitoes was heralded by their peculiar hum from the border of papyrus between the garden and the lake. It always reminded me of an orchestra tuning up—slightly discordant and anticipatory, but here, it had a sinister edge. Once we saw or felt the first mosquito land on an arm, we headed indoors, regardless of the time or the view.

Absent-mindedly washing breakfast dishes one morning, I paid little attention to the small group of local workers heading towards the lake in their shorts and rubber boots, each carrying a machete. It was a typical morning that engaged the senses in that peculiarly African way: pungent smells of charcoal cooking fires and rotting tropical vegetation, rising heat on my skin, the rhythmic pounding of mortar and pestle for ground-nut sauce, punctuated by the strident calls of hornbills and the communal chatter of weaver birds. Gradually my mind registered that something was different.

An unfamiliar noise seemed to be growing louder, and I went outside to investigate. The farm workers were standing by the fence at the edge of our yard, casually looking on as a raging fire swept through the papyrus and other foliage near the lake. As I watched in horror, the flames raced across the grass and leaped at "my" palm tree. I ran toward the cluster of men, yelling at them to put out the fire. But I was too late. As I reached the fence, the beautiful green fronds were suddenly ablaze, and just as suddenly were limp and charred, leaving only a blackened asparagus-shaped stub.

"Why did you set the fire?" I cried.

"It was necessary for the garden, Madam," was the casual reply.

I asked, "But why did you let it burn the tree?" The men shrugged their shoulders awkwardly as they observed my obvious distress.

"Don't worry, Madam," one said. "You can always plant more trees."

In frustration and anguish, I sobbed, "But I won't be here to see them!"

For weeks afterwards, I avoided looking at the lake, not wanting to see the charred stump that ruined my postcard view. The black trunk seemed only too clearly to symbolize the ruin of my early hopes and anticipation of impacting lives in Uganda. It was almost more than I could bear. Not only did we deal with constant threats to our personal safety, but there were numerous other difficult circumstances that suddenly seemed overwhelming. The frequent visits of deadly snakes on our compound, sometimes even inside our house, the challenge of home-schooling three bright children without adequate resources, and the ongoing difficulty of providing nutritious meals for my family on a very limited budget and without household help, all threatened to drown me. The loss of the palm tree and what it represented took its toll, and I skated on the edge of depression and despair.

My circumstances were inescapable; we were only midway through a two-year commitment to our task in Uganda. As I fought discouragement and hopelessness, I finally realized that I faced a choice. Would I succumb to self-pity, letting it suck me into the black bog of despair and fear, or would I again embrace the truth of God's love, protection and provision? I can't say it was an easy, straightforward, or painless choice. But somehow I knew that the only way out of the dark pit was to trust that, regardless of the fire of my circumstances, my loving Heavenly Father would bring good and growth into my life. So I slowly began to subdue and replace the negative thoughts, and once again looked for beauty in the middle of disorder and difficulty. I planted a new flowerbed, figured out how to "bake" cookies in a frying pan over a propane burner, and moved gradually away from the edge of despondency.

Our situation didn't change significantly. Life really didn't get any easier, but it became bearable, with new moments of joy. Then one day a month or so later, I was astonished to see a green sprout coming out of the top of the burned palm stump. Gradually more fronds emerged, and a pleasing silhouette began to reappear. In just a few weeks, the branches were shapely and symmetrical, and my favorite vista was restored. Now, however, it was not only a symbol of beauty, but also a symbol of God's faithfulness and His grace for overcoming devastation.

~Carolyn L. Wade

Find Your Happiness

Jumping Off
the Hamster Wheel

*As you grow older, you'll find the only things you regret
are the things you didn't do.*

~Zachary Scott

What If You Won the Lottery

*Obstacles are those frightful things you see when you
take your eyes off your goal.*
~Henry Ford

At the early stages of my career, I totally hated my job. "I have no idea what I want to do. I cannot stand banking," I whined to my brother.

He replied, "Imagine that you just won the lottery! What would be the first thing you'd do?"

Without even thinking, I blurted out, "Oh my God! Move to Italy!" I had dreamt of living there since childhood. Me living in Italy. Impossible! Debt-ridden, I couldn't even afford to take a vacation.

But what a fantasy. Italia. My mouth became a Fountain of Trevi envisioning my antipasti (appetizer) of fresh mozzarella and tomatoes, followed by homemade pasta: farfalle al salmone or maybe spaghetti drenched in a rich pesto sauce. Was there any Italian food I didn't love? No matter what I chose for my primi piatti, I always had room for dolci (dessert): tiramisu or an ice-cold strawberry gelato. La dolce vita! A deliciously rich espresso slid down my throat.

I chuckled. My overactive imagination took off like a Formula One Ferrari. I visualized the gorgeous hotel concierge as I, albeit in terribly broken Italian, asked him to please fax a resignation letter to my boss. *Per favore.*

"Then do it! Move. I'm sick of hearing that you hate your job. I'll come visit." My brother's voice brought me back to reality.

"I don't have the money. And I don't speak Italian."

"Jennifer, if you wait until you learn the language, you'll never do it. Moving there will force you to learn Italian quickly. You know, money or lack thereof, has always been your obstacle. Why are you letting it hold you down?"

"I have a ton of debt," was my stubborn answer.

"Well then, do whatever it takes and get out of debt. Start saving. Focus on moving to Italy. Call it a birthday gift to yourself. Hang up with me and call your buddy who lives there. Ask him if he'll help you find somewhere to live. Goodbye."

The dial tone drowned out my, "But..."

Before I chickened out, or realized that it was rather late in Milan, I grabbed my address book and punched in Piercarlo's number. What was I doing? This was insane!

Being the epitome of a charismatic Italian, even half asleep, Piercarlo told me to book a flight and he'd meet me at the airport. He even offered to introduce me to his friends and help me get an apartment. My hand quivered as I hung up the phone. This was more doable than I thought. But I had to figure out how to pay off my credit card obligations.

By focusing on my specific goal of moving to Milan by November 1st (or sooner), I threw all my energy into getting out of debt. I stopped carrying cash and put my credit cards in my freezer so I couldn't use them. That halted my impulsive spending. I brought my lunch to work, stopped going out for dinner and went to the library to check out tapes on how to speak Italian. Curtailing my spending helped reduce my outstanding credit card balance faster. I found all kinds of ways to save. I cancelled magazine subscriptions, cable TV and my health club membership and took the money refunded and threw it at my debt. My brother was right. Nothing was as crucial as getting to Italy.

What did I need to do before I moved? I made a list of everything and started doing tasks daily. While physically I may have been in Los Angeles, mentally I was in Italy. My usual work stress was greatly diminished as I ticked off the days on my calendar. I packed my suitcase! I put my passport inside and every time I saw it in my bedroom, I was reminded that this was actually happening. The more actions I took, the more my dream became reality.

Sometimes the timing isn't perfect. My deadline got pushed up when Piercarlo called to say that I only had until October because then he was moving to Sierra Leone to work for the United Nations.

Out-of-my-mind terrified, I boarded the plane to Milan with about $1,200, more money than I had ever saved before, a few days before Piercarlo left. I didn't know what would happen in Italy, but one thing was for sure, even on its worst day, it had to be more interesting than my boring life as a stressed-out, debt-ridden banker.

So, imagine. If you won the lottery, what would you do? My imaginary lottery win forced me to listen to my inner voice and that imaginary lottery ticket turned into a real plane ticket. Deciding to move was a turning point in my life. My brother Sean knew that money had always been my obstacle. He simply removed money from the discussion and asked me to envision a different reality. Because so many of us use money as an excuse not to do something, I love this way of thinking and still use it when I'm trying to decide my next steps.

~JC Sullivan

New Rewards

He is rich or poor according to what he is, not according to what he has.
~Henry Ward Beecher

took a huge pay cut when I began working in a library. I had a college degree, was working on a master's degree, and had worked in the media business for four years in New York City. But my work in Corporate America wasn't satisfying. I found myself "working for the weekend" and spending a lot of after work time at the mid-Manhattan branch library, poring over stories about happier, more satisfied people, and trying to figure out what it would take for me to be happy at work.

It turns out, what was making me happy outside of work could also make me happy at work.

So, at twenty-seven years old, I moved back home to Indiana and became a Page — the lowliest of the low-paid in libraries — and my new career with a minimum wage paycheck began.

This also happened to be around the time that the economy crumbled and people began losing their jobs in record numbers. Our library was in a neighborhood that was already poor, so we found - more and more people flooding in to learn how to file for unemployment and how to apply for new jobs. Some of them were also simply looking for a good, free movie to lift their spirits. People who hadn't noticed the library before were now appreciating all the ways we could help.

Although I enjoy helping the adults, what really makes my

workdays rewarding is working with the children. During the school year, they come through the doors at 3:30 p.m., looking for a positive escape from the dire situations they face at home. Most of them are in to use the computers, but some of them are in to pick up a new book. And then there are the few who are there to talk to me and the other library staff members, to share with us their triumphs and their hopes for a brighter future.

Many of my friends think I read books all day and then alphabetize the shelves. Well, sometimes I do alphabetize shelves. But more often than not, my job title could be "friend." Or just simply "caring ear." Public librarians are often part information seekers, part social workers.

Although I've been working at a library for almost four years now, I don't think I was completely certain that this is the fulfilling career I'd been looking for until one of our regular ten-year-old patrons saw me enjoying a dinner break at the picnic table outside the library last week. He gleefully called my name and ran over to join me. We shared casual conversation until it was time for me to return to work. As I told him I'd see him back in the library, he looked pensive for a moment.

"I'm glad I can always see you in the library."

Teachers are often rightly praised for all they do for our children. But there are others out there who are working to make the youth of today a happy and productive generation of tomorrow. And I'm proud to say I'm one of those "others" providing a positive environment for many wonderful children who are full of promise.

I know that I will never be rich in money in this career. But, I also know that I won't soon be leaving this career because the wealth of compassion and good I see and help to spread each day is worth much more than any paycheck. And knowing I've made even one person's day a little better because I've said hello? That is one of the greatest blessings in my life.

~Carrie O'Maley

Rewriting My Future

Not until we are lost do we begin to understand ourselves.
~Henry David Thoreau

From third grade on, when asked, "what do you want to be when you grow up?" my answer was, "a writer." I wrote through elementary school and treasured the "Good Job!" stickers my teacher put on my stories. I wrote through middle school, often turning my stories into sketches for "Talent Days." I didn't do anything in high school (except develop an interest in boys) but by college I was back to writing. I wrote a humor column called "Becky's Corner" and a weekly Top 10 list called "Well Heck—It's Beck!" for student newspapers. I also worked for the *Americus Times Recorder* where I wrote assignments ranging from accounts of soldiers coming home from Desert Storm to a Boy Scout nicknamed "Stinky" receiving his Eagle Scout badge. I found nothing more delightful than telling, or being told, a great story.

After graduation, I moved from Atlanta to Los Angeles and began working in the entertainment business, doing everything under the sun—except writing. My first job was as a Client Assistant at a post-production house.

Being a Client Assistant meant that I made cappuccinos for anyone who walked through the door. I made dozens of cappuccinos a day and as I stood steaming the milk, I would remind myself it was a stepping stone to becoming a Hollywood writer. But the truth is, except for writing down lunch orders, I'd stopped writing entirely. Between getting sandwiches for A-listers and trying to remember who would freak out if the deli accidentally put a tomato on their sandwich or allowed a pickle to touch their bread, my dream of becoming a writer took a backseat.

Fortunately, I went from making cappuccinos to being a Post Production Supervisor within a year. It started when a star editor asked if I would help move his family from Valencia to Beverly Hills. I did, and it went well. He was impressed with my organizational skills and asked if I wanted to be a Post Production Supervisor on an Eric Clapton project with him. I didn't know what a "Post Production Supervisor" was, but it sounded better than being a cappuccino maker so I agreed.

Flying under his wing, I learned a great deal. Suddenly I was working with top executives at Warner Brothers Records and was eating lunch with editors and clients rather than serving them cappuccinos. I was nervous and overwhelmed, but I worked day and night and managed to keep up.

The project went well, so the next phone call I received was from a producer asking if I'd like to work on a Madonna music video. I played the phone message twice to make sure it wasn't actually just a friend inviting me to McDonald's! The producer verified that my last gig had been the Eric Clapton project, and that was good enough for him. Fortunately he didn't ask what I'd done before that, because the answer would've been that I'd probably served him a cappuccino.

The Madonna music video was hard for me. I was working with Mark Romanek, who is one of the most talented (and demanding) directors in the business. I know there were times when Mark was irritated by my lack of knowledge, but since we were editing the music video where I'd served cappuccinos, I managed to get through the project with the editors and in-house producers surreptitiously teaching me in the hallways and at the lunch tables.

Going through this baptism by fire left little time for me to think of becoming a writer. I worked around the clock, often sleeping on couches. Even when the others went home I'd stay so I could pore over the telecine film transfers, logging every bit of footage so I could answer Mark's questions intelligently and efficiently. I was sleep deprived but excited, exhausted yet exhilarated, and the only thought in my mind was, "If I work hard enough, I can do this."

That was my mantra for the next ten years as I worked on projects like *American Idol* and *Scooby Doo II* and for companies such as IMAX and National Geographic. The entertainment industry is a notoriously demanding business where ninety-hour workweeks are the norm. I liked it—you could even say I was addicted to it, given the excitement and good paychecks, but I always felt numb. I felt as if I was running on a hamster wheel and that life was passing me by. Yet it was hard for me to unplug, and I started wondering what it would take to make me pursue my dream of becoming a writer.

That question was answered in the form of an autoimmune disease that came on suddenly, out of nowhere, attacking my eyes and joints and making it hard for me to walk or see. It quickly became impossible for me to drive, so I couldn't go anywhere, and I couldn't work. I was housebound and very frightened. I was restless and agitated the first few weeks and my mind raced, but the wonderful thing about a horrible illness is that it brings your purpose, passion and joy into serious focus very quickly. As I settled into the quietness and the stillness of being alone with my thoughts, the silence brought me clarity. I re-remembered that what I really wanted to be was a writer.

Weekly, I'd press my optometrist to tell me when my eyesight would return. She'd say, "I'm not sure; we have to keep evaluating your condition." After a month of this, I began to panic. What if my eyesight never came back? I thought, "If I can't see, I'll never become a writer." I would fill with sorrow, thinking how I'd spent my twenties doing film and television work, but not developing my passion for writing. I wondered if I'd missed catching my dream, not understanding how short life can be.

Sitting alone in the apartment all day was the perfect time to begin writing. I had to start somewhere. First, my husband made the font on my computer very large and bought me a magnifying glass. Though I couldn't see the letters clearly, I could make out their shape. I began submitting stories regularly to *Redbook* magazine and Chicken Soup for the Soul and while I was writing I felt peaceful, calm and full of purpose.

A second wave of panic happened when, thinking the worst was over, the disease began attacking my fingers. I started crying and bargaining with God, saying "Not my fingers. I need them to type. My legs and hips can hurt, but not my fingers. If you'll leave me use of my fingers, I promise I'll write every day except Sunday."

Eventually, with rest and medicine, the swelling in my joints subsided and my eyesight returned. I also got the great news that two of my stories were going to be published in *Redbook* and four of my stories were going to appear in *Chicken Soup for the Soul* anthologies. When I saw my stories in print, they meant more to me than any music video, television show or film I had ever worked on. They made me feel that if I died today, my last breath would be peaceful.

~Rebecca Hill

Last Call

Begin at the beginning and go on till you come to the end; then stop.
~Lewis Carroll

The ring of our home phone jolted me from my reminiscing and forced me back to reality. My husband was asking if I had made the calls. He was busy, serving up the last supper for his faithful customers, and it was my job to extend the invitations for last call to family and friends. With each phone call, I could feel my throat swell and my stomach tighten. I managed to stifle my tears and keep the phone conversations short and light, even cheery.

Soon it was time to go to the restaurant. When I arrived, my husband was still finishing up the dinner hour. Our guests trickled in looking a little shell-shocked. We put them at ease, maintaining our position as hosts. This night was for savouring our memories and making new ones, a night to party like it was the good old days.

It was a night of lasts. There was one last dance on the table, one last night for the kids to fill their own fountain drinks, and eventually, one last call. Throughout the evening we all had our cameras out. We sat, we talked, we joked and we laughed. It was a bittersweet night we'll always remember fondly.

We had known for some time that it was inevitable. After seventeen years, the time had come to close the doors of our family restaurant. We had longed for a miracle but the recession had been the nail in the coffin.

Seventeen years earlier, the restaurant had just been a new, friendly roadhouse that was close to my office. For the owner it had been an exciting new business venture. After frequent visits, it became obvious that the place had a magical charm. It was difficult to drive by without stopping in. I didn't know it then, but the owner, a large, loud man with rogue Irish charm, would one day become my husband.

Before we settled down to child rearing and marriage, there were many late nights of unabashed good times. If we weren't dancing to the jukebox hits, or singing karaoke, we were sending requests to the live performers. The music and the dancing were just the icing on the cake. What made the place truly great were the people. The distinction between staff and customers was fuzzy. We were all friends. Often you'd find the staff on the other side of the counter on their days off.

Times change and people move on. Such is the nature of the business. Many people drifted through and as life circumstances changed, so did the faces of the staff and customers. It seemed one day my daughter was playing pranks on the staff, and before we knew it, she was one of them. When our first son was born our late nights were curtailed, and instead, many afternoons were spent in "our booth." When the next baby boy arrived the first one was ready for a high chair. From pabulum in the beginning to ordering their own whole lobsters as teenagers, these boys ate well.

It was also the venue for many celebrations, including my wedding shower, our sons' christenings, many birthday dinners and of course, New Year's Eve. St. Patrick's Day was a favourite celebration and often we would host an Irish band to put us in the celebratory mood. Even the year we couldn't secure a band to play the Irish ditties, the Caribbean calypso band somehow worked. It was also the last stop for many customers on Christmas Eve, and it was there that the magical calm of the evening would hit us. There were other, more solemn, celebrations.

How could we part with our past, our present and what we thought was our future? When we finally did come to grips with the fact that closing was our only choice, we did not belabour the decision. Once made, we were catapulted into a cyclone of surreal events that spun much too quickly. Through it all, and behind our masks of optimism, we feared for the unknown and reflected lovingly on the past.

It has been a year since we shut down the restaurant. Closing a business you've put your heart and soul into for so many years is really tough. But when it is no longer profitable, no matter how much you love the place, you have to let it go. The digital images from that last night already appear distant and detached. We are looking forward to new beginnings, new endeavours. Life is full of many twists and turns. We've learned to enjoy everything we have and not lament over what we don't. We've learned how important it is to just keep moving—keep dancing—since last call comes much too quickly.

~Maureen Flynn

95

When I Grow Up I Will Be a Professor

The other day a man asked me what I thought was the best time of life.
"Why," I answered without a thought, "now."
~David Grayson

I just hate the job. And there's never enough money. I finally got the hospital paid off. I just don't know what to do."

"That's exactly what you said the last time we had lunch," Gypsey said.

I realized that she was right.

After I was widowed, I had moved to Oklahoma, where I had lived for several years. It had been rough financially for many of those years, as I'd been laid off three times and had spent months job hunting. When I did get interviews, half of them said I was under-qualified while the other half said I was over-qualified. Meanwhile, I had collected unemployment when I could, and had gone through a good deal of my savings.

I was now working at a small newspaper after a particularly long period of unemployment. The editor was an unpleasant man and disliked by everyone, and the salary was dreadfully low. It was a dead-end job, but it was somewhat secure after months of no income, and I had stopped exploring other possibilities.

"I told you before and I'm telling you now: do something about it," urged Gypsey. She was frustrated with me and she was right. We had known each other for years and when we both ended up working in Oklahoma City, we occasionally had lunch together.

She had gone back to school and graduated with a Master of Library and Information Studies. She secured a position at the Langston University library on the Oklahoma City campus and she was very happy.

"What can I do?" I whined. I hated it when I whined, and knew my friends must be sick and tired of hearing me complain.

"Go back to school. Get a library degree." I must have looked as dubious as I felt, just as I had when she first suggested I go back to school a few months before. "Look, could you live on $30,000 a year?"

"Sure."

"That's probably what you would make in a library, especially an academic library. I know you love books. It would be ideal for you."

"Who would hire me? Even if I started school tomorrow, I'd be sixty-two when I graduated. That's retirement age for most people. No one is going to hire a sixty-two-year-old for an entry-level job. And what about the expense? Tuition, books, fees. I don't have the money and I don't want to go further into debt."

"There are student jobs all over campus," explained Gypsey. "They don't pay much, but it's something. But first, try to get a graduate assistantship. They pay better. You get some tuition waived, free student insurance, and a thousand a month."

"Really?"

"Oh, yeah. Plus there's the experience you get over and above what you learn in the classroom. Volunteer for projects and other work, too. That looks good on your résumé. Get all the experience you can."

"You make it sound possible."

"It is, Cary. You need to take control of your life and stop drifting from job to job and always needing money. It can be done."

"But at my age..."

"Dammit! Forget about your age. You don't put your age on a résumé."

I knew that, but with all the jobs I'd had, it was clear I was no spring chicken.

She got up to leave. "Do what you want to do. Just don't complain about where you are when you can make things better." She leaned over and kissed my cheek. "Call me. I'll give you a letter of recommendation."

I nodded and she left. That weekend, I seriously considered what she had said about taking control of my life. I couldn't be much worse off, even with a student loan. If I were lucky enough to get a graduate assistantship, that would make everything much easier. After studying the list of classes on the website, I considered the possibility of continuing to work at the newspaper since most of the classes in the library school were at night and on weekends. No, I decided, I would make a clean break from the paper. I needed to get out of there. Plus I would need to concentrate on studying.

The next week I called Gypsey and got more information. Much of it was online—phone numbers, e-mail addresses, names of various people—but she had bits of inside information that were helpful.

Monday I called the School of Library & Information Studies and they mailed me an application. I immediately filled it out and turned it in, afraid that if I hesitated I would lose my nerve. The very next week, I met with my faculty adviser and the week after, I was interviewed for a graduate assistantship.

I voiced my concerns to one of the professors about finding a job at my age. He pointed out that a lot of librarians were also approaching my age.

"There will be a lot of retirements in the next few years," he said. "Then, too, it's the one field where age matters less than experience and ability."

That gave me pause, and I considered what he'd said. Here I was, getting ready to start a new career when most people of my generation were planning on retiring. On further reflection, though, I couldn't imagine my life without having a job.

I started my first class in the middle of August. We met Friday nights and Saturdays all day, and the course was completed in four weeks. In September, when the fall semester started, I had a graduate assistantship in the library, but in January I started a second one in the congressional archives on campus. I had found what I wanted to be when I grew up: an archivist. Much of my library studies concentrated on computer-related information management. But I wanted to work with papers.

In my second year, my final class was a week in Santa Fe, New Mexico, where we visited the state library, tribal libraries, and pueblo libraries. It was the only time since starting graduate school that I had fought for something I wanted, as my adviser didn't believe the class would be of much benefit in my job search.

When I finally started getting interviews, one was at New Mexico State University in Las Cruces. The southern part of the state is very different from the northern, but it has its desert beauty. The position was as the Political Papers Archivist and was tenure-track faculty. When I was interviewed, one of the archivists I had been working for told me, "I didn't think there was a chance for you to get it and I was so worried about how disappointing that would be."

I knew what she meant. I had just received my master's degree and had less than two years' experience, and that only as a graduate assistant. Also, the collection that was the core of the archive was that of a very important U.S. Senator who had served for six terms. There were more than 2,100 boxes of material.

One of the happiest moments of my life was when I got the phone call offering me the job. I'd had my doubts just as my colleague had. But by August of that year I was in Las Cruces, beginning my career as a congressional archivist and an assistant professor. I was sixty-two and as excited as a kid.

~Cary G. Osborne

96

I Chose Love

Chains do not hold a marriage together. It is threads, hundreds of tiny threads which sew people together through the years.
~Simone Signoret

I often wonder what roles little girls of today assume when they are playing pretend. Are they astronauts, doctors, chief scientists and CEOs? When I was a girl, I was always the nurse, never the doctor. Although I am almost two years older than my brother, in our role play, he got to be the boss, the Indian chief, the policeman, and I contented myself with being the helper, the wife, the assistant. My only act of rebellion in this role allocation was that when we played with other kids, I insisted on being the companion of the most notorious boy in the neighborhood. His name was Hermann. He had red hair and freckles and he was always missing a tooth or two. He was the wildest, the scariest, and the most admired—and I was his bride.

When we played cops and robbers with other kids, I would be the jailer in charge of our prisoners. I would be kind and bring them extra food and special treats to make up for Hermann's roughness. When we played cowboys and Indians, I was the squaw engaged to the courageous chief. I would get special gifts and was allowed to ride the fastest horse (bike). When we played family, I was the stay-at-home mom waiting for my husband to come home from his important work, a delicious grass and herb dinner ready on the kitchen table.

I never questioned this set-up. I actually enjoyed playing the "supporting role." It never occurred to me that I could be the hero, the boss, the captain. I still influenced the outcome of our games in my own way, by being the secret advisor to the "chief" behind the scenes. That was enough for me.

When I went to college in the late seventies, I studied French literature. Reading Simone de Beauvoir, I realized the role my gender had played in shaping my identity. I was mad at myself for the limitations I had not only accepted, but actively chosen, as a girl. It was time to claim my power. I cut my hair and dyed it red. I banned skirts from my wardrobe. I primarily read female authors wherever my syllabus allowed and chose the few women professors over their many male colleagues wherever possible. I broke up with my boyfriend when he wanted to get married because I felt too young to settle down. Although this turned out to be the right decision, it was highly influenced by my new misconception that family was a prison and only an independent working career would bring forth my liberation.

I landed a great job and got a taste of the life of a career woman. I jet-setted through Europe, attended important meetings, and signed significant contracts. But while my agenda and my bank accounts were getting fuller, my heart was getting emptier.

The reality of my working lifestyle and a couple of years of unsuccessful dating brought the possible bliss of love and marriage back into perspective. When I met Rob, it was love at first sight. He was a colleague and a rising star on an international career path. So against the advice I had given to so many young women before and without a second thought, I quickly conceded, "I'll go where you go! I am flexible." And I was. I did not consider arranging my life around his a sacrifice. Instead, I felt that my life story was yet to be written and I was happy for it to be co-directed by Rob. I was open to doing different work in different places. I wanted to be with the man I loved, be loved in return and do what was necessary to help him be successful and us to be happy.

Our life became an exciting ride. We got married and together we moved from Belgium to Italy to the U.S. to China and back to the U.S. Although Rob's career was the driver of our moves, I managed to both have my own satisfying work in each location and to create the environment in which our love could flourish. Today, twenty-five years later and happily retired in Florida, we look with gratefulness at the amazing life we have had, the places we have seen, the friends we have made and—above all—the enduring love we have for each other.

For a long time I believed that I had once again contentedly chosen what I considered the supporting role. But Rob never saw it this way. In a rare moment of doubt, I told him that I did not like standing in his shadow. He looked at me in complete puzzlement and said, "How can you stand in my shadow? You are my sunshine." I was amazed at the imagery. And then I smiled. I slowly nodded my head. He was right. And he had reminded me of the true motive for my life choices. As Khalil Gibran said, "Love, if it finds you worthy, directs your course."

~Rita Bosel

97

A Paltry Price for Personal Peace

For peace of mind, resign as general manager of the universe.
~Larry Eisenberg

Working hard comes naturally to me. Even at that, slaving like a hamster on a wheel took some time to perfect. I took the bait though, hook, line, and bonus check.

The medical billing company I work for hired me as a claims researcher and in one year promoted me to head of the Northeast Region Follow-Up Team. It was never my intention to be the best, or the fastest, or even the highest achiever. My ambition thrived on getting through each assignment from start to finish without disappointing one single person in the chain of command. I promised success and by God I would deliver.

In the first twelve months of my employment I proved one thing with absolute certainty. I had no idea how to say "no" when asked to take on a project. This characteristic alone rendered me ripe for the plucking when a management position became available, and I grabbed the ball as soon as it was tossed in my direction.

Every day I rolled up my sleeves and set about the business of leading my team in resolving the issues that prevented emergency room physicians from being paid by insurance companies. I stepped right into the ring and took on the fight while collecting a large salary increase, an annual bonus check, a nice office, and an extra week of vacation every year as my prize. Yep, this was living and I had worked hard earning every perk.

Fast-forward nine years.

"When are you going to finish?" My husband Joe grumbled as he climbed into bed, navigating around a sleeping dog and an ocean of paperwork.

"In a few minutes," I replied.

My track record offered Joe little reason to believe me. Finishing was always just a moment or two away. Then after I knew he was sound asleep, I'd gather my paperwork and move to the kitchen table and work for a few more hours. Later I'd crawl into bed exhausted, knowing that in five or six hours the curtain would rise again on the three-ring circus of stress I called my career.

Somewhere along the way, amid a string of successful insurance appeals, employees that competed for a spot on my team, and a senior management lineup that truly appreciated my efforts, my enthusiasm for living was replaced with grinding drudgery that robbed me of both peace and pleasure. As the company expanded, so did my client base, and with it the chains of responsibility that shackled me to my work grew heavier every day.

One night in particular I remember pulling the covers up to my chin and whispering into the darkness, "Please God, help me find the path back to peace and happiness."

The next morning as I drove to the office, I wondered how long it would take me to gather my courage and resign. Resigning would end the madness and Joe encouraged me to do so daily.

"Just do it Annie. Quit. We'll make do and you'll find another job. You're heading for a breakdown."

Resign, resign, resign! Not now though, I had a client presentation to prepare for and a conference call to attend in about an hour. Later, later, later!

Then an incoming e-mail bubble bounced across my computer screen and the phrase "position available" caught my eye. When I opened it the words "administrative assistant for senior vice president" glowed like a neon sign. Nah, I thought. They'd think I was crazy. Who in their right mind would step back to a secretarial position from a management position?

At home that evening my interest in the job persisted. I had ten years of experience as an executive secretary long before I ever arrived at the company. They didn't know that, but I did, and I knew how much I loved it too.

The next morning I summoned the nerve and told my boss I intended to apply for the job.

"You're in for a huge salary cut, and you'll lose your bonus, not to mention you'll be bored out of your mind," he said. "You're a leader, Annmarie, not a follower. How is it you think this makes any kind of sense?"

"Well," I said. "I imagine it makes no sense at all from your point of view but from where I'm sitting I have a few choices to make. I can choose to give up on this company and resign, or I can look at this secretarial position as an opportunity and try it. If it's not right for me, I'll resign and find something else."

"You're crazy."

"Not yet," I said. "But if I stay in this position much longer, I'm pretty sure I'll end up that way."

Admittedly the manger of human resources was stunned too, but from a budgetary standpoint it's hard to say no to someone who's asking for a salary cut and a decrease in benefits. That's pretty much a novelty you don't run into every day.

I brought to the table a skill set that boasted nine years of in-house experience, which included a working knowledge of every department in the operations area of the company. Though I negotiated to a salary I felt was reasonable for what I was offering, the lost bonus and salary cut brought me to a twenty percent decrease in my income, not including the vacation time I surrendered. Even I was starting to think I had lost my mind.

I closed the door to my office that last day with very few regrets about leaving my management position, but with one whopping load of anxiety about whether I made a mistake taking a job that would look like a demotion. By the end of my first day in the new position I knew I had made the right decision.

No office, staff, salary, or bonus check can ever replace this new feeling of waking up every morning and actually wanting to go to work. I enjoy that pleasure every day. The tasks I perform and the responsibilities I manage aid one vice president in particular and add to the smooth running of the department in which I work. When I leave at the end of the day, I take nothing with me but my desire to come back tomorrow knowing that I am respected and appreciated for the contribution that I make.

My husband always tells me you can't put a price on peace of mind, but divorce attorneys are plenty expensive. It looks likes my path to peace turned up none too soon!

~Annmarie B. Tait

98

What Do You Do?

The life of every man is a diary in which he means to write one story,
and writes another.
~James Matthew Barrie

"We think she has pneumonia again—you need to come get her," said the day care provider.

"I'm on my way," I assured her, and turned back to my computer screen. Staring back at me was an incomplete sales proposal I was preparing for an upcoming pitch. My first thought was, "Come on... how am I going to get this proposal done in time?"

I got in the car and tears rolled down my face when I realized how wrong I was. My eighteen-month-old daughter was sick again and she needed me. It was the second time she had pneumonia in two months, after six months of ear infections, high fevers and a persistent cough. She was ill and she needed her mother—how could I be thinking about anything but her? I began to cry that day and I scarcely stopped for two weeks. I soon realized it was a combination of postpartum depression, worry for my child and guilt about work that led to my mini-breakdown. Even then a part of me knew I had to give up the career I loved.

Our doctor recommended a short leave of absence from work to give me a chance to gain strength and help Zoey recover from pneumonia. After a few weeks, Zoey's lung specialist said she was improving but there was some lung damage and the best way to get her healthy would be to keep her away from germs. That meant staying home. I knew what I had to do. My husband and I discussed our choices, reviewed our finances and I left my job.

I felt like I was walking off the edge of a cliff. I didn't know who I was without my career. It had been such a huge part of my life for twenty years before I had a child. Who was I without the challenge, the adrenaline, the relationships and purpose? The answer seemed simple — I was Zoey's mom — but I felt like a square peg trying to fit in a round hole. My depression got worse. I cried every day, but my daughter did get healthy and thrived at home with me.

I didn't fit in anywhere. My work friends didn't know how to relate to me as a stay-at-home mom. They began to communicate with me differently — they stopped asking my opinion of business scenarios and I felt they no longer had respect for my opinion. I tried moms' groups but they only wanted to talk about their children, diapers and the best place to buy groceries. I wanted stimulating conversation, challenging debates and something to keep my adrenaline pumping. I wasn't getting what I needed anywhere.

I loved my daughter. Her very existence was a miracle. But I was raised to believe a woman could do it all and that was the life I wanted. The problem was finding a way to get what I wanted for myself while still giving my family what they needed. After several months of therapy and medication, my new life began to come into focus. I realized that I was so much more than my career.

I started by asking myself what I would do if money were no object. I would care for my family, write, travel, help people who needed it, and spend time with the people I loved. I began to review the journals I had always kept, especially during the tough times. I started to organize them into manuscripts. I wrote some short stories and made my first story submission to a publisher.

For two years I continued writing, did volunteer work in my community and for charities that had touched my life in some way. I had a second child. One day I received a call to do a project for a former colleague. The project took several weeks; I put my kids in day care part-time and was very stimulated. My kids loved having other children to play with at day care and my husband, once again, saw a smile on his wife's face and a sparkle in her eye.

Today, I still struggle to achieve the right balance, as we all do, but I'm getting there. I care for my family. I walk my daughter to school and am home to help her with homework in the afternoon. I am home with my kids if they are sick and don't feel guilty about a job I can't get to. My friendships changed. Some adjusted, some went away and I found some new community friends who share more of my beliefs and interests. I volunteer at my daughter's school and help a few charitable organizations. My husband and I have a weekly date night and we travel as much as we can. Most surprising of all, I published the one and only short story I ever submitted—and you can find it in *Chicken Soup for the Soul: Grieving and Recovery*. I continue to write and submit stories to publishers for consideration.

Before I left my career, people would ask me what I did and I would answer, "I run sales and marketing for a small software company." When I first stayed home with Zoey the reply became, "I used to be a software executive but my daughter got sick and I am home getting her well." Now the answer is, "I do lots of things; I care for my kids, love to travel, do volunteer work, I'm a business consultant, a wife, daughter, sister, friend, I love to write... should I go on?"

Here's what I learned—what I do is more than the title on my business card. My gravestone will not say the kind of businessperson I was but how I lived my life. I want it to say "she lived it to the fullest," and that is how I try to spend my days.

~Sheri Gammon Dewling

99

Ripe for a Change

Find a job you like and you add five days to every week.
~H. Jackson Browne

For my fortieth birthday, my daughter gave me an empty glass jar on which she had written the word Happiness. "When you find what makes you happy, you can put it in here so you don't lose it!" she explained.

The gift nicely summed up the vast majority of my life: a search for happiness. I certainly was happy as a boy; I can't tell you how many times I've relived boyhood games in my mind. I reminisced about childhood so much that my wife even called me "Peter Pan." Even young adulthood was fun: I loved working at the grocery store, setting up the produce stand, helping customers select the perfect level of ripeness. It was relaxing and I loved interacting with the people I helped. If the real world hadn't beckoned, I could have worked there forever.

But when I became an adult, it seemed that everyone around me had found their correct life, and more importantly, had found happiness in that life. I always felt like I was still searching. I took a job in banking to support my family, but what really made me happy were my two young daughters. When they started growing up, however, I felt lonely and pointless again. My job and the long commute seemed absurd. Pushing papers and meeting deadlines without interacting with clients felt pointless; I'd come home and the girls would be at their friends, or at practice or rehearsal. And I wasn't there to see it.

Thinking about my job consumed more and more of my free time. Over the years, the banking industry had been heartless, and various mergers and acquisitions always left me questioning—and sometimes losing—my job security.

"Just leave work at work," my wife advised. "Come home, find something that makes you happy, and get absorbed in it."

Easy for her to say. She finds happiness in anything—reading, gardening, talking, cooking. In fact, there isn't much she doesn't find joy in—except for watching me mope around the house, miserable.

When the girls moved out, a new bank acquisition sent me away from the stress of New York City into the quiet cities of the South. At first we thought it was a blessing—and it was. My wife and I were now closer to where our daughters had moved. I had a shorter commute. And for a few weeks, I was happy.

But soon the doldrums came again, and my wife declared with frustration, "As long as you're working, you're never going to be happy, Peter Pan!"

A blessing in disguise closed the office, and the company offered to move us back to New York. My wife was horrified that I might accept the offer and frightened about what might happen if I didn't. We considered it carefully, and we decided we didn't need a lot of money anymore: our home was nearly paid off and our girls were out on their own. We could settle for a modest salary, health insurance, and proximity to our daughters.

I declined the offer.

I loved the first few months of being jobless. It was everything I ever thought I wanted. I repaired every problem with the house. I pruned the trees. I created built-in shelves in all the basement storage areas. Crown molding, recessed lighting... I did it all.

Once the adrenaline wore off, however, that tiny seed of worry sprouted in my soul. Why hadn't I gotten any calls from sending out my résumé? I knew the economy was bad, but I expected a handful of interviews by now.

"All the jobs are in New York," my wife sighed one night.

"I won't move back there," I insisted.

My wife understood, and she was glad for the decision, but she was starting to worry. She watched our checkbook carefully. She started cutting corners at the grocery store, buying store brands and skimping on her favorite treats.

Two years went by, and although my wife wouldn't say it, I knew what she was thinking: she wondered whether finally, now that I didn't have to work a job I hated, I was happy. I saw the anger growing in her face as she left for work each day and glared at me as I sat on the couch sipping coffee and watching television. I wanted to tell her that the joy of it had worn off after a matter of months. That I only continued repairing our home so that I'd have something to do. That now I felt useless and old. I had run out of job prospects and home-improvement projects, and the days blended together.

I wanted to work.

I wanted to be happy.

It took two years of résumé revisions, of unemployment workshops, of promising interviews that for one reason or another just "didn't pan out." My cover letters were lackluster. I realized the drive that had helped me through my early career had been my desire to provide for my family. Now, they were provided for. My epiphany came when I realized that, for the first time in my life since childhood, I could worry about ME.

One day at breakfast, my wife eyed me over her coffee. "You know," she said, "when we were younger, you always used to tell me that your favorite job was working at that grocery store, stocking produce. A few times you even mentioned that, money aside, that would be the only job that would make you happy. Do you remember?"

I smiled. "Of course I do. I can still see those lettuce heads, those glistening apples. I still remember the particular weight of a cantaloupe just begging to be sliced and enjoyed, the feel of a tomato that will be ripe in time for dinner. Helping people instead of pushing paper..."

My wife smiled. It was a relaxed smile, a smile I hadn't seen in a few years.

"What made you remember that?" I asked.

"I saw they're opening up a new supermarket in the next town over. It just made me think of—well," she said, trying not to be too blunt, "I saw an advertisement for a produce department manager. I just thought—"

But she was too late. I had already retrieved a cover letter and résumé from the kitchen desk. "I sent this in three weeks ago," I said. "I've already had a phone interview with the store manager, and he says there are a few positions he'd like to see me fill. My interview is next Tuesday."

Weeks later, happily in my new position, I gazed at the "happiness" jar on my dresser. It was now filled with all my favorite snapshots from my life, from the birth of our daughters to their graduations and weddings.

I may have lost it, but I found it once again. "The love of family," I think to myself each night before bed. "That is what my happiness has always been."

And tomatoes.

~Martin Walters

100

My Secret Love Affair

You've got a lot of choices. If getting out of bed in the morning is a chore
and you're not smiling on a regular basis, try another choice.
~Steven D. Woodhull

The co-worker who sat behind me was getting married. He proudly tacked the corners of his engagement photo onto his cubicle wall. He looked over at me and observed, "Did you ever notice that what people put up in their office space is a reflection of what they care most about?" I realized that my cubicle was the only one in the office that wasn't covered with photos of chubby babies or other loved ones. In fact I didn't have any family photos on display. My show and tell was a collage of postcards from cities I longed to go to and places I had already been. Puzzled by the difference, I asked him what my area said about me. He matter-of-factly responded, "You want to escape."

How was it that a work acquaintance knew me better then I knew myself? It should have made me question myself, at least a bit. I'm not sure why I ignored the red flag, but at the time I was in the business of missing the obvious. After all, I had carefully crafted every aspect of my life, from the city I lived in to the company that I worked for. I'd actively pursued a career in advertising. I put myself in a graphic design master's program and graduated at the top of my class, all in an effort to live the dream of working for a big advertising agency and living in a fast-paced city. For all of that, I wasn't happy.

I didn't know that the majority of people in the world didn't cry themselves to sleep at night, the way I was. In fact, my tears even crept into my workplace. I thought it was normal to cry in the bathroom. The fact that I had lived in five different cities in a span of three years didn't seem odd to me. Or the reality that everyone I knew was collecting wedding registry lists and picking out house paint colors, while I was far more interested in collecting new passport stamps. It never dawned on me that my real happiness was waiting for me elsewhere.

After my co-worker opened my eyes, I decided to figure out why I wanted to escape, and why I was alone and loveless while everyone else was planning weddings and having babies. I figured there might be something to this love thing; I should give it a try. I finally got up enough nerve to ask myself out on a date.

The first encounter was simple; I took myself to coffee along with my laptop. Within seconds of typing my first sentence, I knew. Like any transformational love affair I wanted to spend every waking moment with the object of my affection. I hadn't taken any sick days or vacation in over four years, but all of a sudden I was calling in sick so I could spend the entire day with my new love—my writing self.

I had found my passion. It was time to declare my love to the world, so I took my writing on a honeymoon. We arrived in the most romantic city in the world, Paris. I spent two glorious weeks on this honeymoon, filling it with exploration, amazement and awe. I wrote every day.

On a whim I sent some of my travel blogs to editors and book publishers. A few months later I received a letter from an editor that read, "Congratulations, your story has been selected to run in our upcoming book." Before I could finish the letter, my knees collapsed and I fell to the floor! For the first time in my entire life, tears of extraordinary happiness poured through me. There was a light at the end of my dark tunnel. I was going to be a published author. I hadn't known that this was a dream of mine until my heart sang out.

I knew what I had to do—it was time for me to break up with advertising. Like leaving any involved relationship, I got scared. I worried about finding money to pay my bills, and where I would live as a travel writer. So I stayed where I was, miserable and depressed. Finally I got lucky and I was laid off from my job and I received a healthy severance that gave me the confidence to launch my new career and to travel the world.

~Shannon Kaiser

A Final Word

Editor's note: Angela Sayers died on July 15, 2011 as this book was being completed. She had already edited the story "My Epiphany" that appears first in this book and she was thrilled that it was going to be published.

Angie lived half a year longer than the doctors predicted and was active and involved right up to the end. She left a final letter that her parents found after she died. It was an extraordinary gift for her family, friends, and fans.

We were lucky to have Angie on our writing team and we are honored to publish this final letter from her. Angie embodied the spirit of "happiness" right to the end, always looking at the bright side, being grateful, and thinking positively.

Dear Friends and Family,

I cannot tell you how many times I've written this letter in my head and across my heart. I both want and feel like I should bestow some great wisdom upon you, and tell you all kinds of great and amazing things. I want to comfort you too, and tell you that everything will be alright. And it will be; you're not there yet.

Even though I would like to wipe away every one of your tears, come back and hug you one last time, I can't. And I'm sorry. I'm sorry for leaving you. I won't begrudge you your tears. Not now. After all, I would cry and hurt and shed tears for you too, if the situation were reversed. No, I understand all too well how time and life plays tricks on us in the moments of our deepest sorrows. So, I want you to cry and hurt and yell and scream if you need to.

But I don't want you to cry forever. I want you to turn around when you're ready and seize life with all you've got. I want you to remember, if anything, for my sake, that life goes on and you're a precious part of it. I take comfort in the fact that even though I'm gone, each of you is not, and that I will always continue to live in your memories and in your hearts, because I will never have truly left you.

I'm there when you breathe in a sweet drop of spring air. I am the splash of a raindrop across your window. Whenever you think of me and are reminded of the way I lived—I will be there with you. Hold me and your memories of me close to your heart. But never forget to live, laugh, and move on. Mourn me gently and deeply but then dry your eyes, take a deep breath, and *live*. Live, cherish, and *love*.

In my mind's eye I envision myself up in Heaven as this is being read. Perhaps, it is only in my imagination but I am dangling my legs, yes *legs*, off a silver-lined cloud looking down upon you. I'm sorry for your tears, sorry that I left you. But as I sit there, encompassed in white, I remember that every cloud has a silver lining and mine does too.

This image of me is so very clear. It is a healthy me. That's the silver lining. The version of me sitting upon that cloud not only has two legs, but is skinny, blond, and rosy-cheeked—the picture of health.

I am healthy in this new body, no longer chained to a body that has been abused beyond recognition and belief. The irony is that the Angie upon a cloud is the answer to every prayer that has been spoken in my name over the past five years. We prayed for healing over and over again and I am healed! God has granted me health, on his terms, in His time, and using His method. He may not have answered our prayers in the way we expected, or perhaps wanted. But I still cannot deny the fact that now, the moment you are reading this, I am healthy. I am okay.

You might be wondering how I can be so optimistic all of the time. People do ask me that a lot. I'm not optimistic all of the time. I have my dark days. But I am also, you see, exceedingly fortunate in all other things in life. I have a wonderful family, amazing friends, and a faith in a God that is bigger than the cancer in me. Optimism and perspective are nearly the same thing.

Sometimes life just needs a new perspective and to be optimistic you must teach yourself to see the good in every situation. I choose to envision myself as being fairly healthy at the moment. But when I think of it, I could pull out a host of complaints, of what hurts, my fears about what is growing where, and a million other incessant complaints that sometimes worm their way into my thoughts.

I think believing in the best is the only way that I could bear this journey. It is the only way I could ever stand to leave. The only way that I can deal with the challenges of these living moments is to believe with all of my heart that the dying moments will bring me the peace and happiness that I've always yearned for. It comforts me to know that eventually I will no longer be stuck in this body of mine. I hope, with all of my heart that this comforts you too. My heart and my soul are now free and *that* is the miracle we've been wanting all along.

Love Always,

Angie

Meet Our Contributors

Because of her experiences on her first trip to Bolivia, **Linda Allen** returns annually to work with medical and construction teams. She enjoys writing about her experiences and "second family" in Bolivia. E-mail her at lindaeallen@sbcglobal.net.

Shannon Anderson has her Master of Education degree and lives in Indiana where she enjoys spending time with her family, running, writing, teaching, presenting, and learning. She taught first grade for sixteen years and is currently an elementary literacy coach and high ability coordinator. E-mail her at shannonisteaching@gmail.com.

KT Banks has been an avid reader since childhood, reading all types of genres, and she still does. She believes in paying it forward and loves helping other people. Her novels are in the thriller genre, with lots of action, adventure and romance. Learn more at www.KTBanks.com.

Shinan Barclay is a ceramic artist and writer. Her first love is gardening. She is the co-author of *Moontime for Kory*, a rite of passage adventure, and she has been published in three other *Chicken Soup for the Soul* anthologies. She lives on the Oregon coast.

Valerie D. Benko received her Bachelor of Arts degree in Communications from Slippery Rock University in 2002, where she studied journalism and creative writing. She writes from western Pennsylvania and is a frequent contributor to the *Chicken Soup for the Soul* series. Visit her online at http://valeriebenko.weebly.com.

Sarah Bergman is married to the man of her dreams and resides in her hometown with their three incredible children. She has been a classroom teacher, freelance writer, and has been involved in children's ministry for most of her life. She loves to help kids come to know the love of Christ.

Rita Bosel, a native of Germany, lives in Flagler Country, FL. After more than two decades of work in a multinational company that took her to many countries, she enjoys capturing the defining moments that shaped her life's stories.

Teresa Brightwell, award-winning writer, speaker, and former "woman at the well," is passionate about sharing the hope of Christ. After a disastrous first marriage ended in adultery and the tragic death of her son, Teresa has a passion to empower others to become soul-healthy.

Alexander Brokaw received his Bachelor of Arts degree from Emory University in 2011. He currently lives in New York City, where he is working on his first book. E-mail him at alexander.brokaw@gmail.com.

Maureen Bruschi is a freelance non-fiction, travel and sports writer and photographer. Her articles appear in a number of publications including *GoNOMAD*, *BootsnAll Travel*, *TravelLady Magazine*, *Offbeat Travel*, *Real Travel Adventures*, *50Plus.com*, *Lovin' Life After 50*, *Budget Travel*, *40plus Travel and Leisure*, *The Writer* and USTA Middle States newsletter. E-mail her at mbruschi@embarqmail.com.

Georgia Bruton, a freelance editor and writer of children's books, received her B.A. from University of North Dakota. Currently, she lives in Florida with her husband, Steve. A mother of two and grandmother of three, she spends time enjoying her family, working with children, walking, writing, and reading. E-mail her at gjbruton@yahoo.com.

John P. Buentello is an author who has published many works of non-fiction, fiction and poetry. He teaches college classes in creative writing, and is currently at work on a book about writing fiction. E-mail him at jakkhakk@yahoo.com.

Jane Congdon is the author of a memoir, *It Started with Dracula: The Count, My Mother, and Me* (October 2011, Bettie Youngs Books). A native of West Virginia, she graduated from Concord University in Athens, WV, and was a textbook editor in Cincinnati, OH, for thirty years. Contact her at www.janecongdon.com.

Courtney Conover is a writer and yogini who resides in Michigan with her husband, Scott. And this fall, baby makes three: Their first child, Scotty Jr., is due in September. This is Courtney's fifth contribution to the *Chicken Soup for the Soul* series. Visit her online at www.courtneyconover.com.

Freelance writer and speaker **Julie B. Cosgrove** leads retreats, workshops, and Bible studies. She writes regularly for several Christian websites and publications. She has published three Bible studies and one fiction book. Julie has one grown son and lives in Fort Worth, TX, with two cats. Visit her website at www.juliebcosgrove.com.

Jeannette de Beauvoir is an award-winning author and playwright whose work has appeared in fifteen countries and has been translated into twelve languages. She lives and works in an old sea captain's house at the tip of Cape Cod, MA, with one bat, two lovebirds, and thousands of books.

Diana DeAndrea-Kohn is a small business owner and writer. She has three boys, Kenny, Alex, and Brodie. She would like to thank her husband Scott for being so supportive of her writing.

Sheri Gammon Dewling, a former software executive, runs a small consulting business, while raising two small children in Markham, Canada. Sheri aspires to turn her life lessons into stories that will inspire others. E-mail Sheri at sheri@justmomsense.com.

C.M. Downie received her B.A. in Psychology from the University of Arkansas in 1961. She balanced a thirty-five-plus-year career in information technology with an M.A. degree in English/Literature from the University of Minnesota in 1992 and various dabblings in print. She enjoys scuba diving, wilderness camping and several of the arts.

Danielle M. Dryke is a program evaluator and researcher with an M.S. degree in International Development from the University of Amsterdam. She has lived in Mali, Lebanon, The Netherlands, Denmark, and her native Minnesota. Danielle enjoys salsa dancing, socializing and retreating at ARC Retreat Center to work on her memoir.

Although **Janet Perez Eckles** lost her sight, she gained insight to serve as an international speaker, writer, columnist and author of *Simply Salsa: Dancing Without Fear at God's Fiesta* (Judson Press, August 2011). From her home in Florida she imparts inspiration at www.inspirationforyou.com.

Shawnelle Eliasen and her husband Lonny raise their five sons in Illinois. She home teaches her youngest children and writes about their adventures. Her stories have been published in *Guideposts*, *MomSense*, *A Cup of Comfort* books, *Christmas Miracles*, *Christmas Spirit*, and several *Chicken Soup for the Soul* books. Learn more at Shawnellewrites.blogspot.com.

Malinda Dunlap Fillingim enjoys writing, walking, and wondering what will unfold in her life next. Recently she and her husband David relocated to Wilmington, NC, and she hopes to have found a job as a minister by the time you read this. This will make it her twenty-sixth move and she hopes her last. Happiness is contagious!

Judith Fitzsimmons is a freelance writer and business consultant who lives in middle Tennessee. Her hobbies are aromatherapy, yoga, and fitness, but her passion is being a Mom.

Maureen Flynn is a Canadian working mother of three. She expresses her creativity through her writing and painting. She currently writes a weekly column titled "View from the Crow's Nest" for a local newspaper and continues to pursue work on her murder mystery/ghost story novels. E-mail her at grrrumpychick@hotmail.com.

Betsy Franz is an award-winning writer and photographer specializing in nature, wildlife, the environment, and human relationships. Her articles and photos reflecting the wonders of life have been published in numerous books and magazines. She lives in Florida with her husband Tom. Learn more at www.naturesdetails.net.

Jennifer Gauthier is currently studying Social Services at Laurentian University. She plans to one day work with children and teenagers. Jennifer could not have made it this far without the help of her mother Lynn, Janyk, Anne, Helene and her grandmothers: Gillette and Rachelle. E-mail her at jengauthier@hotmail.com.

Carol Gibson completed the Christian Writer's Guild Apprentice Course in 2010 and is a registered nurse with the State of California. She is the author of the book *Walking as Children of Light*, a devotional currently being offered for publication.

Pamela Gilsenan is the mom of five adult children and various grandchildren. She graduated from Stephens College with an English degree. She hangs around bookstores and libraries looking for story ideas. E-mail her at Rhubarbwoman5@gmail.com.

Michael Gingerich lives in Hershey, PA, with his wife Kathy and his son Matthew. He is also the father of two other sons—Adam and David. He is an author, counselor and pastor. E-mail Michael at michael.gingerich@hotmail.com.

Nicole Guiltinan is a first-year college student in Northern California. She plans on entering the field of social work, and works on writing poetry in her spare time. Nicole enjoys reading, poetry, and art. E-mail her at nguiltinan@yahoo.com.

Chelsey Colleen Hankins graduated from the American Academy of Dramatic Arts in Los Angeles, CA, in 2010. Chelsey enjoys acting, traveling, snowboarding, writing, and directing. She currently resides in Los Angeles and is working on her first book and writing a web series. E-mail her at colleenhnkns@yahoo.com.

Judy Harch spent many years editing medical journals. As a freelance journalist, she contributed to *The Philadelphia Inquirer* and other publications. She is co-author of the book *Alzheimer Solutions: A Personal Guide for Caregivers*. Judy has written a novel and hopes to have it published. E-mail her at judyharch@verizon.net.

Nancy Hatten grew up in Belvidere, IL, where she enjoyed the change of seasons and fell in love with the Chicago Cubs. Now she lives in beautiful Austin, TX, where she often battles the heat but no longer snow and ice.

Miriam Hill is a frequent contributor to *Chicken Soup for the Soul* books and has been published in *Writer's Digest, The Christian Science Monitor, Grit, St. Petersburg Times, The Sacramento Bee* and Poynter Online. Miriam's manuscript received Honorable Mention for Inspirational Writing in a Writer's Digest Writing Competition.

Rebecca Hill is delighted to say that she is now in good health and is keeping her promise to God to write every day. She is the author of a children's book called *Don't You Worry, Don't You Cry* and a novel entitled *Confessions of an Innkeeper*. E-mail her at rebeccahill1969@hotmail.com.

Abigail Hoeft received her Bachelor of Arts degree in English from the University of Wisconsin-Stevens Point. She plans to use her passion for writing and her own personal experience with schizophrenia to make a positive impact on the lives of others living with disabilities.

Erika Hoffman writes essays, non-fiction narratives, and mysteries. She lives with her true love (yes, that is her husband!) and also with her dad, who provides her with funny stuff!

Ruth Jones lives in Cookeville, TN, with her husband Terry and a very fat cat named Annabel.

Marsha Jordan is no stranger to hardships and suffering. But through it all, she's kept her sense of humor. She shares her hard-earned wisdom, along with a few laughs, in her book, *Hugs, Hope, and Peanut Butter*. Visit her website at www.hugsandhope.org or E-mail Marsha at hugsandhope@gmail.com.

Shannon Kaiser is founder of playwiththeworld.net, a wonderland of adventure, fun and fulfillment. A full-time travel writer, author, and adventure junkie, she inspires people to "love their life to the fullest" and make the most out of every moment.

Nancy Julien Kopp grew up in Chicago and now lives in Kansas. She began writing late in life, but has been published in eleven *Chicken Soup for the Soul* books, other anthologies, e-zines, magazines and newspapers. Once a classroom teacher, she now teaches through the written word. Visit her blog at www.writergrannysworld.blogspot.com.

Victoria LaFave is a writer and Marketing Coordinator for nine Catholic schools in Michigan's Upper Peninsula. She's been published in *Chicken Soup for the Soul: Thanks Dad*, and *My Teacher Is My Hero*.

Her stories have also appeared in *Parents*, *FamilyFun* and *Woman's Day* magazines. E-mail her at vrlafave@sbcglobal.net.

Jeannie Lancaster, a freelance writer from Loveland, CO, finds happiness in simple things. She writes from her heart about the experiences that have defined her life. A graduate of the University of Northern Colorado, Jeannie has been a life-long lover of words and the power within them.

Lisa McManus Lange is a receptionist by day and writer by night in Victoria, BC, Canada. While writing towards publication in humorous women's fiction, her work can be found in national and international magazines, as well as a writing reference book. E-mail her at lisamc2010@yahoo.ca or visit www.lisamcmanuslange.blogspot.com.

Dina Leacock has been writing for twenty years and has 200 short stories and two books published. When not writing she's a senior citizen center director. The mother of two sons, Dina resides with her husband and her cat on the edge of the Pine Barrens in Southern New Jersey.

Laurie Leal holds a master's degree in elementary education and teaches third and fourth grade in Massachusetts. Laurie enjoys scrapbooking, Tae Kwon Do, whitewater rafting, visiting with friends, and caring for animals. She is in the process of getting her first novel published. E-mail her at dragonspirit28@comcast.net.

Craig Learn recently graduated from Buffalo State College with a B.A. in Journalism. Craig is trying to break into the industry and hopes this can be his first break. He loves writing human interest stories, as well as sports stories. E-mail him at learncw@gmail.com.

Linda Lohman, a frequent contributor to the *Chicken Soup for the Soul* series since retiring in 2005, also writes a column for *Miss Kitty's Journal*. She thanks God daily for a bounty of supporting friends and family. Living in Sacramento, CA, she loves life as a Red Hat Society Ambassador. E-mail her at laborelations@yahoo.com.

Rita Lussier's column has been a popular weekly feature in *The Providence Journal* for twelve years. Her essay, "A Sign of the Times," took first place in the 2010 Erma Bombeck Writing Competition, an honor she also won in 2006. Her essays have appeared in *The Boston Globe* and NPR.

Gloria Hander Lyons has channeled thirty years of training and hands-on experience in the areas of art, interior decorating, crafting and event planning into writing creative how-to books, fun cookbooks and humorous slice-of-life stories. Visit her website to read about them at www.BlueSagePress.com.

Shawn Marie Mann is an amusement park geographer and historian living in Pennsylvania with her husband and three children. She loves sharing information on Pennsylvania's amusement parks through her website www.amusementparkmom.com. This is Shawn's fourth story in the *Chicken Soup for the Soul* series. E-mail her at www.shawnmariemann.com.

Tim Martin's work has been featured in numerous *Chicken Soup for the Soul* books. He is the author of *There's Nothing Funny About Running* and *Wimps Like Me*. Tim had two children's novels due out in 2011: *Scout's Oaf* and *Summer With Dad*. E-mail him at tmartin@northcoast.com.

Sara Matson lives with her husband and ten-year-old twins in Minnesota, where she enjoys writing, reading, cooking, and home-schooling her kids. She has previously written about her family in *Chicken Soup for the Soul: Twins and More* and *Chicken Soup for the Soul: Tales of Christmas*. E-mail her at saramatsonstories@hotmail.com.

Debra Mayhew is a pastor's wife and home-schooling mom to six children. After faith and family, her greatest passion is writing for children. Debra loves good books, long walks, and an empty laundry basket. E-mail her at debra@debramayhew.com or visit www.debramayhew.com to learn more.

Ian McCammon is an outgoing guy from Sugar Land, TX. This story is for him as well as the many people who will be inspired to be themselves and not let anyone get in their way.

Heather McGowan is a wife, mother of two young children, and owner of Sounding Board Marketing & Communications in Folsom, CA. Heather blogs about her experiences as a working mother on hvmcgowanmakingendsmeet.blogspot.com.

Caitlin McLean lives in the Midwest, where she is now a writer, mother, and wife. When she is not writing, Caitlin enjoys other forms of creating, particularly cooking, sewing, knitting, and shooting pictures.

Kimberly Misra lives in western Massachusetts with her husband and four children. Her interests include writing, reading, home-schooling the kids, keeping chickens, and exploring New England. She is currently working on her first novel. E-mail her at kmmsra@gmail.com.

Richard Nakai is a graduate of the University of La Verne. His interests include Japanese history and European medieval history. He has two cats named Shadow and Tama. Richard is an Aspie. E-mail him at rulerofworld14@hotmail.com.

Janice Flood Nichols earned her B.A. degree from Seton Hill College and her M.Ed. from the University of Pittsburgh. As the author of *Twin Voices: A Memoir of Polio, the Forgotten Killer* she devotes her time to speaking about the importance of polio eradication and vaccination. Learn more at www.twinvoices.com.

Carrie O'Maley studied Journalism at Butler University and then received her Master of Library Science degree at Indiana University. She has worked for Indianapolis-Marion County Public Library, Muncie Public Library, and Indiana University-Purdue University Indianapolis Library, and hopes to have a lifelong career in libraries. E-mail her at omaleyc@yahoo.com.

Tracey Miller Offutt graduated with a BSN, magna cum laude, from Georgetown University. Her clinical practice focuses on pediatrics. Previously, she was a journalist and editor. She now teaches and is working towards a master's degree. She is married with two wonderful children. E-mail her at TraceyOffuttRN@aol.com.

Cary G. Osborne received her B.A. degree from Mary Baldwin College and her MLIS degree from the University of Oklahoma in 2007. She is the author of six novels and a number of short stories. Currently, she is also the Political Papers Archivist at New Mexico State University. E-mail her at iroshi@aol.com.

Jeannine Ouellette received her Bachelor of Arts degree in Psychology and a Master of Education degree from the University of Ottawa. In 2000, she won the Laura Jamieson Prize for her book on women's ways of learning. She is currently writing on the healing process. Learn more at www.triyana.ca.

Margie Pasero is a musician and Health Rhythms facilitator. She plays clarinet in ensembles and teaches African drumming. Her women's group, Namaste Women Who Drum, performs at summer fairs. She brings the spirit of well-being and joy to retirement homes, senior centers and retreat centers through her Health Rhythms programs. E-mail her at heartbeats@nventure.com.

Faith Paulsen's work has appeared in *Chicken Soup for the Soul: Shaping the New You*, as well as *Literary Mama*, *Wild River Review*, *Open Salon*, several *A Cup of Comfort* books, and *What Canst Thou Say?* She is the co-author of *Fun With the Family in Pennsylvania*.

Donna Paulson lives on the island of Martha's Vineyard with her four children. She enjoys reading, walking on the beach, singing in church and laughing with friends. She plans to write novels based on her experiences as a single mother. E-mail her at dpaulson31@verizon.net.

Marsha Porter has written numerous short stories and non-fiction articles. She co-authored a video movie guide that reviewed 20,000 films. She perfected the 500-word essay in grade school when it was the punishment du jour. Currently she teaches high school English.

Robin Pressnall is Executive Director of Small Paws Rescue Inc., which is featured on Animal Planet's *Dogs 101*. She has been a three-time guest on the Fox News Network's *Fox & Friends* in NYC. Robin lives in Tulsa, OK, with her husband Dale, and their three Bichon Frises.

Karen Putz is a deaf mom of three deaf and hard of hearing children. She is a contributing writer for the *Chicago Tribune*, TribLocal and ChicagoNow blog. She is a speaker and board member of Hands & Voices. E-mail Karen at karen@karenputz.com.

Jennifer Quasha has been a freelance writer and editor since 1998, and she loves to write for the *Chicken Soup for the Soul* series. When she's not writing, editing, or reading, you'll find her chasing after her human and canine family members, or asleep. Learn more at www.jenniferquasha.com and www.smallpawsbarefeet.com.

Monica Quijano is one of those awkward, geeky, high school freshmen always writing in a notebook. She hopes to one day be a full-time writer and is currently working on her first novel. This is her first published non-fiction piece. She lives with her family and two cats.

Jamie Anne Richardson is a freelance writer and editor. She and her husband live in a Dallas suburb where she is working on her first chick lit novel while raising their three young kids. E-mail her at jamieannerichardson@hotmail.com or check out her website at www. jamieannerichardson.com.

Megale Rivera received her Bachelor of Arts degree in English from Florida Atlantic University, and Master of Education degree from the University of Phoenix. She teaches Adult Education to incarcerated individuals. She enjoys spending time at the beach, reading and spending time with her family.

Carolyn Roy-Bornstein is a pediatrician and award-winning writer. Her essays have been published in many medical and literary journals and anthologies including *JAMA*, *Brain, Child* magazine, *Literary Mama* and *Chicken Soup for the Soul*. Her new memoir *Crash!* is due out in October of 2012.

Angela Sayers was a twenty-year-old cancer patient who sought to raise awareness for pediatric cancers, especially osteosarcoma. She loved books, writing, playing online *Scrabble*, and her cat, Charles Fitzpatrick The Third.

John M. Scanlan is a 1983 graduate of the U.S. Naval Academy and a retired Lieutenant Colonel from the U.S. Marine Corps. He is pursuing a second career as a writer. E-mail him at ping1@hargray.com.

Jenny Scarborough holds a M.Ed. degree from Loyola College in Maryland. She has been teaching since 1996 and currently teaches Language Arts to sixth graders in North Georgia. Jenny enjoys singing, reading, fishing, and spending time with her husband Rob and their son Konrad. This is her first time being published.

Larry Schardt, PhD, is a motivational speaker, facilitator, professor at Penn State and Pitt, and writer. Larry enjoys writing, reading, speaking, walking, community, skiing, football, and friends. His current projects are *The Magic in Every Moment* (non-fiction) and *The*

Angel of the Mountain (fiction). Visit themagicineverymoment.com or e-mail him at larryschardt@gmail.com.

Happiness is **Lindy Schneider's** energy drink! She is an illustrator, author and inspirational speaker. She loves to help people find joy in the midst of their struggles. E-mail her at lindy_schn@yahoo.com or visit www.LindysBooks.com.

Patrick Sepe owns a transmission shop and resides in Merrick, NY, with his wife Susan and daughters Allison and Brittany. He is a political junkie and enjoys a spirited debate. He is currently working on a memoir. E-mail him at psepe60@gmail.com.

Leah Shearer is a 2000 graduate of St. Bonaventure University. Having worked in education for ten years, she developed a special affinity for teenagers and their challenges. In addition to her work with Melissa's Living Legacy Teen Cancer Foundation, she shares her inspirational story as a speaker. Visit www.lifesandwiches.blogspot.com to learn more.

Deborah Shouse is a speaker, writer, and editor. She loves helping people write and edit books and she enjoys facilitating creativity and storytelling workshops. Deborah donates all proceeds from her book *Love in the Land of Dementia: Finding Hope in the Caregiver's Journey to Alzheimer's*. Visit www.thecreativityconnection.com and read http://deborahshousewrites.wordpress.com.

Anne Sigmon is a California writer, stroke survivor, and autoimmune patient who writes about adventure travel for people with health limitations. She is currently finishing a memoir about surviving a stroke and traveling to remote corners from Burma to Uzbekistan. Connect her at www.AnneSigmon.com and follow her adventures on www.JunglePants.com.

Tracie Skarbo was raised on Vancouver Island, Canada, and currently lives there with her family. Her stories have appeared in the

Chicken Soup for the Soul: My Cat's Life and *Chicken Soup for the Soul: Just for Preteens*. Tracie's book, *Harmonious Flight*, is available at http://sbpra.com/tracieskarbo or e-mail her at tracieskarbo@gmail.com.

Colonel George Smawley is an officer in the U.S. Army Judge Advocate General's Corps. He wrote "The Lucky One" while serving in Iraq with the 25th Infantry Division. He received his B.A. in English from Dickinson College, and his J.D. from the Temple University School of Law.

Alaina Smith loves a good story. Her true tales appear in multiple anthologies including two other *Chicken Soup for the Soul* books, six *Chocolate for Women* books, five *A Cup of Comfort* books, and more. She enjoys writing, working for a musical theater company, and moviegoing with her husband, Frank.

Michelle Smyth founded Quad Cities Autism Center in 2006. She currently works as Center Director and lives with her husband David, son Jayden and daughter Caitlyn in Moline, IL. She thanks Sheri Zeck of Milan, IL for writing her story! Visit her website www.qcautismcenter.org or e-mail her at michelle@qcautismcenter.org.

Ruth Spiro is a freelance writer and author of the award-winning children's book, *Lester Fizz, Bubble-Gum Artist*. Her articles and essays have appeared in national magazines, and she frequently speaks at schools and conferences. To learn more about Ruth, visit www.RuthSpiro.com.

JC Sullivan is a member of the Travelers Century Club (www.travelerscenturyclub.org). Having worked in virtually every industry, she took her own advice and escaped the cubicle! Now she visits one new place a month and tries to do one thing a day that scares her. E-mail her at JobfreeJennifer@yahoo.com.

Annmarie B. Tait lives in Conshohocken, PA, with her husband Joe

Beck and Sammy their Yorkie. Annmarie has contributed to several *Chicken Soup for the Soul* books, *Reminisce* magazine and the *Patchwork Path* series. Annmarie enjoys cooking, singing and recording American and Irish folk songs. E-mail her at irishbloom@aol.com.

Michelle Vanderwist is a graduate of Georgetown University and currently works for a software company in Madison, WI. She enjoys painting, reading, and playing board games.

Sharon Dunski Vermont is a full-time wife and mother and part-time writer and pediatrician. She received her M.D. degree from the University of Missouri-Kansas City School of Medicine in 1993. Her daughters, Hannah and Jordyn, and husband Laird are the inspiration for everything she does. E-mail her at svermont1987@ yahoo.com.

Carolyn Wade has lived and gardened on three continents. She graduated with a Bachelor of Arts with honors from Portland State University. Living back home in the Pacific Northwest, she enjoys reading, writing, gardening, traveling with her husband, and spending time with her children and grandchildren.

Ray M. Wong is devoted to his wife, Quyen. He cherishes his children, Kevin and Kristie. Ray is studying creative non-fiction in the MFA program at Antioch University Los Angeles. He is working on a memoir about a journey to Hong Kong that changed his life. Visit him at www.raywong.info or e-mail ray@raywong.info.

Meet Our Authors

Jack Canfield is the co-creator of the *Chicken Soup for the Soul* series, which *Time* magazine has called "the publishing phenomenon of the decade." Jack is also the co-author of many other bestselling books.

Jack is the CEO of the Canfield Training Group in Santa Barbara, California, and founder of the Foundation for Self-Esteem in Culver City, California. He has conducted intensive personal and professional development seminars on the principles of success for more than a million people in twenty-three countries, has spoken to hundreds of thousands of people at more than 1,000 corporations, universities, professional conferences and conventions, and has been seen by millions more on national television shows.

Jack has received many awards and honors, including three honorary doctorates and a Guinness World Records Certificate for having seven books from the *Chicken Soup for the Soul* series appearing on the New York Times bestseller list on May 24, 1998.

You can reach Jack at www.jackcanfield.com.

Mark Victor Hansen is the co-founder of Chicken Soup for the Soul, along with Jack Canfield. He is a sought-after keynote speaker, bestselling author, and marketing maven. Mark's powerful messages of possibility, opportunity, and action have created powerful change in thousands of organizations and millions of individuals worldwide.

Mark is a prolific writer with many bestselling books in addition to the *Chicken Soup for the Soul* series. Mark has had a profound influence in the field of human potential through his library of audios, videos, and articles in the areas of big thinking, sales achievement, wealth building, publishing success, and personal and professional development. He is also the founder of the MEGA Seminar Series.

Mark has received numerous awards that honor his entrepreneurial spirit, philanthropic heart, and business acumen. He is a lifetime member of the Horatio Alger Association of Distinguished Americans.

You can reach Mark at www.markvictorhansen.com.

Amy Newmark is Chicken Soup for the Soul's publisher and editor-in-chief, after a thirty-year career as a writer, speaker, financial analyst, and business executive in the worlds of finance and telecommunications. Amy is a *magna cum laude* graduate of Harvard College, where she majored in Portuguese, minored in French, and traveled extensively. She and her husband have four grown children.

After a long career writing books on telecommunications, voluminous financial reports, business plans, and corporate press releases, Chicken Soup for the Soul is a breath of fresh air for Amy. She has fallen in love with Chicken Soup for the Soul and its life-changing books, and really enjoys putting these books together for Chicken Soup's wonderful readers. She has co-authored more than three dozen *Chicken Soup for the Soul* books and has edited another three dozen.

You can reach Amy through the webmaster@chickensoupforthesoul.com.

About
Deborah Norville

Bestselling author **Deborah Norville** credits many of the successes in her life to a positive mental attitude. The anchor of *Inside Edition*, the nation's top-rated syndicated news magazine, the journalist is a two-time Emmy winner.

Deborah is also the author of a half-dozen books including the New York Times bestseller, *Thank You Power: Making the Science of Gratitude Work for You*. *Thank You Power* brought together for the first time the growing body of academic research proving the benefits of gratitude. Similarly, *The Power of Respect* presented research detailing the benefits of respectful behavior with real life stories. She also wrote the foreword for *Chicken Soup for the Soul: Think Positive*.

A lifelong seamstress and crafter, Deborah recently introduced The Deborah Norville Collection, a line of fine hand yarns for knitting and crochet, available at craft stores nationwide.

Deborah Norville is a *summa cum laude* (4.0) graduate of the University of Georgia. She is married and the mother of three.

Deborah can be reached via her website www.DeborahNorville.com.

Thank You

We owe huge thanks to all of our contributors. We know that you poured your hearts and souls into the thousands of stories and poems that you shared with us, and ultimately with each other. We appreciate your willingness to open up your lives to other Chicken Soup for the Soul readers and share your own experiences, no matter how painful or personal, in order to help other people. As I read and edited these stories, I was truly inspired, excited by the potential of this book to change people's lives, and impressed by the self-awareness you showed and your unselfish willingness to share what you learned about yourselves.

We could only publish a small percentage of the stories that were submitted, but we read every single one and even the ones that do not appear in the book had an influence on us and on the final manuscript. Our assistant publisher D'ette Corona read almost every submission, and she was assisted by editor Kristiana Glavin because there were so many submissions! D'ette worked with all the contributors, obtaining their approvals for our edits and the quotations we carefully chose to begin each story. And Kristiana Glavin, along with editors Barbara LoMonaco and Madeline Clapps performed their normal masterful proofreading and made sure the book went to the printer on time.

We also owe a very special thanks to our creative director and book producer, Brian Taylor at Pneuma Books, for his brilliant vision for our covers and interiors. He worked really hard on that rabbit on the cover, who came to us on an all-black background and with a bent ear. We call our cover star "Dude Rabbit" since he has so much attitude. Finally, none of this would be possible without the business and creative leadership of our CEO, Bill Rouhana, and our president, Bob Jacobs.

~Amy Newmark

Improving Your Life Every Day

Real people sharing real stories—for eighteen years. Now, Chicken Soup for the Soul has gone beyond the bookstore to become a world leader in life improvement. Through books, movies, DVDs, online resources and other partnerships, we bring hope, courage, inspiration and love to hundreds of millions of people around the world. Chicken Soup for the Soul's writers and readers belong to a one-of-a-kind global community, sharing advice, support, guidance, comfort, and knowledge.

Chicken Soup for the Soul stories have been translated into more than forty languages and can be found in more than one hundred countries. Every day, millions of people experience a Chicken Soup for the Soul story in a book, magazine, newspaper or online. As we share our life experiences through these stories, we offer hope, comfort and inspiration to one another. The stories travel from person to person, and from country to country, helping to improve lives everywhere.

Share with Us

We all have had Chicken Soup for the Soul moments in our lives. If you would like to share your story or poem with millions of people around the world, go to chickensoup.com and click on "Submit Your Story." You may be able to help another reader, and become a published author at the same time. Some of our past contributors have launched writing and speaking careers from the publication of their stories in our books!

Our submission volume has been increasing steadily—the quality and quantity of your submissions has been fabulous. We only accept story submissions via our website. They are no longer accepted via mail or fax.

To contact us regarding other matters, please send us an e-mail through webmaster@chickensoupforthesoul.com, or fax or write us at:

Chicken Soup for the Soul
P.O. Box 700
Cos Cob, CT 06807-0700
Fax: 203-861-7194

One more note from your friends at Chicken Soup for the Soul: Occasionally, we receive an unsolicited book manuscript from one of our readers, and we would like to respectfully inform you that we do not accept unsolicited manuscripts and we must discard the ones that appear.